FOR THE FIRST TIME IN 11 YEARS, INDY 500 AND NASCAR PICK THE SAME OFFICIAL PACE CAR.

SMART MOVE, GUYS.

You picked a winner. Pontiac's Limited Edition Turbo Trans Am.

A car so well engineered that almost nothing had to be done to prepare it to pace the start of this year's Indy 500. Only the air conditioning was removed, high-speed tires added and the axle ratio lowered to increase top speed.

Otherwise it's the same car that will be in the hands of 5,600 lucky owners. A car that will pace the starts of the Daytona 500 and other NASCAR races without *any* modification.

With the first production turbocharged gas V-8 of the '80s.* Engineered for a

smooth, steady response over a broad r.p.m. range. Trans Ams are equipped with GM-built engines produced by various divisions. See your dealer for details.

Equipped with silvered removable hatch-roof panels. Turbo cast aluminum wheels. Four-wheel disc brakes. Limited slip differential. Tungsten quartz halogen headlights. And special interior trim with a host of luxury extras.

Visit your Pontiac dealer soon and see the Turbo Trans Am. A car so remarkable it's been awarded the rare distinction of pacing both this year's Indianapolis 500 and NASCAR starts.

MORE PONTIAC EXCITEMENT FOR THE GREAT ONES

*Turbo V-8 not available in Calif.

MARK OF EXCELLENCE

GT Radial. The tire that introduced outline white letters to the performance market and then won two IMSA Series Championships* to prove that it offered much more than just good looks.

This year's official Indy 500 Pace Car—a turbocharged Pontiac Trans Am. Its tires: the new Eagle GT,* a special-order, steel-belted version of the Wingfoot Radial.

*Tread reduced to ½ depth for racing.

The first family of

Super

From a long line of winners.

Every one of our Superadials has distinguished itself, not only on the roads but also on the race tracks of America. Born of racing, bred from racing, proved by racing, every single one of them has at least one Championship under its belts. They are truly Superadials.

INDIANAPOLIS 500 YEARBOOK

For those who are at least mentally involved with Championship automobile racing, the mood at the 64th running of the Indianapolis 500 was happily one of tranquility this year as opposed to the legal battles that overshadowed the activities of 1979.

Although the weather checked what promised to be one of the most exciting qualifying sessions seen, the rules for the 1980 race allowed what may only be termed as a great competitive atmosphere. By our estimate, nearly a third of the field might have been bumped by mere hundredths of a second if the rain hadn't arrived.

For one who has always appreciated the flowing bodywork of the classic cars of the Twenties and Thirties, your publisher is glad to see that the Speedway cars of the Eighties shall again appear as fully clothed vehicles with gentle curves blended into a gentle bump here and there. No longer will we see mechanical apparatus jutting out from behind the driver's head in the space where the engine goes.

As we look forward to the decade of the Eighties, it is difficult for us to speculate on the technological innovations that may occur in the 500. We can well imagine that aerodynamics will continue to play an increasingly important role but cannot comment on the types of engines we'll see because we don't have a feel for upcoming specifications. That's fine with us, it adds to the mystique of the Speedway.

Once again we're fortunate to have assembled some of the nation's foremost writers and photographers in bringing you our annual Yearbook. We've tried to bring a blend of old and new this year, as well as a nice piece of fiction. We hope you enjoy our effort as much as we do in producing it.

Volume VIII   Number VIII

Unequalled in Coverage of The World's Most Famous Automobile Race

Publisher	Carl Hungness
Editor	John Mahoney
Historical Editor	Jack C. Fox
Staff Photographers	Tracy Talley
	Phil Whitlow
Circulation	Wilma Steffy

Secretary	Terri Gunn
Production	Justyn Blackwell
	Volney Knopp
Typesetting	Marie Willis
Mailing	Ray Toms

Our thanks once again to Al Bloemker, Bill Donaldson, Bob Laycock, Bill York and the entire Indianapolis Motor Speedway publicity and press room staff for their continuing assistance. Head Speedway photographer Ron McQueeney, his assistant Nancy Chandler, and his staff are also thanked for their annual contributions.

Color Separations by: Kayenay
Printing: Webcrafters

Artist Rich Ernsting of Indianapolis produced our cover.

Contributing Photographers:
John Mahoney
Tracy Talley
Phil Whitlow
Charles Lytle
Ralph Tippy
Jack Fox
Dave Knox
Arnie deBrier
Al Meadows
Steve Snoddy

Steve Margison
Jim Alvis
Don Larson
Ken Coles
Jim Dawson
Gerald Walker
Rick Lane
Robert Rowe
Larry Shuman
Roy Query
Doug Wendt
Danny Laycock

Dave Scoggan
Bob Mount
Ann Miller
Robert Kincaid
Phil LeVrier
Tom Dick
Wayne Nowostawski
Don Gandoff

IMS Photo Staff:
Ron McQueeney
Bob Scott

Jack Householder
Denis Sparks
Frank Newman
Jim Haines
Charles Duffy
Steve "Link" Lingenfelter
Dan Francis
Harlan Hunter
Richard Wallace
Harold Bergquist
Dave Willoughby
Jack Schofer

Bill Watson
Rick Wall
Tom Lucas
Harry Goode
Tom Balistreri
Mike Grove
Marion Thomas
Steve Voorhees
Dale Roeschlein
Dave Thomas
Dale Wines

Contributing Writers:
Jack Fox
Donald Davidson
Jep Cadou
Carl Hungness
John Mahoney
Ann Miller
Fritz Frommeyer
Al Stilley
Dave Scoggan
R. E. Smith
Philip LeVrier
George Peters
John Pell

The opinions expressed in the various articles herein do not necessarily reflect those of the Indianapolis Motor Speedway.

American Auto Racing
Writers and Broadcasters
Association

The Content

The Peeled Eye

By Carl Hungness Editor & Publisher

"I don't think I'll come back here unless it's with a first class operation," the lady said at a meeting of the nation's most respected auto racing writers and broadcasters.

The scene was the annual breakfast given by the American Automobile Racing Writers and Broadcasters Association (AARWBA) and referred to by the membership as Ah-roo-bah. The breakfast is a highly anticipated event held each year the morning before the race. It is usually attended by not only the membership, but many high-ranking Speedway officials, owners, drivers and sponsors. As far as Indy car racing is concerned, there aren't too many important types who don't attend. Consequently, if you are accorded a shot at the microphone, what you say may very well have some impact. Master of ceremonies this year, for example, was Paul Page, Voice of the 500.

The lady who stood before us and told us that she just might not be back unless she was in a first class operation was none other than Janet Guthrie. A couple of years ago she claimed that if she had Al Unser's car and his chief mechanic, she too, could win the race. Thus, cocky little Sherman Armstrong, the car owner from Winchester, Indiana who likes to walk around the Speedway with a grin and a straw hat that says "I'm the Boss" on the brim, promptly went out and bought Unser's car and hired his chief.

Janet made the show and looked like she dropped anchor when Starter Pat Vidan dropped the green flag. Nobody asked her why she didn't win, we all figured she was doing a damn admirable job admist all the heckles and jeers she had to put up with from the red-necked race fans who didn't take too kindly to seeing their male turf invaded. Through it all Janet remained not only a lady but a capable driver as well. And sorry Janet, but we do have to use the word driver, for a racer you're not.

For more than a couple of years now we've stood behind you, next to you, in front of you and witnessed your conversations and your performances. You are definitely a good driver, but then again so are dozens of others who would dearly love a ride like you had at the Speedway this year. You were driving for Lindsey Hopkins, a true example of a fine old Southern Gentlemen who has been entering cars in the 500 for some three decades.

Lindsey and Janet have one thing in common at the Speedway: neither of them have ever won the race. We don't doubt that Lindsey could buy the place if he wanted and run a weekly Saturday night show here if he took a mind to. The only reason we can think of that Lindsey has never won a 500 is because he's too much of a gentleman. There were times throughout his career as a car owner when he could have gone through the process of hiring and firing drivers and mechanics and playing musical chairs. But Lindsey is one of those old timers who honors his word more than he craves a victory. We've never heard him make a threat and he likes to see people do precisely what they want to do.

Back in 1961, for example, his driver Tony Bettenhausen was grabbing headlines every day in *The Indianapolis Star* as being the man to beat. It was a sure bet he would be the first man to top 150 mph in qualifying and seemingly had the pole sewn up, several miles per hour faster than his nearest competitor. It looked like old Lindsey was going to have himself a winner. His operation consisted of a standard Offy-powered roadster with a capable Jack Beckley as mechanic.

The day before qualifying Bettenhausen walked up and said, "Hey boss, Paul Russo is having a hard time with his car... how about if I take a few laps in it for him?"

Lindsey and Beckley allowed as how they'd rather he didn't, but they both knew how much Bettenhausen liked Russo and wanted to help out an old racing pal. They never saw Tony again. They put him in the ground the following week. Somebody forgot to tighten up a steering control bolt on Russo's car. It fell out and Bettenhausen was killed in the ensuing crash.

Now this year, Tony's eldest son Gary came to the Speedway without a ride. He hadn't called up the first car owner and offered him a nickel for a ride. Matter of fact he didn't even call up a car owner and ask for a ride. This is the same Gary Bettenhausen who had the 1972 "500" won hands down until late in the day when the car quit. The same Bettenhausen went to the nation's most prestigious dirt Sprint race the day the Speedway opened and set a new track record. The following week he was blowing their doors off at pavement race.

Finally Sherman Armstrong told him, "Hey GB, you can have this old Offy... it ain't exactly new, but with a little ingenuity you can probably put 'er in the show."

The Armstrong garage is not exactly described as being run by a computer. There are cars on the left, on the right, one or two in pieces up against the wall and the term "Chinese Fire Drill" is usually heard when a passer-by glances in. Bettenhausen blended into the Armstrong scene just fine, called up old Sprint car pal Willie Davis, asked engine wizard Herb Porter for a little advice and by the skin of his teeth slid the four-cylinder in the program.

Here's an interesting parallel Janet: Can you imagine how many car owners would call you up had you set a track record at Terre Haute... and then later led the field at Indianapolis Raceway Park? You wouldn't have to go to New York and drum up a single sponsorship dollar. Roger Penske himself would probably ring you up and offer you a ride. Yet it is his very involvement in Sprint cars that keeps Gary Bettenhausen out of most first-class operations. Penske himself will admit that if Gary weren't a Sprint racer he'd probably still be driving a Penske machine. Bettenhausen isn't even driving a Lindsey Hopkins machine. He was simply lucky to land himself a back-up ride.

(Continued On Page 202)

[6]

Monroe makes this pledge to gain your allegiance.

"If in 60 days you don't agree four Radial-Matic® shock absorbers give you the best ride you ever had, Monroe will replace them, no charge, with any comparably priced shocks."

It's one thing to make a great shock absorber like our new Radial-Matic. But it's a whole different ballgame to back it with a revolutionary pledge like the one above.

You see, we're making this pledge because we're sure our Radial-Matic shocks can give you the most comfortable ride you've ever had. And for good reason. Radial-Matic is the first shock to combine five proven ride control features in a single shock: A one and three-sixteenth inch bore. Nine-sixteenth inch rod. Full displacement piston. Nylon piston skirt. And larger reserve tube. Together they add up to a ride that's so comfortable, you won't believe it until you try it.

A ride that great adds up to a whole lot of customer satisfaction. And that's the reason you owe it to yourself to try a set of Radial-Matics on your car. When you do, we're confident Monroe will have won your allegiance forever.

AMERICA RIDES MONROE®

Monroe Auto Equipment TENNECO
Division of Tenneco Automotive

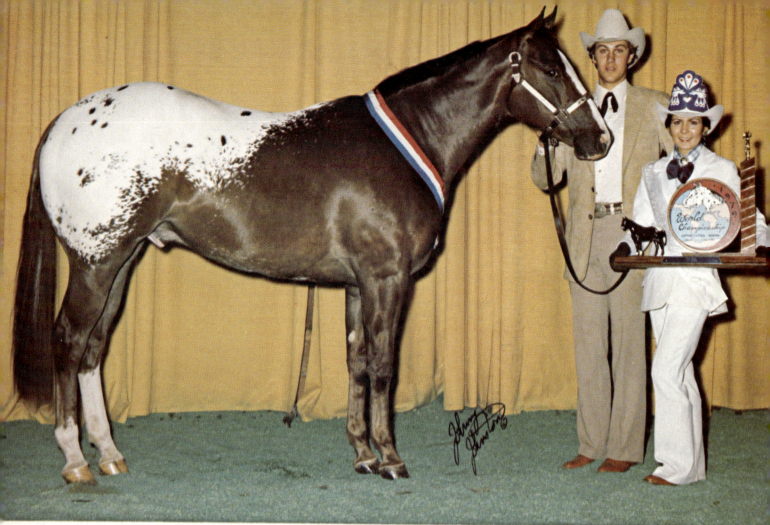

HORSE POWER
"Any Way You Look At It"

Whether it is the Indy 500 or the World Championship Appaloosa Horse Show, the Diamond Head Ranch will always be headed towards the winners circle. Congratulations to Gordon Smiley for your fine job in this year's Indy 500 and for carrying the Diamond Head Ranch colors.

Dave Anderson's
Diamond Head Ranch
1022 Terminal Building
Lincoln, Nebraska 68508

Diamond Head

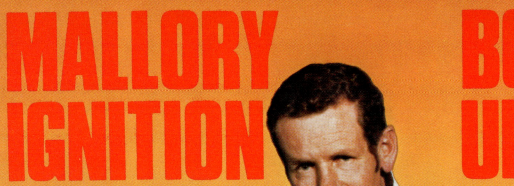

Tim Richmond

Rookie Tim Richmond said it best himself in describing his month of May: "Man, this is great . . . it's more than I ever expected . . . I'm just really very lucky . . . and I want to come back for many, many years." Richmond's first year at Indianapolis was indeed storybook. He hit on a mechanical combination with Chief Mechanic John Barnes that allowed him to be not only the fastest rookie, but one of the fastest drivers all month long. If central casting were to design a young, handsome and aggressive race car driver, Richmond would fill the bill. This year he hitched a ride to victory circle with winner Johnny Rutherford, but we imagine he'll drive there under his own power in the not too distant future.

Loctite. No team goes to Indy without it.

Loctite high perform-
ance adhesives and sealants help
hold cars together. Even at 200
miles an hour.

Loctite products keep nuts and bolts from
shaking loose. And stop leaks in over 100 places
on *your* car. That means lower maintenance costs,
improved safety, more consistent performance.

For more information on how you can use Loctite products to improve
the performance of your car, write to Norm Kirby, Loctite Corp.,
4200 Commerce Court, Lisle,
Illinois 60532.

Available from major automobile
dealers everywhere, and your author-
ized Loctite Industrial Distributor.

Sugaripe

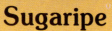

Easy going car owner Jerry O'Connell and his compatible crew didn't have anywhere to go but up at the start of the 1980 "500". They had been relegated to start last after crashing their already qualified car. The crew, and especially driver Tom Sneva became the crowd's darling when he progressed from 33rd to 2nd. We can well imagine that when this team reaches victory lane they'll say, "It's about time . . . and it's sure been fun getting here."

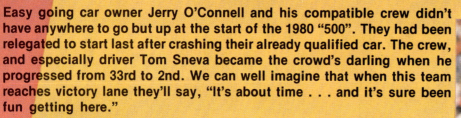

Day-By-Day

Indianapolis 1980: Many Crashes, No Injuries, Lots of Rookies... A Good Year.

Scoggan

Rookie Bill Tempero had the honor of being the first driver on the track.

Editor's Note: Our thanks once again to the many who assist us in compiling our comprehensive day-by-day report. The folks at True Value Hardware who provide an invaluable daily report ably produced by writer Jep Cadou and assistant Sue Jordan are to be commended for their continuing support. The Indianapolis newspapers, STAR and NEWS are used extensively as well as the Indianapolis Motor Speedway's public relations staff.

by Jack Fox

The 1980 Indianapolis 500 pre-race activities started on a much more optimistic note than had those of the previous year. The USAC-CART feud, while not entirely resolved had at least been quieted with the formation of the new Championship Racing League which combined their forces under the overall sanctioning of USAC to supervise a series of championship events for 1980 of which Indianapolis would be the first. (A previously scheduled event at Texas International Raceway was cancelled due to a surprising lack of entries.) If it was to be only a shotgun marriage between the pair the Indianapolis ''honeymoon'' could be indicitive of things to come. The "minister" of these nuptuals was John Cooper, who in the off-season had taken over the IMS presidency from Joe Cloutier. Big John was certainly no newcomer to motor racing nor the Speedway for that matter as he, as NASCAR's Bill France had done years earlier, had been a member of at least one Indy pit crew. (M.A. Walker's car driven in 1953 by Rodger Ward). His love for racing had led him to a number of jobs including one as the first paid member of the newly-formed USAC office staff in 1955. The Hulman-Cloutier management of the past 26 years since the death of Wilbur Shaw, while usually

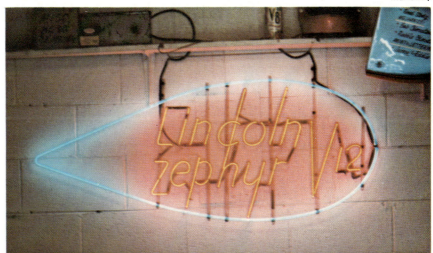

Mahoney

Car owner Bob Olmsted has been an antique car buff for years and he let passers-by know of his interest with this great looking neon sign. We need more like him.

efficient, did not always represent the aggressive leadership which could come from real "racers." Tony Hulman loved the Speedway and in his capacity was a steadying influence on racing in general and Joe tried to carry on the traditions of his boss but somehow you always had the feeling that they were just what they admitted to being . . . very successful wholesale grocers who just happened to own the Speedway. They had purchased it to keep the Hoosier tradition alive but they really intended for Wilbur Shaw to operate it. When Shaw died tragically in

an airplane accident Hulman just sort of slipped into the position of management when no dynamic leader of Shaw's stature and acumen appeared available from within racing. While Tony hadn't originally sought the position and the responsibilities of controlling the "Greatest Race Course in the World" and its attendant responsibilities to motor racing in general he did the best they could while running a multi-million dollar, totally-unrelated, corporation. With Cooper's appointment a "racer" is once again in charge. His suggestions

and leadership may be just the stabilizing influence that the Championship Racing picture needs to win back the fans who were disgusted and disinterested with the name calling, petty ego trips, back biting, and legal battles indulged in by the warring factions of CART and USAC. At any rate this was how things appeared when Chief Steward, Tom Binford, announced at one o'clock on the afternoon of May 3, "THE TRACK IS NOW OPEN FOR PRACTICE!"

SATURDAY, MAY 3
Warm and Clear

Before the track was officially opened there were some ceremonies up by the starting line as well as in downtown Indianapolis. The annual Mayor's Breakfast was the morning kickoff and at noon 500 Festival Queen, Joan Pearson, and her court participated in the trackside opening along with the Speedway president, John Cooper, Mary Hulman, Mari Hulman George, Rick Mears, Howdy Holmes and Indianapolis Mayor William Hudnut III. Johnnie Parsons, driver of the Pontiac Trans-Am pace car joined the gathering as did officials of General Motors' Pontiac Division. This is the 30th anniversary of Johnnie's victory in the rain-shortened 1950 race. His winning car has been restored figured in pre-qualifying and pre-race activities.

If there were only a few of the name drivers on hand it was probably because they were over at Terre Haute's Action Track for the annual Tony Hulman Sprint Classic. Eddie Leavitt was the winner of the televised 40-lap feature with Steve Chassey second and 500 veteran, Pancho Carter, third. On the tube it looked like the track was a bit slick . . . it would benefit greatly from

Chevrolet power made for an extremely clean Gurney entry. With some additional development work we think this might be the wave of the future at Indianapolis.

some lights so night racing could be held as it is almost impossible to build a dirt racing surface which will hold up for a successful afternoon of racing.

Binford had earlier announced that a 170 mph speed limit would be in effect but with a large and classy crop of rookies ready for drivers' tests and refreshers that didn't last long and before the afternoon all restrictions were off and the annual quest for speed and the games of doing head trips on your fellow driver was under way.

First driver on the track, prophetically, was a rookie, Bill Tempero, a big blond lad in his mid-30s from out in Fort Collins, Colorado. His light blue and yellow No. 65 Eagle/Chevy is one of the more attractive cars in Gasoline Alley which last year was plagued of various combinations of red, white and blue cars ad infinitum, ad nauseum. It seems that this year's crop with a few exceptions are a little more colorful and imaginative. Tempero took four laps just to inagurate the month's practice session and then later went out and breezed through the first phase (160 mph) of his test. Before the six o'clock yellow light he had also gone part-way through his second at 170 and up.

Young Tim Richmond from over in Ashland, Ohio didn't disappoint the many railbirds who have been tabbing him as a new superstar. After quickly disposing of his 170+ refresher test he

Badge in center in genuine, but the counterfeiters were out again this year.

The business-like appearing tower is functional, air-conditioned and does all the things it's supposed to do . . . but the old Pagoda sure had more class.

[17]

IMS-McQueeney

Far Right: The gentle clip-clop of the Budweiser Clydesdales brought a welcome sound to the Speedway's pavement.

Right: The beautiful Hall of Fame has been re-arranged to better display the great collection of antique and race cars.

clocked an amazing 186.4 to become the afternoon's fastest mover and gain points for the Rookie-of-the-Year honors. He has a fine ride in the No. 21 Mach I Enterprises Penske/Cosworth, a nice appearing red and white car with yellow and black slashes to set it off. Tim's speed barely beat out Jerry Sneva, one of only two veteran drivers to hit the track. Jerry was in one of Sherman Armstrong's cars but you wouldn't know it from the grandstand. Unlike all of the other AMI cars which are black with orange and white trim, Jerry's is white with black sides and blue trim. It's a Lola/Cosworth.

Howdy Holmes, in another AMI car, a brand new English-built Orbiter II/Cosworth, was out for a few laps but an oil line let go and it was back to the AMI garages (which, incidentally, are adorned with pretty little hanging baskets from which grow light green plants with yellow and black flowers . . . said Armstrong to an admirer "Glad you like 'em . . . some guy gave me $5,000 to put them up).

Other drivers on various stages of their tests and/or shake down cruises were

Spike Gehlhausen (driving other than the family car this year), Bill Alsup, Dennis Firestone and Frank Weiss who was driving an ex-Frank Fiore McLaren/Offy. Fiore sold his San Carlos, California-based team to Buddy Boys of Calgary, Canada who, with his son, Trevor, are regulars on the USAC Midget circuit. Buddy had planned to drive the team car but USAC officials didn't feel he had the necessary experience in Championship equipment and suggested he try another year.

SUNDAY, MAY 4
Warm and Clear

One new change in the operation of practice periods went into effect when it was announced that cars on the track may remain (at reduced speeds) while a car is being towed in. It eliminates the necessity to dodge into the pits every time some minor problem occurs on the course.

Spike Gehlhausen was the "official" speed leader of the afternoon with the

timers catching him at 189.235 on the electric eye although later in the day when the timers were busy checking out rookie tests, George Bignotti's crew's watches clocked their driver, Tom Bagley, at 190.2 in their blue and white No. 70 a Wildcat/Cosworth.

Jerry Sneva got into the 180 bracket with a 182.3 but most of the veterans on the track were posting slower times on shakedown cruises. Among these were Billy Vukovich, Gordon Johncock, Howdy Holmes and Larry Cannon.

Bill Tempero became the first rookie to pass his entire 40-lap driver's test in his stock-block Chevy. Other drivers on the early stages of their tests were Dennis Firestone the 1979 USAC Mini-Indy champion, Herm Johnson, Ron Shuman, one of the hottest Sprint drivers in the game, Pete Halsmer, and Tom Frantz. Tom was on the track quite a bit in 1979 but failed to qualify for the race.

MONDAY, MAY 5
Warm and Sunny

The first driver to go over 190 in the 1980s and the decade's first wall job were noted on this third day of practice.

Johnny Rutherford, who has seen the checkered flag twice, cranked out a 192.472 in Jim Hall's bright yellow Pennzoil Chaparral/Cosworth. Picked as one of the pre-race favorites, if not THE favorite, Rutherford had been out most of the day trading fast runs with the surprising Spike Gehlhausen and his

Query Photos

The parking lot displays a few personalized race fan license plates every year.

Chuck Kopache,
Chief Alignment Technician,
Bear Championship Race Crew,
10 year veteran of the
Bear Indy 500 Race Service Center.

"Whether aligning an Indy 500 race car or a car in Waterloo, Iowa, I use only Bear."

"The Golden Bear Telatronic Alignment System, impressed me so much at Indy that I bought one for my shop.

"It's 100% electronic instrumentation, and performs total alignment.

"I can set the toe once and get it right. The steering wheel is centered the first time.

"With this professional alignment center, I've cut my work time and watched the profits grow.

"Bear means business.
"Put extra profit in your shop with a Golden Bear Telatronic Alignment System. Why don't you contact your Bear jobber, or call me at 319/232-9991."

Wheel Service Equipment
BEAR. ⏻ APPLIED POWER

Automotive Division, Applied Power Inc., P.O. Box 27207, Milwaukee, Wisconsin 53227

#M-9634

"Lone Star J.R." has found a perfect combination with the Chapparal team.

Mount

quick lap came just before the track shut down for the evening.

Both Tim Richmond and Howdy Holmes got into the high 180s but most of the other boys were in or near the 180 mark. Phil Caliva and Herm Johnson finished their driver's tests and Dennis Firestone finished the second phase of his in the dark red Scientific Drilling Controls Penske/Cosworth.

Tony Bettenhausen, son and namesake of the Speedway great who lost his life in a practice session crash in 1961, had the season's first wall-job when he lost it coming off the south chute, made a half spin and slid 240 feet up to the outside wall where he banged the rear of the car and then slid down 380 feet to the inside of the track. The car which was sponsored by Gordon Van Lieu's Vita-Fresh Fruit Juice (an old Speedway sponsor who used to push orange juice in the '60s), was pretty badly wrecked but is possibly repairable.

Tony was getting warmed up for his test which, in the old days would have immediately banished him back to the minors for a year or so, but things are much easier now for the rookies if they have had even a minimum of rear-engined experience. Likewise, the tests are much easier compared to the times when a driver was required to run the forty laps plus or minus one mile an hour of the specified speed and any minor goof-up could register a failure for the aspiring rookie. Of course, you rarely had a rookie who wasn't nationally known applying for a test.

TUESDAY, MAY 6
Hot and Sunny

With 34 cars out of the 59 quartered in Gasoline Alley on the track taking practice runs Johnny Rutherford was again fast for the very warm day with 191.449. As yesterday, his opposition was Spike Gehlhausen who some railbirds are beginning to take seriously after several years of watching him being plagued with mechanical troubles and concrete walls. This year the handsome young Spike has abandoned the family operation and has a fine ride in one of Bob Fletcher's cars. The difference is noticible. Barely nosing out Spike was '79 winner, Rick Mears in one of Roger Penske's Cosworths with 189.7 and Mario Andretti in another Penske was right behind Gehlhausen's 188.758. Mario's car is quite striking in appearance with a red, blue and silver paint job. His speed was 188.6.

Tom Bagley ran 187.3 but most of the others including former winners Bobby

500 Festival Queen Joan Pearson took part in the opening day ceremonies.

Unser, and Gordon Johncock were in the low '80s and A.J. Foyt shook down his Parnelli/Cosworth at somewhere near 175. Al Unser was out taking a check ride in Ron Shuman's No. 78.

Dennis Firestone, who recently passed his rookie test, ran just over 182 which indicates his ability to find some early speed. Janet Guthrie was just a tick over 180 in the white and pink Texaco Lightning/Cosworth, a white job with hot-pink stripes. Rookies Ferguson and Alsup were also slightly over 180.

WEDNESDAY, MAY 7
Cool, Sunny and Windy

The weather began to cool off somewhat but the action on the track was just about as hot as it could get with three drivers crashing in a quest for speed. A breezy day greeted the spectators who, if they came out to see action, were not disappointed.

First and most serious of the accidents occurred just before four o'clock when Frank Weiss, driver and mechanic for Buddy Boys' two entries got low coming out of the northwest turn, spun and skidded 540 feet into the outside wall, hitting the left front of the car, it did a half spin and after getting slightly airborn slid across the track hitting the inside wall. It was a spectacular ride. Frank was pinned in the wreckage until the Hurst rescue tool separated the bent metal so that he could be extracted. After an inspection at the field hospital he was flown downtown to Methodist Hospital by helicopter. It was determined that Weiss had sustained a fractured left knee and fractured right ankle. The car was a total washout.

A half-hour after the Weiss accident Sheldon Kinser got out of shape coming out of the first turn and slid 540 feet in a half spin and clobbered the outside wall with the left side of his Genessee Beer Wagon and then slid 420 feet to the middle of the track. Sheldon wasn't injured and was released after the mandatory trip to the infield hospital for a checkup. The left rear part of the car was a bit battered and when the incident happened the crew deserted the pits causing team driver, Billy Vukovich to inquire as to their whereabouts. Dr. Tom Lucas, now on the Speedway photo staff, quipped "In surgery!"

Dennis Firestone came along a half-hour after Kinser (it was a REALLY hectic two hours) and bent up his dark red Scientific Controlls No. 18. It appeared that he got down on the grass of the infield and committed the blunder of trying to drive the car back on the

track. When the right wheels took hold on the asphalt the car executed a quick right turn and hit the wall with the left side of the car and then slid 65 feet down the track. Firestone wasn't injured, but the car was bent some although with a lot of night work it might be possible to repair it.

Once again Johnny Rutherford was fast for the day with a 191.489 in his

Rookie Frank Wiess removing the traditional rookie stripes.

Indianapolis Mayor Bill Hudnut.

The handsome Parsons, dad and son.

Calm Chief Steward Tom Binford.

[22]

ROGER PENSKE

Roger Penske will surely go down in history as one of Indianapolis' most successful car owners. If an outsider visits the Speedway and wants to see how to "do it right," all they need do is amble by one of the many Penske garages and you'll find a near antiseptic environment filled with glistening hardware. Penske treats racing as a business and his success is evidenced by the length of time he is able to satisfy his sponsors. This year he brought the super-team of Rick Mears, Bobby Unser and Mario Andretti (below) to Indy and each was considered a potential winner.

backup car temporarily numbered 4T although officially it is No. 49. Bobby Unser clocked in next to Rutherford with a creditable 190.034 in the Norton No. 11. Just under the 190 mark was Tom Bagley in No. 70. Tim Richmond, the classy rookie, who is beginning to make the female fans' hearts go pitty-pat was quick with 188.4 just a bit faster than Mario Andretti and Howdy Holmes.

There were 39 cars on the track with Greg Leffler passing his drivers' test and Pete Halsmer still on his. Of the 99 cars entered only 62 have put in an appearance although more are supposed to be en route. Naturally not all of the entries will be here with some 20 being only to secure garage space or cars which might be pressed into service should the primary car be destroyed. While some of the teams do have their backup cars on the track, they have little intention of attempting to qualify. Others might just be unassembled tubs and or assorted parts.

THURSDAY, MAY 8
Cold and Partly Cloudy

It was a good day for Mario Andretti who got in a few very hot laps topped off with a lap of 190.880 to put him right up near Johnny Rutherford as a candidate to win the pole on Saturday. It was a particularly bad day for Gordon Johncock. He got out of control in Pat Patrick's No. 20 coming out of the first turn and executed a half spin into the outside wall hitting with the left side and inflicting extensive damage. The car got slightly airborn and then slid backwards along the wall for over 500 feet.

Johncock was extracated from the car and an air cast was applied to his injured left leg. After a checkup at Dr. Hanna's infield hospital, he was transferred downtown to Methodist Hospital with what was believed to be a hairline fracture of his ankle. It didn't appear to be serious enough to prevent him from making a qualification attempt. The car, however, was another matter and would take a somewhat longer time to heal than Gordy.

Despite Andretti's hot lap, Rutherford was again fastest of the day with 191.898.

HOME ON THE RANGE...

OR RUNNING 200 MPH AT DAYTONA...
A.J. FOYT CHOOSES CRANE CAMS

There's a lot of difference between running 200 mph down the backstretch at Daytona and climbing hills at 40 mph down in South Texas. But four-time Indy winner A. J. Foyt insists on Crane Cams for both!

A. J.'s famous race cars always run up front. That takes horse-power and reliability...the kind A. J. knows he gets from Crane Cams.

Back at his Houston, Texas ranch A. J.'s Crane Gripper HT cam puts more bottom-end torque and mid-range power into his personal Chevy pick-up.

A. J. knows that a Crane Gripper HT cam improves both low-end and driveability, and makes driving across a Texas-sized spread a whole lot more fun...even with today's emissions engines and fuel economy gearing.

Although you can't run side-by-side with A. J. at Daytona, you can find out what a Crane Gripper HT cam can do for your everyday street vehicle, on the highway, or home on the range.

Crane Cams®

P.O. Box 160-17
Hallandale, Fla. 33009
305/457-8888

CRANE LIFTERS BRING OUT THE BEST IN YOUR CRANE CAM!
Ask for Crane Cams' hydraulic or mechanical lifters. They're designed to deliver all the performance designed into your cam.

Snoddy

Query

Tim Richmond

The teeny-boppers (and their big sisters) found themselves a hero in the form of young Tim Richmond. Although he spent a fair amount of time posing with the ladies, Tim managed to communicate well enough with his Chief Mechanic John Barnes to top 193 mph and prove that he's just as much go as he was show. Richmond, along with a healthy crop of other rookies, was definitely a welcome sight at Indy this year.

IMS-McQueeney

Meadows

This was the fourth straight day he won those honors.

Johncock had been running 187 shortly before his wall-banging incident, which was just about the same as A.J. Foyt had clocked in his backup car, No. 14T. Actually as USAC Champion, Foyt rates No. 1 on his car but he has had much more luck with 14 which he now uses as his more or less permanent number leaving the single digit up for grabs.

Although he had no official USAC points Rick Mears put it on his car, possibly on the basis that he was the defending IMS Champ. Plus, Mears is also the champion of the CART series which ran in conflict with the usual USAC Champ series last year.

The 186 bracket had some well-known names in it which included Tom Sneva, Pancho Carter, Tom Bagley and the surprisingly low-profiled Danny Ongais who hasn't made much of a splash speedwise this year. On the track he seems much more conservative without those spectacular bursts of speed and a driving style which reminded some veterans of the late Billy Vukovich. Possibly he has realized that the race is for 500 miles and broken cars or blown engines don't finish so well.

Mears was running an unspectacular (for him at least) 185.5 and Janet Guthrie produced the first speed she has shown car owner Lindsey Hopkins when she finally ran over 184. Al Unser was also slightly over 184 in the No. 5 Dairy Queen Longhorn/Cosworth from Bobby Hillen's stable. His brother, Bobby, was third fast for the day (which was cut short by Johncock's accident) with 189.155.

Pete Halsmer passed his drivers' test and Billy Englehart, who suffered a broken leg attempting to qualify last year, got the OK on his refresher and immediately pushed his Beaudoin Racing No. 29 up to 180.2. This is one of the more unattractive cars on the track with a slightly sick-looking yellow paint job set off by navy blue and white. It's Tom Sneva's car from last year and the crew has plans to paint it soon. Don Whittington, who has run some sporty-car road races also passed a refresher in his No. 96.

ESSEX

At the 500 we see attractive cars annually. But every once in a while a team comes along that simply has the word "Class" written all over it. Roger Penske brought the folks from Essex Petroleum to Indy this year with Mario Andretti as driver and they were definitely the class of the field in the looks department. Mechanical failure put Mario out of the race, but we certainly hope to see Essex back in 1981. Auto racing in general is better by their presence.

Roger Rager

Roger Rager spent a good many years criss-crossing the United States with a Sprint car hitched up out back. And each time he even got close, his thoughts would drift toward the Indianapolis Motor Speedway and someday racing there. He still has the "stand-on-the-gas" attitude that has won him Sprint races from the Banks of Belleville, Kansas to the swampland of Florida. He and his closely-knit crew bolted a Chevrolet engine in an old Indy car and qualified right up there with the best of them. Lots of determination and a little support from pretty wife Gail helped the operation. Nice job.

Mahoney Photos

FRIDAY, MAY 9
Mild and Sunny

Most of the superstars who searched for speed all week finally found it on the day before the opening day of qualifying and some of those who seemed stuck down in the mid-180s broke into the 190s for the first time.

Several years ago 190 wasn't fast enough to raise many eyebrows but with the decrease to turbo-charger boost, 190 is now the barrier which the hot dogs shoot for.

Johnny Rutherford cruised at 193.009 (his fastest of the month). A.J. Foyt got 192.555 and Spike Gehlhausen (not quite of the superstar calibre yet . . . he will have to get some high finishes with

consistency for that) ran 191.939. Rick Mears did 191.737; Mario Andretti 191.652 and Bobby Unser 190.476 to give notice that the Roger Penske team is ready and Danny Ongais finally got up to 190.921 in Teddy Fields' black No. 25.

With a half-hour left before the six o'clock yellow flashed, personable young Tim Richmond went out and blew the other boys out of the box when he cranked on a hot lap of 193.507 which made him the fastest driver of the month and set historians to remembering other red hot rookies like Jim Hurtubise (1961) and Walt Faulkner "The Little Dynamo" (1950) who was aided somewhat by a stuck throttle.

After things shut down for the day the

traditional drawing for opening day qualifying order was held in front of the Tower. Sheldon Kinser whose car was still recuperating from a wall job drew No. 1 spot followed by Rick Mears, "Little Joe" Saldana and Tom Bigelow.

SATURDAY, MAY 10
Cool, Partly Cloudy,
Rain and Hail

The somewhat less than capacity crowd who came out to see the first day of qualifications were greeted by a cool 66 degree morning with the prediction that there might be some showers in the late afternoon. Whether this, the gasoline prices, the general economy or

AMERICAN ENGINE-UITY ™

That's AMS/OIL for you!

Men on the moon, high-speed computers, faster race cars — American ingenuity at its best! When you want the best for your car, rely on products of American ingenuity, AMS/OIL synthetic lubricants.

On or off the track, AMS/OIL synthetic lubricants and performance products help your car, truck, farm and recreational equipment operate at peak performance to last longer, give better fuel efficiency, and lessen our dependence on foreign oil.

That's what we call American engine-uity. That's AMS/OIL for you! AMS/OIL Inc., AMS/OIL Building, Superior, Wisconsin 54880.

the realization that even the fastest qualifying run would be something like 10 mph slower than Tom Sneva's track record held the crowd to something like 125,000 (about half of what the attendance they used to expect).

Qualifying for the 500 has become rather run-of-the-mill in the past few years much like the time trials of any lesser race. Maybe the shortened practice period and, necessarily, shortened ballyhoo time, has lessened the spectators' interest. Of course there are those that just always go to the time trials. Neither gas, lack of speed, or weather will deter them. It's just what they do almost automatically but the marginal fans have to have a little more incentive and any one of the aforementioned factors can keep them home. Also, Indianapolis isn't in the most affluent section of the country and the $5.00 admission can escalate to $25 or $30 depending on how big a family a man has.

Only in the "Snake Pit" do things seem unchanged. The kids (and adults, too) get drunk, play in the mud (if any) smoke their pot (much less openly than do Californians) and yell for well-stacked young ladies (?) to "Show us your T...!" Take it from a "Snake Pit" addict. A trip through this area can liven up an otherwise dull afternoon but such a trip is only for the adventurous and definitely not for the faint of heart.

The pre-qualifying practice period opened right on the stroke of nine and six minutes later the yellow flashed on for the tow-in of car No. 92 driven by John Mahler. A few minutes later it came on again when Janet Guthrie's No. 55 lost a left front wheel coming out of the second turn. The car made no contact nor did it spin. She merely coasted to the inside of the track.

A little after 10:00 the Snake Pit spectators got a big thrill when Tim Richmond looped out coming out of the first turn and slid 600 feet on the short chute before hitting the outside wall. After impact the car slid an additional 375 feet and finally stopped in the middle of the track. Tim, who had just turned a lap at over 190, was checked at the infield hospital and released. Unfortunately the car sustained a bent tub which

Mahoney

The inimitable J.C. Agajanian.

IMS-Schofer

The 500 Festival Parade should be on every race fan's agenda.

Scoggan

Jim Hall spruces up for official front row photo.

Talley

Dirt car owner, Tim DelRose.

IMS-Hunter

Artist Ron Burton and wife Diane.

IMS-McQueeney

Al Sweeney, Donald Davidson and John Cooper.

Scientific Drilling Controls

Columbus, Indiana car owner Jack Rhoades has to be applauded for his efforts in bringing not one, but a pair of Rookies to Indianapolis. Along with the help from the folks at Scientific Drilling Controls, an L.A. based firm, Rhoades' operation looked good. Team manager Max Luther was kept extremely busy as both drivers crashed in practice, but enough midnight oil was burned to get Dennis Firestone's car in the show. Rhoades himself enjoyed the month despite the bent equipment and says, "For sure," when asked if he'll be back next year.

Ouch! Rain is something you expect at Indy in May, but this year there was a hailstorm that was memorable.

is not easily repaired. The accident certainly took the head off any possibility of a rookie repeating Hurtubise's or Faulkner's feats.

Of the unofficial times kept during the practice session Mario Andretti was tops with 191.2 followed by Foyt (190.9) and Richmond. Johnny Rutherford at 187.0 in his backup car was only eighth fast which goes to prove either something or nothing depending how you read it.

Sheldon Kinser didn't take the opportunity to be first out so the honors fell to Rick Mears in Roger Penske's blue and white Gould Charge Penske/ Cosworth. His first lap under Duane Sweeney's green flag was 185.758 but his next three were progressively faster and his fastest was his last (188.838) for an

average of 187.490. While it didn't look good enough for the front row, Mears seemed happy with the speed. With the Pace Car on the track during yellow light periods, a front row starting spot isn't as important as it once was.

The next half-hour was an exercise in futility with Joe Saldana in No. 69; Tom Bigelow, No. 3; Dick Simon, No. 8 all taking their three warmup laps without asking for the green and Howdy Holmes in No. 43 came in after three laps ranging from 177.4 to 184.5. Rookie Dick Ferguson whose mouth got him a lot of bad press last year, tapped the wall on the north short chute on the second lap of his run but still was able to average 182.880 which is about as fast as he had run all month. A lot of people didn't feel

Jim Gilmore, long-time A.J. Foyt sponsor is running for Congress in Michigan. If he's able to meet the voters individually, he's a shoe-in.

What's this? A 1979 photo in the '80 Yearbook? Right, but it's just to show the Ditzler Paint Award winning car owned by Russ Polack.

Grant King

Grant King is one of the most unique individuals in a business that is made up of unique people. He's an around-the-clock racer. For over 20 years Grant has devoted his every waking hour to automobile racing. There was a time when he was a car builder in the Pacific Northwest and dreamed of coming to the 500. Since moving to Indianapolis he has successfully built every type of oval-track racer imaginable and is considered one of the most successful independent race car owner-builders. He has now become an advocate of the stock-block engine and we look forward to seeing many of his creations at the Speedway during the 1980's.

this would be fast enough although Ferguson and his crew on the Aero Electronics Penske/Cosworth a white and red No. 26 believe so.

Jerry Karl took three warmup laps in the Tonco Trailer No. 38 a McLaren/stock-block Chevy and came in and then Danny Ongais blew his engine when on his third warmup. Spike Gehlhausen got an average of 188.344 in Bob Fletcher's red and white No. 35 with one lap at 190.114. It, temporarily at least, gave him the pole although it would take several well-placed miracles to keep him there.

Janet Guthrie in Lindsey Hopkins' Lightning/Cosworth was averaging 184 but Lindsey had instructed the crew to wave off anything less than a 185 average so the yellow came out after the first three laps. Will they be candidates for the "Jigger Sirois Award?"

Al Unser got in the race with a 186.442 in Longhorn Racing's Dairy Queen Longhorn/Cosworth and then the loquatious politician from Illinois, Larry Cannon, settled for a 183.252 in his yellow and blue No. 95 a Wildcat/DGS (similar to an Offy but with certain modifications by Dale Drake, Leo Goossen and Art Sparks, who was in the pits . . . the first two have been deceased for several years). "Boom-Boom got the needle into several local businesses who had turned him down for sponsorship. "Eat your hearts out," was his message.

Tom Sneva became the sixth qualifier with a creditable, if unspectacular, 185.290 in the blue and red No. 9 Phoenix/Cosworth mechaniched by the veteran Jud Phillips and owned by the San Jose, CA trucking tycoon, Jerry O'Connell.

Mario Andretti, former World's Road Racing Champion upped the pole speed

Hard-working Dick Simon is versatile.

Three decades later: 1950 winner Johnny Parsons poses with his winning car and a field full of fine looking Pontiacs. John thoroughly enjoyed himself in May.

Morales crewman Kevin Doran gives Pancho Carter a hand with his helmet.

Mechanic Johnny Capels and Pancho Carter made a strong combination in '80.

to 191.012 in the No. 12 Essex Penske/Cosworth. Essex is a European petroleum company and are noted for their dramatic and high-toned promotional presentations. For a banquet to be given selected members of the racing and media fraternities they are supposedly importing one of France's better-known chefs.

Fifty-two year old Jim McElreath, the Texas-based former Sprint car star who became the oldest driver to ever drive in a 500 last year, was safely in the race with a 186.249 in his own blue, red and white Penske/Cosworth, quite similar in looks to Tom Sneva's car.

A few drops of rain began falling as Johnny Parsons was on the track taking his preliminary warmup laps so the yellow light flashed on and he pulled in until the track was judged raceable as it was in about 15 minutes. Johnny did a fine job in the white No. 15 Lightning owned by Lindsey Hopkins. His speed of 187.412 was especially good considering that the engine was an Offy and the chassis not considered the hot setup. Rick Muther took his three laps in his attractive red, orange and yellow No. 82 but declined the green.

Tom Bagley got Pat Patrick's No. 20 in the race with a 185.405 but declined to

pose for the official photo as since he and Gordon Johncock had switched cars he preferred to wait until his car could be repainted and renumbered. Bagley prefers to race with No. 40 under the yellow and blue of his sponsor, Kent Oil. Johncock, should he qualify, will retain the blue, white and red of North American Van Lines and his traditional No. 20. A very detailed explanation of Bagley's actions were made to the press and public by Patrick's P.R. man.

Jerry Sneva qualified the first of the large Sherman Armstrong team at 187.852. This is the white, black and blue Hugger Beverage Holder No. 7 which with its different paint job looks like the stepchild of the AMI operation.

Salt Walther, who has also been keeping a lower-than-usual profile this year didn't take the flag in his white No.

Cliff Hucul and Jan Sneva chat.

Bill Alsup had a frustrating month.

Mario's sons with their uncle Aldo.

76 (his backup car?) which nowhere seems to carry the Dayton-Walther name. Supposedly it was financed by Salt this year rather than by the family business over in Ohio which hasn't exactly been getting rich with their racing ventures. Salt may be the only driver in Indianapolis competition who has NEVER won a race of any kind in a four-wheeled vehicle.

Johnny Rutherford, prime candidate for the pole position wheeled out his yellow Pennzoil No. 4 while the ever-dramatic Tom Carnegie prepared the fans for what all believed would be the fastest speed of the year. As he finished his first lap and was heading down the backstretch the famous voice (as if from somewhere on High) pronounced the time and speed for the first circuit. "LISTEN TO THIS . . . FOURTY-SIX POINT EIGHT OH! . . . One hundred NINETY-TWO point three oh eight!" The second lap was 192.226 and on the third lap Carnegie again," It's even FASTER!! 46.73 (192.596)." "That the last lap dropped down to 191.898 meant

little. The average was 192.256. Plenty good enough to oust Andretti from the pole. A few years ago it would have been only an average run but as all things are relative the fans were just as excited (or almost) as if he had run over 200 mph.

Of course, there were still at least two drivers still in the line who might go faster but I doubt that many of the fans thought they would.

One of the remaining superstars followed Rutherford. It was Bobby Unser, and his 189.994 would be good enough for the outside of the front row.

If any of the remaining drivers still in line could get a spot in the front row the

John Gordon and Bill Smock, left, helped Jerry Sneva's successful 1980 effort.

Danny Ongais and mechanic Phil Casey had hoped they'd arrive with a Porsche.

best bet was A.J. Foyt but he pulled in after taking one lap on the flag with some undisclosed problem, the most obvious being that he just wasn't going fast enough. Apparently neither was Salt Walther who was back out for the second time in his white No. 76 and came in after three warmup laps.

Pancho Carter made a very consistent run whose four laps varied only .13. His average was 186.480 in the Morales Brothers orange and white No. 10 Penske/Cosworth. The Moraleses are in the Mexican food business out in California and have owned race cars

(most of which were called "Tamale Wagons") since Legion Ascot Speedway was running along about 47 years ago . . . pre-dating J.C. Agajanian's entry into racing by a couple of years.

Roger Rager was next away in perhaps the most authentic stock-block Chevy-engined car in Gasoline Alley. Roger claimed that the block had run some 70,000 in a school bus up in Minnesota. Housed in a Wildcat chassis (an update from his aged Eagle of 1979) Roger had complete confidence in the machine and although his qualifying speed was a phenominal 186.374, he claimed that he still had a lot more throttle. In any case, he soon came up with a manufacturer of school busses as a sponsor. Joe Saldana was averaging in the mid-183's when his crew called him in after three laps and Dick Simon had two laps in the 184's when Rolla Vollstedt displayed the yellow.

Rookie Don Whittington didn't take the green in his yellow No. 94 and as he was the last car in line the track was opened for practice at 3:30.

A few minutes later, John Mahler's car was seen spraying some liquid on the track and the practice session was shut down until Howdy Holmes decided to make an attempt in No. 45, another of the AMI stable. He could do no better than 178.5 in two laps.

After another short practice period under lowering skies, Foyt gave it

"Let's see now...first we make this run..."

Somebody should have hired Krisiloff.

Frank Weiss

Frank Weiss suffered through this grinding practice day crash when he lost control coming out of the fourth turn. Weiss had to be pried from his twisted car, suffering breaks in both legs.

Lane Sequence

Mechanics tied up motel keys, along with a $20 bill and hoped that some female passers-by would provide some companionship later in the evening. No takers found.

Vern Thornburg was on the AMI team.

another shot and had one lap at 186 before some rain drops were felt on the premises and he was temporarily flagged in. The attempt didn't count against "Supertex" and he got back in line until things dried off. By this time the proceedings were being televised on ABC and Tom Carnegie was able to narrate a hailstorm which hit the track at 4:33. "Well, we've had just about everything here today but now IT'S BEGINNING TO HAIL!" Everyone withdrew to shelter until the small pebbles of ice moved elsewhere and then, with one minute remaining before the closing gun the officials determined that the course was open and Foyt again roared away. His average wasn't very impressive — 185.500 — but A.J. didn't seem too upset. At least he was fast enough and early enough to start with the first day qualifiers rather than behind all of them should he have waited until Sunday.

It was announced that Mach I and Roger Penske made a deal for the purchase of a new PC-7 tub to replace the one damaged by Tim Richmond in the morning. It will be trucked out from Reading, PA so that mechanic John

Barnes can start rebuilding the wrecked machine in time for next weekend's time trials.

SUNDAY, MAY 11
Warm and Partly Cloudy

If only about half the expected number of fans were at the track for the Saturday qualifications then only a small percentage of that number came out for the Sunday trials which weren't particularly impressive.

Maybe the most interesting thing to happen was Dana Carter's crash which took place during the morning practice period. He was tooling his Scientific Drilling Controlls No. 19 through the second turn when he got low and spun with the right front of the car clobbering the outside concrete for a distance of 420 feet. After another 180 feet he came to a stop. He was uninjured but the car was a washout.

Only 16 cars took advantage of this practice session including several who had qualified on Saturday. Danny Ongais had the fastest unofficial laps in the 188 bracket followed by Gordy Johncock (in

No. 40T) and Hurley Haywod running 185 and 184 respectively.

Ongais was the first of the group to attempt to qualify and he was successful with an average of 186.606 to become the 17th driver in the race. No one else was ready and practice held forth until 12:42 when Haywood got in three laps, two in the 185's and one in the 183's, which brought out the yellow from his crew. About an hour later Johncock, sore foot and all ran 186.075 in the Kent Oil No. 40 which will switch paint jobs and numbers with his teammate Tom Bagley. George Bignotti will have to petition USAC to switch numbers but undoubtedly his request will be granted despite the fact that neither driver earned USAC points in 1979. At 5:00 Don Whittington took out his No. 96 and ran 183.927 which should put him safely in his first race.

This was to be the last car to make the lineup as Howdy Holmes went out twice in No. 43 but didn't complete either run (only the first was on the flag). John Mahler and Joe Saldana both warmed up but didn't request a flag from Duane Sweeney. With the first weekend history, nineteen cars were in the field and their average speed was 186.752.

MONDAY, MAY 12
Mild and Rainy

There wasn't much activity on the

J.R.'s chief, Steve Roby.

Ferguson's chief, Jerry Eisert.

Engine man Rick Long.

Spike's chief, Derek Mower.

Dawson

Tom Bagley looped his Kent Oil #40 during carb tests.

IMS-Haines

Dana Carter's month ended against the second turn wall.

Gandolf

Howdy Holmes brushed the back straightaway wall in trials.

Margison

Sheldon Kinser skinned his Genesee #24 in the south chute.

Dawson

The third turn wall inflicted moderate damage to Caliva.

IMS-Scott

Jan Sneva crashed in turn two during his rookie test.

Margison

Rick Muther had a good lap going when he spun in quals.

IMS-Householder

Dennis Firestone got into the infield grass, then the wall.

Walker

Tony Bettenhausen crunched during his refresher test.

Capable chief Mike Mullins.

Dr. Harlen Hunter checks out x-ray of Paul Page's old helicopter injury.

Pat Patrick left, and George Bignotti.

track with only eight cars running between the showers which finally closed it down for the day shortly before 3:00.

Already qualified Bobby Unser was fast for the day with 191.002. Mario Andretti, Rick Mears and Spike Gehlhausen also took some laps while the remaining four cars were Midget and Sprint ace, Rich Vogler, in the blue No. 50, an ancient Antares/Offy. Ron Shuman in No. 78, Joe Saldana, No. 69 and Bill Whittington, who completed his refresher test in No. 94.

If there wasn't much action on the track there was perhaps the finest party of the month on tap in the evening with the annual Monroe Rookie Recognition bash down at the plush Columbia Club. A lot of the conversation at the party was centered around the blast that Johnny Parsons had made in the morning press regarding the ability (or lack of same) of his teammate, Janet Guthrie.

While many of the things he said were undoubtedly true, most felt that it wasn't his place to say so in such a manner particularly when they were both driving

A racer crosses the yard of bricks.

for such a respected gentleman as Lindsey Hopkins.

WIFE Sports Editor Paul Scheuring, on his hard-hitting and often controversial sports talk show which concentrates largely on racing during May, made the point that making such statements often tend to "Jinx" a driver as, in truth they had to Ms. Guthrie in 1979 when she ran only a few laps after popping off in '78 that she could win the race if she had the same chassis and engine in which Al Unser had won. Sherman Armstrong got her both (as well as Al's chief mechanic) and then she did absolutely nothing. It remains that even with her big buck sponsorship from Texaco she isn't really a competitive driver (or at least she hasn't proven to be one yet) and never seems to enjoy the best of relations with her various crews. A suggestion for 1981 . . . how about Janet teaming with Salt Walther . . . might be interesting.

TUESDAY, MAY 13
Mild, Partly Cloudy and Windy

Those fans who come out to the Speedway every afternoon to watch the practice sessions had a pretty slow day so far as speed was concerned, but to the rookie drivers attempting to pass their

tests it was a very important afternoon. Officially this was the next to the last day for the tests and it was almost imperative for the runs to at least get started.

Several drivers got their final OK from the officials and the driver-observers who watch the final phase from spots in the turns. By six o'clock Gordon Smiley, Rich Vogler and Ron Shuman were certified as being able to make a qualifying attempt. Vogler, National USAC Midget champion in 1978 is one of this division's most consistant performers. He has won a lot of Midget and Sprint races including a number in Australia and New Zealand. Rich was driving the old Antares/Offy which Eldon Easmussen surprisingly qualified for the 1979 "500." Shuman is an Arizona boy whose most notable victory was in the 1979 Turkey Day Midget Grand Prix at J.C. Agajanian's Ascot Speedway, the oldest and most prestigeous event (dating back to 1934) in Midget Racing. He also is the only driver to have won the "Triple Crown of Outlaw Sprint car racing."

Jerry Sneva at the Art Pollard picnic.

Champion's Jerry Grant is rain ready.

Gordon Johncock

The south end of the track claimed another driver when Gordon Johncock plowed into the wall with his new Wildcat. Gordy suffered a slight fracture of his left ankle.

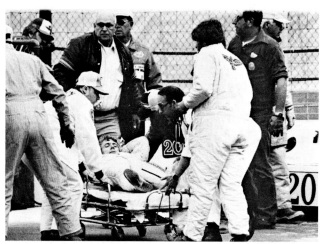

Larson Sequence

Gary Bettenhausen

When the month of May arrived, one of America's most determined race car drivers, Gary Bettenhausen didn't have a ride. Then Sherman Armstrong came through and GB wound up 3rd!

Wife Wavelyn hugs her man.

Clowning at the last row party.

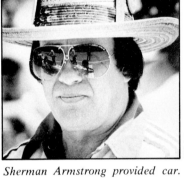

Sherman Armstrong provided car.

Old Sprint pal Willie Davis helped.

Brother Merle shared some joy.

Gary found time to help Tony.

Waiting for the car.

Getting needled by Vukovich.

A talk with old pal Larry Dickson.

[41]

Tim Richmond

A *first* turn practice session crash on the first day of qualifying ended Tim Richmond's "best and worst week of my life." Tim qualified a twin car and went on to Rookie of the Year honors with a ninth place finish.

Margison Sequence

Denny Ebert, in suit, again brought a group of drivers and pretty Susan Lilovich to Riley Hospital to visit the kids.

Bear's Keith Andrews pastes one of his company trademarks on defending champ Rick Mears. Keith is an Indy regular.

Smiley is a road-racer from the SCCA ranks who somehow secured an excellent ride in Pat Patrick's stable and did quite well on his test.

For Jan Sneva, yet another of the famous Washington family of race drivers, and Salt Walther it should have rained. Salt had assigned Jan to his No. 77 and he was familiarizing himself with the car and track when he lost control in the second turn and slid 120 feet down to the infield grass where it slid an additional 100 feet and then went across the track for another 180 feet before it hit the outside wall. The car was too badly wrecked to make repairs practical although Jan wasn't hurt and took a big ribbing from brother, Tom, on the latter's evening TV show.

John Wood, another road racer finished the first phase of his test in the Mergard No. 42, a white and orange machine which hasn't shown much speed in the past few years it has been entered.

Other than the rookie activities, there wasn't much of interest going on. A number of the unqualified drivers cruised in the 170 bracket and Rick Mears and Tom and Jerry Sneva ran in the low 180s. Mears was fast for the day with 185.644.

WEDNESDAY, MAY 14
Mild and Partly Cloudy

If Tom Sneva got the needle into brother Jan the previous evening about his wall-job, it was Jan's turn when Tom ran over something on the track and blew a front tire. Tom's already-qualified No. 9 shot into the wall after a 420 feet slide, skidded along the wall for some 230 feet which ground a number of expensive things off the chassis and then went back across the track to the infield grass for 600 feet. There seemed to be no hope of salvaging the car in time for the race so USAC officials gave Tom his choice of three options: 1) try to repair the car, 2) substitute the team's backup car or another similar machine and start from 33rd spot (a new procedure which was instituted late last year), or 3) withdraw the wrecked car and attempt to qualify the backup car which could start the backup as high in the field as 19th or even higher depending on how many cars from the opening weekend get bumped. Of course if Tom failed to qualify the backup he would sit out the race.

Owner Jerry O'Connell and chief mechanic, Jud Phillips, will have only two or three days to make their weighty decision.

Of those as yet unqualified, Pete Halsmer was fast with 184.0 in the No. 34 Wysard Wildcat/DGS. Engelhart was close with a 183.8 in the Beaudoin No. 29.

The Armstrong Mould Team, which hasn't been graced with particularly consistent runs, finally got all of their cars (at least those which they plan to race) into the 182's. Greg Leffler, Tom Bigelow, Howdy Holmes and Gary Bettenhausen were all just about the same speed with Greg having a slight

Long-time pals Foyt and Snider.

A.J. never misses a chance to rib Bobby.

Getting in the mood, on a Wheel Horse.

Conroy

Tom Sneva

One day after younger brother Jan had a second turn skirmish with the wall, Tom Sneva's right front tire blew, sending him into the south turn wall with terrific force. Tom required a few stitches; the car was given last rites.

Bill Engelhart

Several seasons back, mechanic Danny Jones and Bill Engelhart campaigned a Midget and talked about coming to Indy. This year they made it and you couldn't find a happier pair.

edge with 182.852 in the No. 44 stock-block Chevy.

Herm Johnson, Salt Walther and Sheldon Kinser were others in the low 180's.

THURSDAY, MAY 15
Mild and Partly Cloudy

Tim Richmond had his No. 21 all healed after his brush with the wall last Saturday and after shaking it down he got up to 186.877 which proved that neither he nor the car has lost much speed and should be a cinch to qualify on the coming weekend. Gordon Smiley did even better in running a lap of 187.891 in one of Pat Patrick's cars the numbers of which are too confusing at this point to even try to record. Phil Caliva, one of the few drivers in Speedway history to sport a beard, was the day's only "wall job" when his deep orange No. 47 got away from him in the third turn and spun. He then slid 570 feet and struck the wall with the right front. He was able to keep coasting to the pit entrance despite severe damage to the right front of the car. He had just been clocked at 182.

Tom Sneva and Jerry O'Connell apparently made a deal to replace the wrecked No. 9 in the starting lineup with No. 81 which is owned by Wayne Woodward, the "Bad Boy" of last year's race. The Woodward stable is fresh out of engines while O'Connell is short one chassis. Al Loquasto, whose record for making the starting field hasn't been particularly impressive, supposedly will be given his choice of Woodward's cars for the remainder of the season.

Vern Schuppan had the other O'Connell car out and up to 187. Obviously the reason that O'Connell has opted for the Woodward car is that Schuppan has come complete with his own sponsor (and sponsorship money). Quite possibly, it is cheaper to rent the Woodward car than cancel the sponsorship on Schuppan's car.

Bentley Warren (L) and Sheldon Kinser.

Al Unser was fast for the day in his No. 5 Joe Saldana was fastest of the unqualified cars with 185 in No. 69 and Bill Alsup got a 184.2. Salt Walther ran 183.5 in his remaining car. The AMI cars were in the low 180's with Rich Vogler and Janet Guthrie in the 181's.

Tony Bettenhausen, his wrecked car now rebuilt, and Roger Mears finished refresher tests. Mears was in the Grant King-J.C. Agajanian stock-block Chevy No. 97 a long, low blue job which hasn't seen much track time.

Another car which hasn't been on the track yet but which is having a lot of visitors in its garage is the V12 Volker-powered Olmstead/Eagle. While the car has been entered for a number of years it hasn't made it to the track yet although Olmstead fires the big engine up occasionally for spectators in Gasoline Alley. It has a very attractive paint job on its Eagle chassis with various shades of blue and orange and a flamboyant Eagle design.

Yet another car made a belated appearance in its garage. It was the new machine sponsored by the International Machinists Union and supposedly built completely by union labor. It caused a lot of laughter by arriving two weeks late still not quite ready to race. The assigned

Query
Larson

IMS-Householder

Crafty wrench A.J. Watson.   *The Mears brothers relaxing with their radio controlled cars.*   *Leffler removes his rookie stripes.*

driver is Phil Threshie and it is really a beautiful job painted ivory, red and blue. A stock-block Chevy is under the hood. Maybe non-union labor would have had it to the track on time! It recalled the time when the Joe Hunt Magneto Special retired from the race with mag trouble and the Cop-Si-Loy Brake Special crashed due to brake failure.

FRIDAY, MAY 16
Mild and Rainy

Twenty non-qualified drivers managed to get out on the track during the brief one hour and six minutes the track was open between rainstorms. It was the last times they could get in laps not under qualifying day conditions.

Billy Englehart was the fastest of this group with a lap of 183.9. Spike Gehlhausen was the fastest overall driver in Bob Fletcher's No. 35. Phil Caliva was a surprise practitioner (or is it practicer) in his hastily rebuilt No. 47 which he had wrecked the previous day.

Howdy Holmes will be the first qualifier on the morrow as he was next in line last Sunday. He will be followed by Dick Simon and Caliva.

Shortly after noon, the clouds came in and it started a steady, light rain which caused Tom Binford to suspend operations for the day along about 3:35.

SATURDAY, MAY 17
Mild and Rainy

Not a wheel turned due to the steady rains and had they done so, very few railbirds would have been around to see them. Even the Snake Pit had only a few cars and drunks in it and the grandstands appeared deserted. The few tickets to the trials which were sold were to be honored on Sunday which, weather

permitting, will be the last day of trials.

Should Sunday also be rained out some rather complicated rules to fill the field were announced. Every year there are plans and rumors of how an extension of the trials would be held although it seems this year's seem to be the most fair to all contestants.

SUNDAY, MAY 18
Mild, Partly Cloudy,
Afternoon Rain Showers

With a do-or-die situation because of the improved weather conditions, some 40 cars took the track for the pre-noon practice session. After one of several yellow light periods there were actual traffic jams when large groups of cars tried to get on the track at the same time. It looked like 16th Street a half hour after the checkered flag on race day. There were, however, no serious incidents during this period although a blackbird came out second best in a collision with a race car.

Several cars which have been quartered in Gasoline Alley made their first appearances on the track in the morning practice period although cars coming out this late have practically no chance of qualifying which should have been obvious to the car's owners. The Threshie Union-made No. 30 finally got out but ran only two or three laps before an electrical switch broke (no wonder Datsuns and Toyota's sell so well).

Tom Bigelow was first away from the line when the track was opened for qualifying at noon (wonder why it is traditionally 11:00 on Saturdays and noon on Sundays?). Tom cruised the No. 45 Armstrong Lola/Cosworth at 182.547 and begins to sweat as this is a bit less than the boys were settling for last weekend.

Dick Simon followed Bigelow out and beat him slightly with a 182.788 in his yellow Vollstedt/Offy.

Phil Caliva had his repaired No. 47 out next but was flagged in by officials two laps later when an observer reported that he was spraying some kind of liquid on the track. He was allowed to go back out after a checkup but the best he could do on his run was 178.873 which looked pretty doubtful unless some rain would come along in the late afternoon. Bill Alsup became the second slowest qualifier with 181.919 in his No. 41 Penske/Cosworth and Billy Vukovich seemed content with his 182.741 in Ralph Wilke's No. 2 Watson/Offy, a blue white and red No. 2.

Rick Muther, who hasn't been on the scene for several years, was running a strong 184 when he looped coming out of the first turn on his third lap. He made no contact but he had blown an almost sure chance to make the race. Sheldon Kinser took the checker to record an unspectacular and shaky 181.196 in the Watson car which he had earlier wrecked.

Hurley Haywood the good looking Jacksonville, Florida resident, did a nice job qualifying Lindsey Hopkins white No. 99 at 183.561. It has a Chevy Turbo 6 engine in the Lightning chassis, the first of its kind to ever qualify for the race. Jerry Karl in a McLaren/stock-block Chevy with some years on it, did quite well with an average of 183.011.

John Mahler could go no faster than 177 in the two laps he ran in his No. 92 a Finley/Offy before he was given the yellow.

Tony Bettenhausen accepted a slow 176.410 which only the most optimistic felt would make the race to become the 28th qualifier and then Mike Mosley ran a 183.449 in the Teddy Yip-Dan Gurney

Eagle also with a stock-block Chevy powerplant. It is a big long white noisy machine carrying Dan's traditional No. 48.

Lee Kunzman could do no better than 178 in two laps in one of Gus Hoffman's cars. This was a Lightning/Offy No. 59 which is sponsored by George-the-T-Shirt Man who produces some of the more original and humorous bits of wearing apparel seen around the track.

Another rookie, Pete Halsmer's speed was only 181.351 in the Wysard Wildcat DGS No. 34 but the most publicized rookie, Tim Richmond, lived up to his press notices when he cranked on an average of 188.334 in his rebuilt Penske/Cosworth. The popular driver got in a dig at the Iranians during his post-qualifying interview thus drawing loud applause from the rather sparse crowd.

The third rookie in a row was Herm Johnson, a lanky blond from up in Eau Clair, Wisconsin but he stalled on the backstretch and had to be towed back to the pits.

Salt Walther qualified his remaining car No. 76 at 181.726 but with a number of good cars still in line this looked somewhat shaky.

The classy rookie, Gordon Smiley, filled the starting lineup as he became the 33rd qualifier and signalled the starting of the bumping process. His speed was 186.848 second fast of the day so far.

John Martin, who has only had a few laps on the track this year ousted Tony Bettenhausen from the lineup with a 181.956 although that didn't put him too safely in the race. Martin was driving the red and white Wildcat/DGS No. 37. Roger Mears wasn't fast enough to make the grade as his best lap was only 179.2 and his crew called him in. Roger was in No. 97 sponsored jointly by Guiffre Bros. Cranes and J.C. Agajanian.

Billy Englehart was definitely a qualifier as his speed was 184.237 in No. 29 the Beaudoin/McLaren/Cosworth. This bumped Phil Caliva.

Rookie Bill Whittington eliminated veteran Sheldon Kinser with an average of 183.262 in his Sun Systems No. 94 a Parnelli/Cosworth and Dennis Firestone in the Scientific Drilling No. 18 removed Pete Halsmer with his 183.702.

Howdy Holmes rubbed the wall on the third turn as he was warming up the AMI Orbitor/Cosworth No. 43. This new ground-effects model hasn't proved itself this year and time is running out.

The veteran, George "Ziggy" Snider, did an excellent job in A.J. Foyt's backup No. 16, a Parnelli/Cosworth and his 185.385 bumped Bill Alsup and put John Martin on the "bubble".

Martin's bubble broke seven minutes later when Greg Leffler put the AMI No. 44 in the race with 183.748. This was a fine ride for the Sprint car-oriented driver whose father, Paul, turns the wrenches on all of the Armstrong team cars.

Leffler's ride put his teammate, Gary Bettenhausen next on the bump list but most of the best cars had gone and only a few stragglers remained in line as dark clouds began gathering off to the west.

Bob Harkey could run no faster than 174.5 in the remaining Buddy Boys car, a Rascar/Chevy and Bill Tempero, misunderstanding his instructions, pulled his machine off on the backstretch when he realized he was no where near qualification speed. He had been asked to get off the track in such a situation but he took Tom Binford too literally and his parking necessitated a tow-in which, in fact, wasted more time.

Holmes went out and warmed up again but didn't take the flag. Ron Shuman was getting ready to go out at 4:20 when it started to sprinkle. For a while it looked like Ron would get a shot as the track almost dried off shortly after 5:00 but a sudden downpour came along and watered things down making it impossible to resume qualifying. Shuman was still double parked beside Rick Muther when the closing gun went off promptly at six o'clock. Ron was only somewhat mollified with the presentation of the $2000 AMI (Almost Made It) check for being the next car in line at the gun.

Down the line were two cars, 55 and 55T, assigned to Janet Guthrie both unraceable. Her primary car had a blown engine which happened when Johnny Parsons was test hopping for her in the morning. Had the field not been filled and an extension granted on Monday there might have been time to make the necessary repairs but such was not the case and Ms. Guthrie missed her first race since she came to the Speedway.

The usual garage celebrations and garment-rending lasted on into the evening despite repeated threats over the P.A. system that the gates were to be locked.

One of the last to leave the area was Speedway prexy, John Cooper, who was talking racing over the closed gate with Midget driver Jerry Weeks, Paul Scheuring, Gordon Schroeder, of steering gear fame, and historian, and radio personality Donald Davison, who summed up the qualifying and subsequent starting field as "IT'S NEAT!"

MAY 19 thru MAY 24

This is the traditional tear-down week when, if a car is running poorly, the crew tears it down to see if they can find the trouble and if it is running well they take it apart to see if anything has been forgotten or is showing any signs of undue wear.

Racers both; the Voglers, dad and son.

Sheldon Kinser and his lady Susie.

Open wheel racers, Larry Dickson & Rice.

"Honest Ma, we had a real good time."

It is also a period of stepped-up social activity with such events as the annual roast of a driving celebrity, the State of Indiana dinner, the Oldtimers' Club Barbecue and the Last Row Party. The first annual James McElreath memorial bash out at IRP was well attended and hopefully, the first of many. Most of the big names in racing came out to eat barbecued beef and Lloyd Ruby's chili beans.

For those fans who wanted to see more races there were the CORA Midgets on a weekly Wednesday night schedule out at the Indianapolis Speedrome, certainly one of the cleanest and best-lit racing plants in the country with, unfortunately, a rather non-spectacular virtually flat paved quarter-mile track. (Even the infield is paved . . . the whole area between the walls looks like a parking lot). The Midgets run a combo show with Go-Karts. Sprint car lovers have the Hoosier Sprints at the Indiana State Fairgrounds . . . this year the Friday

night event was rained out by a thunderstorm and downpour during qualifying and was rescheduled for the following Monday. The "Little 500" for Sprint Cars up at Anderson is a traditional event and a real thriller (particularly when 33 cars hit the first turn at the same time on the banked quarter. The almost-annual Night Before the 500 was held again out at Indianapolis Raceway Park to the west of the Speedway in Claremont, Ind. It was won (as it has often been in the past by Mel Kenyon.) There were even some jalopy and junker races in the environs during the week.

There were no surprises during the annual "Carburetion Tests" (or, more accurately, last minute practice period) on Thursday although Tom Bagley got in the wall and bent his No. 40. It wasn't badly damaged and was repaired in time for the race.

The first IMS fatality in some time occurred not on the track but in the Snake Pit where a 19-year-old flipped his Jeep as he swerved to miss a mud puddle. His companion was thrown clear but the roll bar caught the unfortunate driver.

Saturday was the second annual Collectors' get together held at the downtown Howard Johnson's. Collectors show, sell and trade their memorabilia and some of it is quite historic.

Ernie Holden displayed the car (beautifully restored) in which Eddie Sachs almost won the 1961 "500" and Southern California historian, Phil Harms, won the Loctite Award for having the best preserved and oldest collection of racing photos.

As usual, the 500 Festival Parade was held under damp skies through the downtown streets and the "Drivers meeting" took place just before noon in front of the Tower back at the track. This

is the time when just about anyone who asks seems to be granted access to Gasoline Alley and, therefore, a darn good time to avoid that particular area as it's something like Coney Island on the Fourth of July.

The Miller Pit-Stop Contest was finally decided on Friday with Greg Leffler's AMI crew winning the grand prize. Some of the crews with only one entry failed to compete but Sherman Armstrong had THREE of his cars in the contest . . . as if Paul Leffler didn't have enough to do to get them ready for the race. Of the FOUR AMI cars in the race NONE dropped out with mechanical troubles and THREE were running at the finish!

In contrast to last years petty wrangling and lawsuits, this year was very quiet and while the CART and USAC people might not have all been friendly their "Shotgun wedding" worked at least for the Month of May. Controversial Wayne Woodward did get in a minor controversy when Jerry O'Connell decided to let Tom Sneva drive his backup car which remained unqualified by Vern Schuppan. Some sort of settlement was agreed upon by the two owners and the matter quieted down before much was said.

In general it was a quiet, though thrilling month, and for all practical purposes, one of mutual cooperation.

The mini-marathon was popular again.

"Oh Fred, I think it looks dangerous out there."

"Quiet, Mary Lou, I wanna see them girls in halters."

The Race

Yellow Submarine Torpedos '500' Field

Ho Hum, Everyone Said Rutherford Would Win . . . And He Did. But Wow! You Should Have Seen The Race For 2nd & 3rd!

Believe it or not, this photo was taken at midnight by the creative IMS photogs.

IMS

IMS-Francis

It was a hot day, but overall, race fans couldn't have asked for finer circumstances.

by Donald Davidson

This year there was no rain.

Not even a threat of it.

Bare chests, halter tops and cutoffs seemed uniform as a noisy beer-drinking crowd occupied West 16th street from Tibbs to Georgetown Road on the night before the race, leering and yelling at the bumper-to-bumper traffic as it inched along for hour after hour almost until daybreak. The good forecast was great news for the local residents, who could look forward to the following evening when this unruly mob would be gone. Their front yards would once more be their own.

Roger Penske looked decidedly out of place dressed in a white shirt, tie and dark suit as he spent something like thirty minutes motoring eastward from the corner of Georgetown Road to the Speedway Motel just before midnight.

There was a smile on his face. Perhaps he was recalling the trip he made down from Cleveland with his father to watch the 1952 event as a 15-year-old. The 16th Street jam-up was even worse in those days, when the road wasn't as wide and the traffic would start lining up at the main gate the previous afternoon. But helmeted, night stick-carrying policemen have kept everybody moving on until well after midnight in recent years.

When it became light and the main gates opened at 5:00 a.m., the show, for many, was over. Some people had come from as far away as New York just to experience the sometimes awesome spectacle of a beer-drinking crowd that numbers many thousands. But when the gates opened to let people into the race track, they were ready to start their homeward trip, while others hung around to see an additional two or three hundred thousand lug their coolers toward their seats in the stands. Some

actually paid admission and entered the grounds!

The sun was bright as the crowd streamed through the gates, mostly scantily clad in anticipation of a hot day. They streamed and streamed and streamed. The bands played, the celebrities waved, and hundreds upon hundreds of well-dressed people jammed the pit area as holders of pit passes. The cars were rolled onto the straight and the front three or four rows were completely hidden from view as the well-wishers circulated them in search of the drivers. But most of the drivers, as usual, managed to make themselves scarce until the last minute!

At 10:15 a.m., Johnnie Parsons took his 1950-winning Wynn's Friction Proofing Special Kurtis Kraft #1 around the Speedway for a lap of honor in recognition of the 30th anniversary of that victory. Thirty years earlier, Parsons had strolled over from his digs on West

[51]

USAC Official Art Myers checked out everything the crews brought into their pits.

had taken great care to make himself appear as he had in his driving days with the exception of a blue driving uniform which he could not locate. But he wore a Cromwell helmet, and even took the trouble to jam a handkerchief between his teeth as was his race track custom. It was a very satisfying sight.

Once the lap was complete, JP then had to change into civilian clothes prepatory to driving the pace car.

The traditional songs were played, and the traditional emotions they provoke were both voluntarily and involuntarily experienced once again. Mrs. Tony Hulman was able to revert to the traditional command not heard since 1976. Janet Guthrie was not among the 33 starters, and so Mrs. Hulman spoke the words as her late husband had done so many times; "GENTLEMEN, START YOUR ENGINES".

Johnnie Parsons moved the main pace car away with USAC Registrar Bob Cassaday as his passenger. Behind them, forming a vee, were two more Pontiac Trans-Am pace cars. One was driven by Robert C. Stemple, Vice-President of General Motors and General Manager of the Pontiac Division. His wife was his passenger. The other car was driven by Tony George, grandson of Tony Hulman, whose passenger was his mother, Mari Hulman George.

14th street with Jack McGrath on the morning of the race. As they walked across the track through the gate just at the entrance to the first turn, which one is no longer permitted to do, they had glanced over at a plot of land that is now underneath an extension of the tower terrace grandstands. Victory Lane used to be there. They were just two fellows strolling along in a happy bustle of people who had no idea that two prominent race drivers were rubbing elbows with them. Parsons and McGrath looked at the plot of land and agreed that one or the other of them would occupy it later in the day. It was Parsons who did, but much earlier than anticipated, as a downpour of rain had ended the race after 138 laps with John the winner.

Parsons, always the showman, waved happily as he drove his winning car around on this gorgeous morning. He

Hurst's personable Linda Vaughn is always a welcome sight for Indy 500 followers.

1950 winner Johnny Parsons was all smiles.

Bobby Hillin, owner of the Longhorn team had a new car with its problems.

TV star Mike Douglas got his share of applause during race festivities.

"Hee-Haw" star Misty Rowe evoked whistles.

Behind them came the 33 qualifiers, all of whom were underway with no trouble. Johnny Rutherford in the blazing yellow Pennsoil Chaparral had the pole. Mario Andretti, a World Champion since he last raced here, was now in the Essex Penske with its smattering of red trim on navy blue and silver. And Bobby Unser had the Norton Spirit, navy with yellow trim. All of them were former winners. Rutherford was on the pole for the third time. Only Rex Mays and A.J. Foyt had done it as many or more times. Unser was on the front row

for the eighth time, and in the outside spot for the fifth time. It was the 16th time in his 18 starts that he had been amongst the top ten qualifiers. For Andretti, in his 15th start, the only time he had *not* been among the fastest ten was in 1978 when rain had forced him to miss time trials and his car was qualified by Mike Hiss, in eleventh.

There were sentimental favorites further back, but surely the winner *had* to be one of these three as they motored around on the warmup and then the parade lap. Astrological enthusiasts had

noted that all three celebrated a birthday within three weeks of each other, Unser on February 20th, Andretti on February 28th and Rutherford on March 12th, all under the sign of Pisces.

The Stemple and George Trans-Ams came off the track to leave Parsons pacing the race alone. Many of the drivers were waving at the crowd as they passed by the main grandstands on this last lap before the start.

The sky was still dotted with thousands and thousands of balloons released during the singing of "Back Home Again In Indiana", rendered this year by Dr. Richard Smith of the Purdue Glee Club. The balloons had drifted south, which was rather unusual.

A small part of the throng that makes the 500 the world's most famed auto race.

The Hurst ladies dressed up the Pontiac.

Sally Bagley and Steve Kent wire up their favorite man.

Dr. Richard Smith of the Purdue Glee Club sings the traditional "Back Home Again In Indiana."

The sight was as beautiful and as moving as ever as the pace car darted though the fourth turn and headed for the pit lane. The field appeared to approach the starter's stand a little slower than in recent years, and with the cars lined up extremely well.

Duane Sweeney, the veteran starter from Wisconsin who replaced the retired Pat Vidan this year, stood ready with a pair of green flags. Suddenly he frantically waved them both in a contra-rotating motion as the 64th Indianapolis 500 Mile Race was on.

Bobby Unser, as expected, got the jump from the outside, but only just.

Rutherford was accellerating just as quickly as Andretti got squeezed back. Unser was first into the turn but Rutherford quickly overhauled him.

Rutherford came streaming by to complete the first lap with a good half-second lead over Bobby Unser and was the only person to complete the circuit in under 50 seconds. He clicked it off in 49.65 seconds for an average of 181.269 mph, which was almost as fast as some people had qualified! Mario Andretti was another half-second behind Bobby, while Rick Mears had come from the outside of the second row to place fourth. It was the first good start that

Rick had had in his three years in this event, having missed a shift from the outside front row in 1978, and having been overtaken by the rest of the front row in spite of starting on the pole last year. The Penske trio were evenly spaced out behind the Chaparral of Rutherford.

Spike Gehlhausen was fifth across the line, all cars being fairly strung out at this early stage. Pancho Carter had picked up a couple of spots for sixth while Jerry Sneva had taken a conservative start from the middle of row two and was seventh. Johnny Parsons was eighth and had a full second over A.J. Foyt, who was ninth after starting 12th.

WKRP's Les Nessman.

It appears as though the sun tan lotion worked very well.

U.S. hockey team goalie Jim Craig was a crowd favorite.

The 500 is a proving ground more than ever now: Computer inside Longhorn garage.

Tim Reid (Venus Flytrap) of "WKRP in Cincinnati" waves to the fans.

Al Unser was 10th, followed by Roger Rager, Tom Bagley, Jimmy McElreath, Gordon Johncock, Don Whittington, Tim Richmond, Gordon Smiley, Danny Ongais, Mike Mosley and George Snider in 20th. Mosley had picked up seven positions. Whittington, Richmond, and Smiley appeared to have latched onto Johncock for guidance through the pack as the quartet had each advanced three positions.

Dick Ferguson had also taken a conservative start and was 21st from 15th, followed by Larry Cannon, who had dropped from 14th, Greg Leffler, Bill Whittington, Dick Simon, Gary Bettenhausen (26th from 32nd) Hurley Haywood, Tom Sneva (28th from last) Jerry Karl, Bill Engelhart, Billy Vukovich and Tom Bigelow in 32nd. Fully six seconds after Bigelow trailed Dennis Firestone, who had evidently suffered some kind of problem at the start. All 33 cars had completed the first lap, which is something that doesn't happen every year.

Firestone had not long disappeared through the first turn before Rutherford was diving into the mainstraight and heading down to complete his second lap at a 187.5 mph clip. His lead had increased slightly over Unser and Andretti while Mears and the rest had fallen quite a distance back. There were hardly any changes in the order except that Al Unser had dropped two positions, allowing Rager to take tenth with the first of the stock-block powered cars. Johncock was 11th.

Mike Mosley and Larry Cannon were slowing down, which caused another minor shuffle and allowed Gary Bettenhausen to advance three more spots as he also passed Simon.

Firestone had picked up speed but still trailed the field, running about three seconds behind Vukovich, who was off the pace. Mike Mosley rolled into the pits with smoke pouring from the rear end and Larry Cannon was rolling slower and slower across the north chute.

Rutherford had relaxed just slightly to 186 mph for the third lap as the gap widened still further. Bettenhausen passed Ferguson, Leffler, and Bill Whittington to sit 20th, thus picking up 12 spots in three laps!

Larry Cannon rolled through the fourth turn as the officials checked his progress. When he stopped just north off the pits, they were obliged to call for a caution and Duane Sweeney subsequently waved the yellow flag for his first time during a race here. For the second year, the "pack up" rule used at all other races

A kid's delight, and adults smile too at the balloon barrage.

Mrs. Hulman gives traditional "Start Your Engines," command.

Fans
In The
Stands

They Come From Far & Near
To Drink Beer and Cheer

Some Watch The Cars
And Some Watch Each Other

As A Rule They're Well-Behaved
And Patient As A Lot

And Without Them
We'd Have To Say

Indy Wouldn't Have
A Very Memorable Day.

Neatly lined in rows of three, the pace car leads the pack.

Pace lap photo gives you an idea of driver skill, trust.

was in effect and so out went the pace car to pick up Rutherford and slow the field down to a nose-to-tail procession.

They had no sooner closed up, which is usually a two or three lap process, than Cannon's car had been pushed down into his pit. Sweeney flashed the green as Rutherford picked up speed to finish the sixth lap. Parsons beat Jerry Sneva to the line and Bettenhausen picked up another position getting by George Snider. Bill Whittington passed Leffler, and Firestone, thankful for the opportunity

of catching up after his disastrous first lap, was by Vukovich, who is not used to running at the back.

Rutherford returned to the 185 mph range by the completion of the seventh lap and began to rebuild his lead over Bobby Unser and Andretti. But the Penske trio had been split as Spike Gehlhausen, who could walk from turn four to his current home in five minutes, had pushed Mears back to fifth.

Tim Richmond, advancing at a more relaxed pace than many thought he

might, took over 15th place from Don Whittington, and Tom Sneva, also progressing at a cautious rate, picked off Greg Leffler.

Rutherford turned up the wick to vault over 188 on lap eight as the distance between most cars began to widen once more. Gehlhausen built on his fourth place over Mears. Johncock moved to 13th over McElreath and Bill Whittington passed Ferguson for 21st.

The race average, which had dipped to 135 mph during the Cannon tow-in,

Rutherford leads a close running group.

Top: Larry Cannon and Dick Ferguson didn't experience the best of days. Bottom: Spike Gehlhausen, 35 and Jerry Sneva both went quick all month.

The Pits

In the old days you'd drive your car into the garage for an oil change and a grease job and the man would say, "Drive it over the pit."

It was a greasy, rectangular hole in the floor, looked like it would hold two coffins end to end.

Today, the Indy 500 driver pulls into the pits nine or ten times for fuel, tires and sometimes a drink. It's illegal to add oil.

The race can be won or lost in the pits. Only seconds are spent there. Crews never receive enough credit for their work. But without them, the 500 wouldn't be the same.

Greg Leffler leads Gary Bettenhausen. The Armstrong team surprised everyone.

Roger Rager had his day in the sun, he started the 500 in the same row with A.J. Foyt and Jim McElreath. Rager's Chevrolet was very popular.

Rookie Billy Engelhart ahead of J.R.

Veteran Jim McElreath found himself in a compromising situation. No injury tho.

returned to almost 150 as Rutherford reeled off his ninth lap at over 186. Foyt fans did a double take when Roger Rager passed the four-time winner for 9th place. Richmond displaced McElreath from 14th and Bill Whittington passed his second competitor in as many laps as he took 20th from Snider. But Whittington was suddenly in trouble. He spun through the second turn and smashed into the wall as pieces flew everywhere. Snider and Ferguson were right behind him and had no time to make any decisions. Snider slithered through the shrapnel but Ferguson was nailed by the careening car and was hurled out of control. He slid down through the grass in front of the V.I.P. suites on turn two and almost flipped. With the nose pointed towards the suites, Ferguson's car reared up on its left wheels during its lengthy slide, exposing the underpan to people sitting in the second turn vista. Just when it appeared

that the car would dig into the ground and barrel roll, it slammed back down on all fours and slid into the rail.

Turn two was a mess.

The yellow was flashed and the emergency vehicles were rolling before the gyrations were completed, a sight which never fails to amaze visiting officials from overseas. There were many such dignitaries in the suites this year, since there was no scheduling conflict with a European event. They had a bird's eye view of the world's most proficient safety crew at work.

Jimmy McElreath may or may not have intended to make a stop at this early stage. As it was, he ducked in very briefly, took on some fuel and quickly rejoined the pack.

With debris spread all over the second turn, Johnnie Parsons's Pontiac pace car held the lap speeds down to 75 mph. Snider and Tom Sneva both pitted briefly while crews with cars near the

head of the pack decided whether it would be advantageous to make a stop this early or not. Most teams were trying to get at least 25 laps out of a tank of fuel, some striving for 30.

McElreath stopped again for a right rear tire and Dick Simon was in for a left rear, possibly having run over some debris. Dennis Firestone and Gordon Johncock made fuel stops as Parsons continued to pace the field at below 70 mph. The race average at 14 laps had dropped to under 114 mph, which pretty well guaranteed that the late Mark Donohue's 1972 average of almost 163 mph would stand for at least another year.

Ferguson was removed from his battered red, white and blue AMS/OIL #26, but LeMans co-winner Bill Whittington was still trapped in the remains of his yellow #94 Sun Systems Parnelli. Ferguson sustained a broken toe which was to cause him to hobble

Pacific Coast Racing

A young and successful Jack Lang decided to become and Indy car owner in 1980 and quickly assembled enough talent to have a successful team. Capable driver Rick Muther was back on the scene after a several year absence and his long-time friend Mark Stainbrook became team manager. Randy Hunter has worked for several years learning the racing trade and was named Chief. Unfortunately, a broken suspension part caused Rick to spin while qualifying. Lang was happy, however, and says he'll be back in '81 with an even better operation.

IMS-Balistreri

A.J. Foyt and Greg Leffler. A.J. wasn't nearly as competitive as most hoped.

IMS-Sparks

Penske cars Unser and Mears lead Spike early in the race. Bobby was early threat.

around for a few days. But he sportingly attended the Victory Banquet at the Indianapolis Convention Center the following evening, which is more than can be said for several drivers who could quite easily have attended but chose not to come. When Whittington was finally cut from his car and taken to the infield hospital, he was found to have a broken leg, which was to curtail any racing activities for a while. He was flown home to Fort Lauderdale, Florida before 24 hours had elapsed.

Larry Cannon returned to the event during the caution but turned just one more slow lap before being declared out of it with a broken connecting rod. Still pitside was Mike Mosley, who now found himself running 33rd, Cannon's latest lap having nudged Mike back to last for the time being.

Danny Ongais stopped and Sneva was in a second time to make a rear suspension adjustment. The more laps completed, the more feasible it became for the lead cars to make an initial stop. There was still quite a bit of work to be carried out in turn two as the wrecked cars and dislodged pieces were swept up. Lap 15 was when everyone decided that the time had come, and the pit lane looked like a scene from a NASCAR stock car race as the pace car passed by the entrance to the pits and half the field peeled off. Rutherford, both Unsers, Vukovich, Engelhart, Andretti, Gehl-

hausen, Mears, Richmond, Bettenhausen, Carter, Foyt, Jerry Sneva, Bagley, Smiley, Don Whittington, Bigelow, Parsons and Leffler all came in within seconds of each other, with the result that next time around, the race leader became Roger Rager! George Snider was 2nd, Johncock was 3rd and Firestone, who had been 33rd at the end of the first lap and who had already made a stop, was temporarily in 4th!

Rager pitted next time around but was first across the line and so won a second $200 prize, the amount paid for leading each lap. Rager got going again just as the pace car's yellow flashing lights were switched off, indicating that it was ready to leave the track. Duane Sweeney stood poised with the green flag and as he unfurled it, George Snider became the leader, thanks to a 13-second stop by the Foyt crew during all the confusion. Jerry Karl and Hurley Haywood made stops, but Haywood's became too long to be routine. Engelhart, having stalled during his first stop, was back in to change a left rear wheel. Puffs of blue smoke were seen from the exhaust of Karl's machine everytime he backed off for a turn, but evidently it wasn't enough to concern the officials.

Snider couldn't hold Gordon Johncock, whose George Bignotti crew are past masters at getting a car replenished as quickly as possible. Johncock was the leader at 19 laps with Snider second. Tom Sneva was 3rd after starting last! Bobby Unser, Simon, Ongais, Andretti, Rutherford, Mears and Gehlhausen were the first ten at this point. Bobby Unser picked up two positions to run second to Johncock on the 20th lap. Snider and Sneva came next, while Andretti and Rutherford also picked up two spots to run fifth and sixth.

Everyone stood up as clumps of cars

headed for the first turn. One group had three abreast with nobody backing off. There didn't seem to be any way that they would all clear the turn. They didn't. Spike Gehlhausen suddenly found himself grabbing handfuls of steering wheel in order to keep from hitting cars as they attempted to merge into single file. Spike tried to avoid hitting a veteran driver, whom he would not officially identify, and found himself out in the gray stuff leaving turn one. He zig-zagged out to the wall and was unable to keep from hitting it as car after car streamed by on the inside. Spike slithered along the wall to stop without

IMS-Sparks

Gary Bettenhausen, 46, on way to 3rd.

Kincaid

Mahoney

Kincaid

Mahoney

SPEEDWAY LADIES

Mahoney

Meadows

Meadows

Gandolf

Mahoney

Spike Gehlhausen was considered lucky that no one hit him in this crash.

anyone else involved, quickly climbed from the car and stormed unaided down to the infield grass.

What easily could have been a multi-car tangle actually eliminated only one car, but the yellow was out for the third time. Johnnie Parsons and Bob Cassaday had hardly breathed a sign of relief before their services were called upon once again.

Hurley Haywood returned to the race after having been delayed for about seven minutes. And Dennis Firestone had replaced a right front flipper. It was quite obvious, since it was painted blue and the rest of the car was dark red! George Snider went one better and had the entire nose cone changed. It was yellow, which contrasted nicely with his Coyote orange paint job. It even carried a different sponsor, that of Sun Systems! What happened was this. George had ripped the nose cone during the Ferguson and Whittington accident but he had kept on going with slightly impaired handling. Since Bill Whitting-

ton was out of the race, he wasn't going to need the spare nose cone that had thoughtfully been placed in his pit. Both his car and Snider's were Parnellis, which were for the most part interchangeable, so Whittington's crew chief, Graeme "Rabbit" Bartils, a former Foyt employee, thought it would be a nice gesture to offer the spare cone for Snider's use. It made for a striking color scheme and an easy distinguishing feature between George's car and Foyt's. The numbers, of course, were different, and Foyt's helmet was red and white while Snider's was jet black, but this nose job made it easier still, and was quite pleasing to some eyes.

The removal of the Gehlhausen car was executed in remarkably short order

and Johncock was given the green as he finished his 24th lap. Bobby Unser and Tom Sneva were tucked in behind Gordy, Sneva's progress being remarkable in that he had made *two* pit stops already. Unser took advantage of the situation and squeezed around Johncock to lead lap 25. Mears passed Simon for 6th and Parsons took 13th to knock Al Unser back another position. A lap later, Gordon Smiley moved into the top ten, passing Ongais, who wasn't running the kind of race he is used to.

Unser's lead was almost three seconds at 27 laps and Rutherford had taken up the chase, passing both Andretti and Sneva in one lap and almost catching Johncock. Simon had a bad lap and lost three positions, dropping from seventh to tenth, as Carter, Jerry Sneva and Smiley all went by. Ongais continued to run off pace and lost 11th and 12th to Foyt and Parsons respectively.

Rutherford displaced Johncock for second on the 28th lap. Foyt and Parsons passed Simon, while Al Unser, not having much of a day, managed to pass Ongais. Shuffling around continued as there were finally a few green laps run consecutively and without interruption. Rutherford turned a 188 mph lap to get within two seconds of Unser's Norton Spirit. Andretti passed Johncock and Sneva for third. Tim Richmond advanced four spots and was running 12th, and Al Unser lost his position to Ongais. They were having a good tussle, even if ten miles per hour off the pace.

The yellow light flashed on for the fourth time at that point and with 30 laps about to be completed the leaders headed for the pits. Unser, Rutherford,

One way to protect your car from dings.

John and Betty Rutherford take a ride in the third pace car he's won.

BACK ISSUES

1973
Regular . . . . Sold Out
Hardbound 8.95

1974
Regular $5.95
Hardbound 11.95

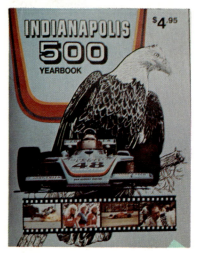

1975
Regular $5.95
Hardbound 11.95

1976
Regular $5.95
Hardbound 11.95

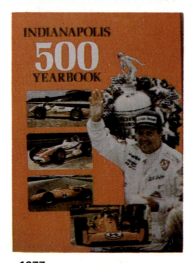

1977
Regular $5.95
Hardbound 11.95

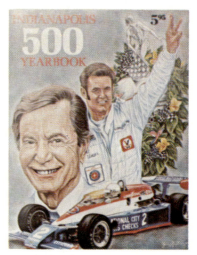

1978
Regular $6.95
Hardbound 12.95

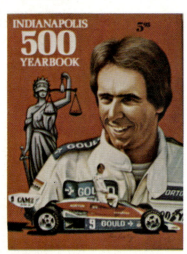

1979
Regular $6.95
Hardbound 12.95

Back issues of each Carl Hungness Indianapolis 500 Yearbook are still available. Supply is short on some years however, and none will ever be re-printed. Order soon.

1981 500 YEARBOOK
Advance Order
Regular $8.95
Hardbound 14.95

Order From:
Carl Hungness Publishing
P.O. Box 24308-Y
Speedway, IN 46224

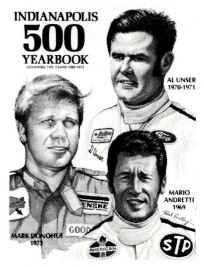

1969 - 1972
Hardbound Only $24.95

Crews giving drivers a last wave before the green drops.

Bobby Unser, No. 11, going around Tim Richmond in the pits.

Andretti and Sneva came in, but Johncock elected to stay on the track. Mears, Smiley, Al Unser, Parsons, and Foyt also stopped during the next few moments. Most stops were for fuel, but Bobby Unser and Sneva had their right wheels changed.

Johncock led the 31st lap as he caught up with the Trans-Am pace car. Pancho Carter had moved to second and Tim Richmond was now third.

The reason for the yellow was a tow-in for Tom Bagley's blue and yellow Kent Oil #40, which had stalled on the track. Teammate Johncock remained on the track, as did Carter and Richmond. Ongais had elevated to fourth and Rager was fifth. Rutherford, B. Unser, Mears and T. Sneva, with pit stops completed, filled sixth through ninth, with Greg Leffler now tenth. Karl, Bigelow, Whittington and Simon rushed off from stops to join the back of the pack as the pace car prepared to come in. Bagley's car had been returned to its pit.

Johncock picked up the pace with the lapped Jimmy McElreath right behind him. Carter, Richmond and Ongais came next and then Rutherford, who beat Rager across the line. Bill Engelhart went back in the race after making his fifth stop. The poor fellow had stalled on his first stop, then flat-spotted a tire in his effort to get away. He had it changed two laps later. He ducked in for a mysterious "check" on his 16th lap, then made two more visits that were unnecessary. He misread a pit board intended for one of the Armstrong team and then picked up another team on the same radio frequency as his, stopping erroneously both times. In spite of all this, the popular Andretti-sized dirt track star was still only a lap down.

Rutherford passed Ongais in pursuit of Richmond. Bobby Unser overtook both Rager and Ongais as racing speed picked up once again. The average speed at 35 laps was 116 mph and had dipped to 103 mph at one point, just before the Whittington/Ferguson accident was cleared up. Evidently Johncock and Carter were attempting to get 28 or 29 laps out of their fuel supply as they had made the early stop during the major accident but none since. Rutherford made it around Richmond and was within a second of Johncock. Mears and Andretti passed Rager and Smiley returned to the top ten once again.

Tom Bagley climbed out of his car after the crew decided that the malfunctioning fuel pump could not be fixed. It was only the second retirement for mechanical reasons, Larry Cannon having left the event shortly after the start. Ferguson, Whittington and Gehlhausen were out because of accidents. Mosley was officially still in the race, although he had only done a couple of laps. The crew were changing a head gasket and had been thrashing for three quarters of an hour with it.

The first "race condition" lead change took place at this point, with Pancho Carter wrestling first position from Johncock. Rutherford, Richmond and Bobby Unser were also flying low and looked like they meant business.

Carter continued to lead on lap 37 but Rutherford and Richmond had both passed Johncock. It took Unser just one more circuit to move up to fourth. Smiley advanced to ninth over Rager. Ongais fell to eighth as Mears and Andretti moved up.

Al Unser returned to the track after a five-minute stop to change plugs, but took only one slow lap and came in again.

Rutherford took the lead away from Carter just in time to lead the 40th lap and complete one-fifth of the event. The average speed was only 121 mph, which meant that no records would be broken unless somebody could run 200 mph for the next couple of hours!

The complete rundown at 100 miles had Rutherford, Carter, Richmond, Bobby Unser, Johncock, Mears,

Always competitive Gordon Johncock leads an anxious pack thru the short chute.

Gentlemen, choose your colors!

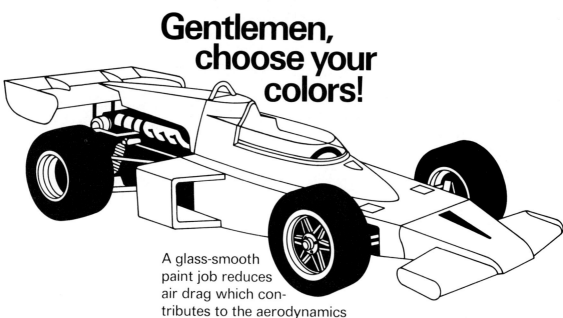

A glass-smooth paint job reduces air drag which contributes to the aerodynamics of an Indianapolis race car. Which is one reason so many entrants this year started with *Ditzler*® paint on their cars. Another reason is a durable deep gloss finish that resists the grueling 500 miles of grit and grime punishment.

And even though you'll never tour the Brickyard with the family car, chances are you've got the same kind of tough finish on your car now. Because PPG Automotive Finishes has supplied the car makers with factory finishes since 1928.

So check with your *Ditzler* Jobber who features the full line of *Ditzler* products the next time your car needs professional refinish work. You're sure to finish a winner!

PPG: a Concern for the Future®

Ditzler Automotive Finishes

PPG
INDUSTRIES

Andretti, Ongais, Smiley, and Tom Sneva as the top ten. Next came Parsons, Rager, Foyt, Jerry Sneva, Karl, Bettenhausen, Leffler, Don Whittington, Bigelow and Simon in 20th. The only other driver in the lead lap was Vukovich, who was about five seconds away from being lapped. McElreath, Snider, Firestone and Engelhart were a lap down. Hurley Haywood was five laps back and Mike Mosley still only had one lap to his credit.

Al Unser was out of the race. The three-time winner was never a factor in this one and he must have had a lot of thoughts about what *might* have been. He had dominated the first half of the 1979 event in the twin to the car that Rutherford was driving in this race. But he didn't see eye to eye with car owner Jim Hall and so the two split at the end of last year. Al turned to an innovation for the third year in a row. He had tried one in 1978 with Hall and had won Indianapolis, Pocono and Ontario in the same year! Last year, in a newer Hall car, he had almost run away with it. This time

Mosley's Chevy didn't last too long.

Dick Simon lost a right front wheel.

he accepted Bobby Hillin's offer to try a new design based on the Frank Williams Formula One car that had won several Grand Prix in the hands of Australian Alan Jones and the Swiss Clay Regazzoni. But since innovations usually take until the second season to work out, nobody could figure why Al Unser would vacate what most people felt would be the winning car of the 1980 race. But his departure was a break for Johnny Rutherford, whose Team McLaren ride of several years had folded because of lack of sponsorship. McLaren had also

The "bunch up rule" under a yellow flag definitely makes leader work harder.

become back markers in Grand Prix competition, and so it was decided to shut down the American operation to concentrate on European racing. The rumors of at least two years became a reality just before Christmas of 1979. It didn't take Hall and Rutherford long to get together, since they had been talking for most of the late summer after Unser had told Hall he was leaving. But Hall didn't want to rob a team of its driver, so he waited for McLaren to close before he would sign the fellow Texan. Ironically, Unser's owner, Bobby Hillin, is from Midland, Texas, which is also Hall's hometown. The two of them had talked about fielding a joint effort at Indianapolis almost five years ago but decided to do it separately, Hillin fielding his first team in 1977.

But Al Unser's gamble with an experiment, futuristic in its approach complete with a computer system hooked up at pit side, had failed, at least for this year. The plainly painted white car with its black numbers was pushed away as Rutherford led the race in the car that Al Unser, but for a personality conflict, would have been driving.

Pancho Carter pitted quickly for fuel on his 42nd lap and Bobby Unser passed the impressive rookie Tim Richmond to take Carter's second spot as Vukovich got lapped. Mears passed Johncock and Smiley passed Ongais as all other moved up a slot with Carter's stop. Rager lost a lap by making a stop under green and Richmond also headed for the pits. Johncock must have cursed his luck. He made a stop for fuel and was no sooner underway than the yellow flicked on!

Johnny Parsons was stalled in the first turn.

That was the sign for wholesale pit stops again, and in they came. Mears and Andretti together, Ongais, Tom Sneva, Smiley (who had climbed to sixth) and McElreath. No sooner had they roared off than the pace car came around having picked up Rutherford, and JR

The "groove" drivers take is clearly outlined in heavy rubber thru the turns.

Whittington-Ferguson

With the race only 10 laps old, Bill Whittington slammed into the south chute wall. Trying to avoid a collision, Dick Ferguson demolished his car against the inside safety fence. Whittington suffered a broken leg while Ferguson escaped with a broken toe.

Margison Sequence

Larson

Margison

Larson

Larson

IMS-Newman

Tom Sneva, No. 9, was tremendous in his 33rd to 2nd drive.

Tom Bagley's day ended in a fashion he hadn't hoped for.

ducked in with Unser right behind him. Jerry Karl found himself third!

The entire Armstrong quartet of Bettenhausen, Jerry Sneva, Leffler and Bigelow stopped on the same lap and were quickly serviced. Foyt and Snider stopped together and so did Whittington and Engelhart.

Andretti assumed the lead on the 47th lap. Pancho Carter was now second under caution, followed by Mears, Johncock, Richmond, Ongais, Unser, a twice lapped Firestone, Tom Sneva, Rutherford and Bettenhausen. Other stoppers at this point included Simon, Haywood, Vukovich and Karl.

Johnny Parsons climbed from his white Lindsey Hopkins entry, ending Lindsey's 30th year of trying to produce an Indianapolis winner. JP's father, who had completed almost as many laps in the pace car as his son had in the Wynn's #15, was partially responsible for the sponsorship. Wynn's sponsored the car which which Johnnie had won the rain-shortened 1950 race and which he had driven for that demonstration lap earlier in the day. A few nights earlier, Wynn's had thrown a 30th anniversary party for Johnnie's friends to talk over the 1950 win. During the course of the pleasant evening, Hopkins and Wynn's representatives had solidified an arrangement to further commemorate the occasion by sponsoring John's offspring. It was a nice gesture.

The green flag was waved once more by Duane Sweeney on the 49th lap and Andretti lapped McElreath for the second time as the pace picked up. Unser and Rutherford beat out Ongais, and Bettenhausen managed to pass Tom Sneva.

A couple of laps later, Richmond and Unser pushed Johncock back to sixth, and a lap later Rutherford caught him as well. At this point, Mike Mosley came rolling out of the pits to complete his second lap! He had been stationary for over an hour.

Thousands of people on the main

straight jumped to their feet at the sight of a blast of white CO_2 clouds as a fire developed in the pits. The car involved was the third Patrick entry, driven by Texas road racer Gordon Smiley, who aspires to Formula One racing. Smiley's first race at Indianapolis was run and seven of ten starting rookies remained.

Rutherford pulled a major accomplishment in squeezing by Bobby Unser, while Ongais found himself being passed by Bettenhausen. Rutherford's surge continued as he took fourth from Richmond a lap later.

Jerry Karl, still puffing miniature plumes of blue smoke at the entrance to the turns, passed Bigelow and started after Don Whittington in 12th.

Rutherford repeated his position-per-

Gary B. dicing with veteran McElreath.

Close competition was order of the day.

lap procedure on the 55th circuit to dispose of Mears. He was now third, but was four and a half seconds shy of Andretti's lead and three and a half seconds behind Carter's second slot.

Gary Bettenhausen climbed to seventh on the 56th lap by passing Johncock just before the yellow came on for the umpteenth time of the day.

It was another accident.

Jimmy McElreath had been struggling with a mishandling machine for some laps. He later complained that it had become very loose. He didn't compensate enough as he left turn two and found himself heading for the wall which he struck. Tom Sneva nipped by on the inside but Roger Rager had an instant decision to make with McElreath right in front of him. Roger veered to the left and found himself out of control. He spun backwards to the infield grass and struck one of the brand new retaining barriers tail first, with enough force to lift the front end high in the air.

Roger angrily extricated himself from the crunched Wildcat and was later quite vocal to the media. He was critical of the officials for placing so much emphasis on the rookies when he felt that the entire starting field should be treated as a whole when preaching caution. He claimed that this accident had been caused by a veteran and not a rookie. On the other side of the coin, there were some drivers and a few respected observers who felt that Roger could have prevented himself from being involved had he followed one of the unwritten codes of the speedway. When you are traveling at a high rate of speed and a car spins directly in front of you, take a deep breath and aim for the spinning car. The theory is that when you get there, it won't be. It doesn't always work out, of course but hind sight shows that, it probably would have on this occasion. McElreath bounced away from the wall after hitting it while Roger was still some 200 yards away. Roger turned to the left in an attempt to squeeze by near the inside

Offer this man $1,500 or a bottle of milk,
and you'd be amazed which one he'd take.

That's Tim Richmond on the left. His 188.334 mph average qualifying speed made him 1980's Fastest Rookie of the Year.

And next to him is Leslie Fishbaugh of the American Dairy Association of Indiana, Inc.

The ADA did a lot to honor Tim. We gave him $1,500 and a plaque. And we engraved his name and qualifying speed on the large ADA trophy, which is on permanent display in the Speedway's Hall of Fame.

But given a choice between all this and a bottle of milk . . . believe it or not, he'd take the milk.

That's because the winner of the Indianapolis 500 always gets a tall, cool bottle of milk in

Victory Lane. It's been a tradition for over 20 years, and this year it went to Johnny Rutherford.

The American Dairy Association of Indiana. We're the ones who honor the Fastest Rookie each year. But somehow, they always want the bottle of milk, instead.

Your Local Indiana Dairy Farmer

Whitlow

grass verge, but the maneuver sent him
spinning into the rail.

Exit two more cars and enter, once
more, the Pontiac pace car.

More drama was about to unfold.

Andretti headed for the pits the
moment he saw the yellow, and this put
Pancho Carter in the lead just as the pace
car was picking him up. Pancho's crew
radioed him to pit on the next lap and
Pancho drew alongside the pace car
through turn one. USAC Registrar Bob
Cassaday was radioed from the tower
that Carter was the leader since Andretti
had stopped, so Parsons and Cassaday
knew they had to pick up the orange and
cream #10 of Carter. Cassaday waved a
couple of cars by as the Pontiac picked
up speed but Cassaday claims he tried to
signal Carter to pull in behind them.
Carter mis-read it to mean that he was to
continue on around. Perhaps he didn't
realize he was leading. Whatever the
reason, it developed into the most
controversial part of the race, and a most
unfortunate one at that. Carter motored
on around the pace car and headed down
the backstretch, hightailing it for the
pits. He made the stop and returned to
the track in fifth place. But the officials
docked him a full lap for illegally passing
the pace car, and that dropped him to
16th.

Mike Mosley was pitted once again,
having been black-flagged for excessive
smoke and possible oiling. He had just
turned a lap of 187 mph, one of the
fastest of the race during his brief blast.

The pits were busy during the next few
minutes as many drivers made stops.
Rutherford and Mears did not, which
elevated them to first and second.

Dick Simon had been in the pits for
about ten laps at this point, which seems
to happen to the poor fellow at some
point during every year's race. The lower
"A" arm had broken and was being
repaired.

Rutherford led at 60 laps under
caution over Mears, Unser, Richmond,
Andretti, Greg Leffler, Ongais, Tom
Sneva, Bigelow and Johncock.

The green was displayed at 62 laps and
Rutherford took off from the Penske trio
of Mears, Unser, and Andretti.

All kinds of swapping around took
place during the next 2½ miles. Unser
passed Mears for second and Richmond
overtook Andretti for fourth. Sneva
moved to seventh over Ongais, while
Bigelow fell from ninth to 12th, and
Bettenhausen picked up two positions to
run 10th.

One more lap found Johncock up from
9th to 7th and Ongais dropping from 8th
to 11th. Bettenhausen moved to ninth
and Jerry Sneva went into the top ten at
Ongais's expense. Greg Leffler's sixth

place was short-lived as Johncock, Tom
Sneva and Bettenhausen each disposed
of him on the 65th lap.

Lap 66 saw Andretti regain fourth
position from Richmond. Jerry Sneva
took ninth from Leffler and their
teammate, Bigelow, moved to within a
second of them as Ongais was relegated
to 12th.

Andretti passed Mears for third and
Sneva dislodged Johncock for sixth on
the 68th lap. Foyt, still in the lead lap,
passed Ongais for 12th, the two of them
much further back than they are used to
running.

Rutherford was running almost 188
when he finished his 70th lap. Bobby
Unser was hanging right with him, but
these two who finished first and second
to each other in 1974 and 1975 were now
almost 12 seconds ahead of third place
after seven laps of green. Mears repassed
Andretti for third and Richmond was
still fifth. Tom Sneva was next, followed
by Johncock, Bettenhausen, Jerry Sneva,
Leffler (in 10th), Bigelow, Foyt, Ongais,

Query

Tim Richmond's crew was new, but very effective all day.

Knox

It was nice to see Wynns back as a Speedway car sponsor.

Left: Hurley Haywood had his share of problems with fire, but no injury.

and Whittington, all of whom were in the lead lap. Carter was 15th, a lap down because of his penalty, Engelhart and Snider being the only others in the same lap with him. Vukovich was way off the pace, running 18th two laps behind, and just ahead of the delayed Dennis Firestone. Hurley Haywood was still plugging along, a constant five laps down since his 16th lap pit problems.

Simon and Mosley were still having their problems worked on, but red-suited Jerry Karl was now a retirement, the clutch on his white Tonco Trailer Company Chevrolet-powered car having given out.

Yet another yellow period came into affect as Mario Andretti, having his best run here in years, slowed to a halt on the track with a siezed engine.

Rutherford, Unser and Mears all streamed into the pits as soon as they came around. The Penske cars both had fresh right side rubber, but Rutherford was dispatched with fuel only.

Several slower cars were in behind the pace car in the meantime. Richmond, a few cars back, actually was the leader as he came across the line on his way to the pits on the next trip. Tom Sneva came up to second and Jerry Sneva was third. Rutherford's excellent stop had him salvaging fourth, while Unser and Mears saved fifth and sixth in spite of the tire changes. Andretti's car was brought back to the pits and the crew looked it over for a short time before pronouncing it out of the race. Mario has had a terrible time of it since winning the World Championship for Lotus in 1978. The 1979 season was a great disappointment and this year has been even worse in Formula One. He had to pass up

Indianapolis last year because of a conflict with the Grand Prix of Monaco, which was a soul-searching decision for him to have to make. He ran well this month and it was nice to see this pleasant man smiling again. But he was not smiling much as the attractive blue, red and silver Essex Penske was pushed away. He grabbed a rag to wipe his face and stared around with his eyebrows arching up with that sad "Why me?" look.

The pace car pulled off and the Sneva brothers were running first and second. Rutherford pulled in behind Jerry and was working on him as they started the 76th lap. Bettenhausen moved up to sixth over Johncock as several drivers had improved their positions by not stopping. Pancho Carter was running just ahead of Tom Sneva to get himself into the same lap and technically would have been leading had it not been for the penalty.

Rutherford took care of Jerry Sneva on lap 76 but found a temporary match in brother Tom at least for the next few laps. Tom led at 80 laps with the average

at over 130 mph but still way off the record. Rutherford was second and Bobby Unser had just passed Jerry Sneva before the 200th mile. Mears, Bettenhausen, Richmond, Johncock, Leffler, Bigelow, Foyt, Whittington and Carter were the remainder of the 13 who had not yet been lapped. Ongais and Snider were a lap in arrears, with Engelhart, Firestone and Vukovich overlapped twice. Haywood, Simon and Mosley were all pit-bound. Haywood now having his gear box worked on.

Carter was driving his tail off to keep ahead of Sneva and Rutherford and stay in the same lap. A yellow at this point would have helped him enormously.

Foyt made up two positions by passing the Armstrong cars of Bigelow and Leffler on consecutive laps. Jerry Sneva gave up fourth to make a stop on the 83rd lap and got going just as the yellow appeared again. This was the one that Pancho had been looking for. He was now permitted to pull away from the Sneva/Rutherford onslaught and close up on the end of the pack. Sneva, Rutherford and Mears aimed straight for

the pits and Unser stayed on the track to take the lead at lap 85.

Pancho lost the lap anyway when he stopped and Unser did not. Richmond

Mears, 1, ran well but didn't challenge.

was Johnny Rutherford.
And so is our 41ˢᵗ.

came up to second and Johncock was third. Sneva and Rutherford were fourth and fifth under the latest yellow.

Don Whittington, who was running 12th and staying in the leader's lap, had spun out of the fourth turn, kept it off the wall and steered down into his pit!

The standings continued to shuffle as just about all of the contestants made their stops. By the time the 90th lap was recorded, things had pretty well sorted themselves out with Unser and Richmond, sans stop, in first and second. Tom Sneva, Rutherford, Mears, Bettenhausen, Leffler, Foyt, Jerry Sneva, Bigelow and Johncock all were on the 80th lap, eleven of them all told. Don Whittington returned to the fray after losing four laps.

Sneva and Rutherford both snookered Richmond on the restart and dropped the rookie to fourth.

Unser ran a 187.5 mph lap on the 92nd circuit but Rutherford turned the fastest lap of the race thus far, 189.195, to pass Sneva. He upped it to 189.514 next time around and Unser's lead dwindled to two seconds. Rutherford's pace backed off just slightly but he was consistently faster than Unser during the next few laps and grew closer and closer. Mears swapped positions with Richmond, and Jerry Sneva knocked Leffler out of eighth. One lap later, Mears was up to third, with Tom Sneva relegated to fourth.

Crews only have precious seconds to check tires: Above is Johncock's mount.

Mahoney

Mears and Andretti were favorites also.

With the halfway mark approaching, Mike Mosley came back onto the track. Last year's third-place finisher hadn't given up yet but was about to. Smoke poured out of the engine compartment, so Mike returned to the pits and that was that. Five laps in one hour and forty-seven minutes.

Final finishing positions could now be applied on an unofficial basis, since Mosley was out. Larry Cannon was 33rd, Mike Mosley 32nd, Dick Ferguson 31st, Bill Whittington 30th, Spike Gehlhausen 29th, Tom Bagley 28th, Al Unser 27th, Johnny Parsons 26th, and Gordon Smiley 25th. Other cars were out, but Dick Simon, who was still in the pits, could still complete a greater distance than had

McElreath, Rager, Karl and Andretti.

Rutherford got to within one second of Unser and then seemed to level off. Bettenhausen passed Richmond to take fifth on the 98th lap. Haywood got back in the race after being absent for nearly half an hour and Don Whittington began a series of pit stops that saw him come in nine times in 23 laps.

Unser was still holding Rutherford at bay with a 185 mph clip as the 100th lap was completed and the half-way point reached. Rutherford, who has been racing against Unser continuously in Championship racing since late 1962, was less than one second behind his rival. Mears was nine seconds behind, in third, with Tom Sneva, Bettenhausen, Richmond, Foyt, Jerry Sneva, Leffler, Johncock and Bigelow still within a lap of

Knox

Ongais, 25 and J. Sneva cross the bricks.

Unser. Carter, Ongais and Snider had been lapped once, Firestone twice, Engelhart and Vukovich three times. The others still in were Whittington, Simon and Haywood.

In the second half of the top ten, Johncock moved Leffler back to 10th and Foyt relieved Jerry Sneva of sixth. Then on the 104th lap, Bobby Unser dived in

for an eight-second fuel stop and was on his way. Mears and Tom Sneva moved to second and third, but Unser, remarkably enough, was able to get going in fourth. Bettenhausen and Richmond both stopped, which juggled the top ten again. Foyt moved to fifth, his best spot of the day so far.

Dick Simon finally got back in the race after a stop of almost an hour. At one point Dick sent an underling running back to the garage area to fetch a certain type of bolt. The poor fellow returned a few minutes later, almost exhausted. Unfortunately, he had brought the wrong thing, so the seemingly tireless Simon ran back himself, reasoning that if you want a job done right . . . etc. The broken "A" arm was repaired and off went Dick to try and salvage some more positions. He made one lap before pitting again, but this was only for a brief check.

Rutherford in the Pennzoil "yellow submarine" continued flogging 185 miles per hour laps with a ten-second lead over Mears. Unser looked in good shape just over 20 seconds back, when he passed Tom Sneva, who had not yet stopped. Unser uncorked a 189.793 on his 109th

deBrier

Rookies Gordon Smiley and Don Whittington.

Spike Gehlhausen

Spike's solid drive with the leaders came to a abrupt halt on lap 21 when things got too crowded in turn one, a disappointing end to his finest month at the Speedway.

IMS-Sparks

Whitlow

Rowe

Jerry Sneva's fine drive ended on lap 131 when he lost control and piled into the first turn cement. Brother Tom #9 slips by on the low side in the first photo.

Jerry Sneva

Tippy Sequence

'The Most Respected Name In Auto Racing'

Automotive Competition At Its Finest . . . .

The United States Auto Club, dedicated since 1956 to providing for its members and fans the very best in Championship, Stock, Dirt Car, Sprint, Midget and Mini-Indy action. The 1979 season will consist of some 100 events, and you can be an informed part of all of them if you'll JOIN NOW!!! The membership fee of $25 will be your ticket to all the races via the USAC NEWS, but that's just one of the advantages to being a part of the finest racing organization anywhere.

Go Racing
With
USAC

❖❖❖

$25 per year

(Special $65 3-year membership
now available)

❖❖❖

SEND TO:

United States Auto Club
4910 W. 16th Street
Speedway, Indiana 46224

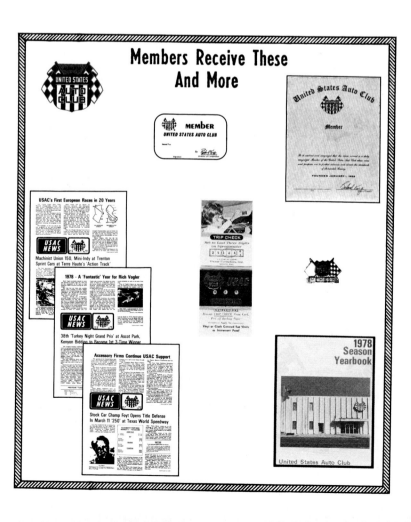

Right: The Jerry O'Connell team came up with bon jour *as a last minute sponsor. Sneva's 33rd to 2nd drive gave them ink.*

lap, faster than Rutherford had gone a short time earlier.

Sneva made for the pits on the 111th lap and Rutherford headed in two laps later. Sneva had right side rubber changed while Rutherford had all but the left front replaced.

Mears came sailing by in the lead, lapping Sneva. Unser moved to second, now eight seconds out of first, and Rutherford found himself 26 seconds back in third. Johncock was the only person in the same lap with them. Sneva and Bettenhausen were able to join them when Mears went in for a 13-second pit stop at 116 laps.

Unser came flying in a lap later, only 13 laps after his previous stop. He got credit for leading the lap but was barely underway before Rutherford went by.

The yellow popped on just as Unser was leaving. Dick Simon's entire right front wheel assembly had come adrift and Simon did a great job of avoiding an accident. He was shortly announced as a retirement and given 22nd place, as he had now traveled a greater distance than Jimmy McElreath, who ended up 24th, and Roger Rager, who was 23rd. Jerry Karl could therefore be given 21st and Mario Andretti 20th, as 19 cars were still in the contest.

Rutherford assumed leadership on lap 118 with Mears second and Unser third. During the yellow there was more excitement in the pits as another cloud of CO2 signalled a fire. This time it was Hurley Haywood's white #99 that had ignited. Fuel splashed over the air vent and flared up on the engine, damaging some ignition wires. Hurley hopped out with a burnt hole on the left buttock of his driving uniform, but the crew quickly went to work to repair the damage.

It took until the 124th lap to clear up the aftermath of Dick Simon's adventure, by which time a number of pit stops had taken place. Rutherford, Mears, Unser, Tom Sneva, Johncock and Bettenhausen occupied the first six positions and were the only ones in the lead lap. Foyt, Jerry Sneva, Richmond, Ongais, Carter and Leffler were one lap down, 7th through 12th. Snider and Bigelow were two laps down, Firestone and Engelhart three down, and Vukovich was four laps behind. Whittington's many recent stops had him 14 laps behind, and Haywood's car, which was

still being worked on, was the only other car still in the race.

Tom Sneva passed Unser and a lap later, Bobby was in the pits again. This was the third time in 22 laps. Bettenhausen and Johncock were hooked together again and Bettenhausen had the best of it this time, moving up to fifth.

Rutherford regained the fast lap honors by raising it to 189.833 on lap 126. Bettenhausen moved to fourth as Bobby Unser was still stationary in the pits. Johncock went to fifth, Foyt to sixth and Richmond to seventh as the two-time former winner sat staring in front of him while mechanics worked on the car.

Hurley Haywood received a round of applause as he buckled in and went out for more. They were to applaud again as Bobby Unser unbuckled and stood up in

the cockpit, through for the day. He climbed from the cockpit and waved to the crowd on the outside of the track, which was a fine gesture. He removed his helmet and head sock, rubbed his head and then waved to the crowd in the area behind his pit. Chris Economaki approached him for an interview on the ABC Wide World of Sports program, to which Unser consented. He also did an interview for the IMS Radio Network, permitting his delightful little chuckle to be heard in both segments. It was a shame that he was one of several drivers who elected to pass up the following evening's Victory Banquet. But it would be interesting to see just how many of the 380,000 people reportedly at the track could have handled the situation as calmly as Unser did. To have raced your

Rutherford's pit stops were rapid and smooth. He couldn't have run a better race.

Two Sprint car racers: Tom Bigelow, No. 43 and Greg Leffler.

Former winners A.J. Foyt and Al Unser weren't contendors.

Chris Economaki interviews a very disgruntled A. J. Foyt.

heart out for almost two and a half hours, have a shot at winning, and be able to smile shortly after that opportunity has been snatched irretrievably away must take a very special breed of person.

The yellow flashed on, amazingly enough, for the tenth time of the day, and it was for another contact with the wall. Jerry Sneva, running eighth and heading for his best finish, lost it through the first turn, directly in front of his brother, and smashed into the wall in the south short chute. The black, white and blue Hugger's Beverage Holder #7 was out as Jerry hopped out unharmed.

Rutherford, Mears and Tom Sneva pitted but Rutherford was able to retain the lead over the other two. Mears took on right side rubber while the other two took fuel only, Sneva taking second place as a result.

Rutherford was first on the 136th lap with Sneva, Mears, Johncock and Bettenhausen running within ten seconds because of the pack-up situation. Carter, directly behind Rutherford on the track, was sixth, a lap behind. Foyt, Ongais, Richmond and Leffler completed the top ten, also a lap down.

The pace car pulled off and Rutherford moved up to 186 mph by the end of 138 laps. Bettenhausen and Johncock swapped fourth and fifth three times in four laps, with Gary getting the advantage on the 140th lap. Rutherford was lapping five mph faster than Sneva during this brief segment and building a six-second lead before the eleventh yellow of the event was displayed as Rutherford completed his 142nd lap.

Rutherford and Mears stopped immediately and both had the same

combination of tire change they had been given earlier, Rutherford having all but the left front changed, Mears, right side only. Rutherford gave up the lead to Sneva but saved second, Mears retaining third as Bettenhausen and Johncock also stopped.

The yellow this time was for Mini-Indy Champion Dennis Firestone, who was stalled on the back stretch. This was the fifth caution period for a stalled car to be towed in, but the crowd still seemed to be accepting the many slowdowns in fine spirit.

The green was given to Tom Sneva on the 146th lap. Ongais and Richmond, a lap down, were directly behind him, followed by Rutherford. Richmond beat Ongais to the line but Rutherford was already on the move. He disposed of Ongais on the 147th lap and in a great move on the 148th took Richmond and Sneva both.

Tim Richmond being dogged by Bettenhausen.

If there were any doubts that Rutherford had the speed to lap the field, he began to display it now, courtesy of the latest tire set-up chosen by crew chief Steve Roby, whom Rutherford brought along when McLaren closed their doors. JR's 149th lap, the fastest of the race, was turned at 190.074 mph, compared with 183 by Sneva. The 150th lap was 187.774, compared to Sneva's 180.7. The result was that Rutherford had built an amazing four-second lead in two laps and was running from the field like a scalded cat.

Hurley Haywood returned to the event after being on the sidelines with a gear box problem that set him back another ten minutes. Another retirement was posted as Dennis Firestone's run was over because of a broken ring and pinion. A rookie no more, the Australian-born Firestone observed a wedding tradition along the way by utilizing something borrowed and something blue in the form of the front flipper, to replace the one that was damaged right after the start. It was also a rookie start for his car owner, Jack Rhoades, a Columbus, Indiana aircraft dealer.

During the next few laps, Rutherford continued to build his lead at about one second per lap as Mears, running slower than Rutherford but faster than Sneva, began to edge closer.

The twelfth appearance of the yellow came as Rutherford was completing his 156th lap, by which time he had built a 13-second lead over Sneva and must have averaged in the range of 187 mph for the nine or ten green laps just completed. Pancho Carter had managed to pass both Ongais and Richmond and was running sixth, directly behind Sneva. Then came

Happiness at Indy is . . .

Mears, who was only one second out of Sneva's second place.

Sneva and Mears pitted, but Rutherford, Johncock and Bettenhausen did not. Sneva and Mears came out of the pits in fourth and fifth as Johncock went to second and Bettenhausen third.

Some debris had been spotted on the track and was removed so quickly that the field hardly had a chance to pack up before the green came out again on lap 159. Rutherford proceeded to do it all over again, and Bettenhausen beat Johncock across the line for second. These two had raced side-by-side almost for the entire race and one had to admire both of them. Johncock had cracked his ankle during practice in a nasty-looking accident that made it hard to believe that he would be racing today. Bettenhausen sustained such severe injuries in a Championship Dirt Car accident in 1974 that he still has practically no use of his left arm. But he was driving like a man possessed on this day, coming from the last row, and doing it in a five-year-old Wildcat that used to be Johncock's regular ride!

The 160 lap, 400 mile mark had Rutherford leading Bettenhausen by two and a half seconds, with Johncock, Mears and Sneva, the rest of the top five, all crossing the line within four seconds. Pancho Carter was sixth, tucked in behind Rutherford, a lap down. Ongais, Richmond, Foyt and Leffler completed the top ten, all being on their 159th circuit. Snider and Bigelow were on their 158th lap, Vukovich was four laps behind in 13th and Engelhart trailed by five laps. Whittington and Haywood, both co-drivers on winning cars at LeMans, were still running, but many laps behind.

Mears passed Johncock on the 161st lap and Sneva was also trying to find a way around the '73 winner. Rutherford had three miles an hour on anybody at this point. Mears was making the second best progress and passed Bettenhausen on the 163rd lap, but was still losing a second a lap to Rutherford. The lead was ten seconds when Bettenhausen gave up third place for a fuel stop on his 168th lap. Johncock and Sneva moved up in the standings, but both had faded to at least a third of a lap back.

Rutherford came in on his 171st lap, took fuel only and was away in 19 seconds, which was, for his crew, a long stop. But they didn't plan to make anymore. They were confident that they could go the remaining 29 laps non-stop, but it was contingent upon squeezing every last drop possible into the 40-gallon tank.

Mears led the 172nd lap with Rutherford trailing by 23 seconds. If there were no more yellows, than Rutherford appeared to be in great shape. Mears had last stopped on his 158th lap and would have to be making a another visit soon. Sneva had advanced to second when Rutherford and also Johncock had stopped.

Rutherford made up three seconds in one lap and was 20 seconds behind Mears at 174 laps, then down to 19 seconds at 175 as A.J. Foyt began a lengthy stop.

Rutherford knocked off another second next time around and was within four seconds of catching Sneva for second when the yellow came on for the 13th time. Just as it was coming on, Hurley Haywood was bailing out of his car near the south end of the pits. It was on fire again. Once again spillage from the overflow vent had splashed down into

Richmond's team was first class effort.

the engine compartment and caused a small fire. Hurley hopped out and began to head on foot the two hundred or so yards back to his north end pit. In the meantime, members of his crew were running southward to meet him before he had walked far. He then went with them to find out what damage had been caused by the latest problem.

The reason for the yellow this time was that A.J. Foyt's car was stalled on turn three and was being towed in.

Mears stayed on the track, but Sneva came in for fuel and right side tires as he had on his previous lap. Mears was still catching up with the pace car when he headed for the pits on the next lap. He took fuel in only ten seconds and scurried off to catch the pack. Bettenhausen made a ten-second fuel visit and Johncock, who had stopped only six laps earlier, was in again.

Rutherford moved up to the lead on the 179th lap, just as the green came out. Sneva had come up to be the very next car in line and so was only a matter of a few feet from the lead. Pancho Carter, a lap behind, was next (but might have been third had it not been for the penalty, although that "might" was strictly speculative), followed by defending winner Mears, who was three seconds back.

Rutherford lapped at 184 mph on his 180th circuit and put one second on Sneva. Mears, Bettenhausen and Johncock were all within eight seconds of leading the race with only 50 miles to go.

Hurley Haywood's crew found more electrical wires burned in the fire, and so his V-6 Chevrolet-powered Sta-On/ Guarantee Auto/KISS 99 Lightning was through. Hurley stood on the pit lane sipping a drink as the burned hole on the left buttock of his uniform reminded one of his eventful day. George Snider's 16th "500" was also over as his crew were unable to refire the stalled engine on his Gilmore Racing Team #16. The orange-suited, black-helmeted George climbed out and the orange Coyote, with yellow Sun Systems nose cone, was pushed away.

Haywood's aborted attempt at leaving the pit actually gave him one lap more than had been completed much earlier by Bobby Unser. Unser could therefore be declared as finishing 19th on an unofficial basis, with Haywood 18th and Jerry Sneva, whose wall smacking incident had occurred three-quarters of an hour before, with enough laps to be ranked 17th. Snider's ranking was still

McElreath-Rager

Struggling with an ill-handling car, Jim McElreath #23 lost control at the south end of the track and bounced off the wall. Roger Rager's evasive action eventually sent him into the inside rail. No injuries.

Margison

Larson

Margison

Margison

Larson

Margison

Margison

Whitlow

Whitlow

Whitlow

[81]

Rick Mears about to challenge Richmond. Mears' car was a beauty, just a tad slow.

uncertain as Don Whittington was still lapping the track at a slower pace and was quite a way back because of a noteworthy 20 pit stops.

The complete rundown at 180 laps had Rutherford, Sneva, Mears, Bettenhausen and Johncock running in the same lap. Richmond was sixth, ahead of Carter and Ongais, with 179 laps. Leffler, two laps down, was ninth, and Bigelow, right behind him, was tenth. Next up was Engelhart, who was four laps behind Bigelow! Vukovich also had 174 laps in. Another lap down was Foyt, who had been in the pits for about five minutes. Whittington was the only other competitor still running.

Rutherford once more opened up his lead, going from two and a half seconds at 181 laps to four seconds at 182, nearly six at 183, seven and a half at 184 and eight seconds at 185.

Meanwhile Mears had stopped under green, only four laps after he had previously been in, and changed right-side tires. He had been four seconds out of first at the time, but once he had returned to speed, both Bettenhausen and Johncock had overtaken him. Rutherford just barely managed to get a lap on him at the start/finish line of the 185th lap. If the yellow were to come out now, there would be no way that Mears could repeat his 1979 win.

A.J. Foyt gave up with engine trouble and stormed angrily down the pit lane from the north end. He stopped to grant an interview over the public address system and vented his anger by making some very unfortunate comments about the mentality of anyone who would enjoy an event such as this. He made reference to the drivers being "a bunch of turtles going 30 miles per hour." No one would argue that the pace was slow, but in spite of the fact that thirteen yellows had bogged it down, the average was still over 140 mph. Even as Foyt spoke, Rutherford was lapping at 188, and earlier had been within four miles per

hour of the race lap record. Foyt later suggested that the team which wins is the one which cheats the most, which was rather a thought-provoking statement from the person who has won more Championship events and more 500 mile Championship races than any other driver in history. Foyt's unfortunate blast over the P.A. did not go down at all well and was met with a lot of booing. A quick check through a set of field glasses at a few thousand faces in the stands indicated that they were thoroughly enjoying their day at the Speedway. An angry and disappointed Foyt stormed back to the garages. But four weeks later he'd be at Pocono, qualify for the front row, and lead much of the first half of the race.

Still the lead built. Nine seconds at 186 laps went to eleven at 187, twelve and a half at 188 and fourteen at 189, as Bettenhausen dropped off at a slighter pace and was only five seconds behind Sneva. Tim Richmond stopped and Pancho Carter climbed to sixth.

Rutherford's lead was almost 15 seconds at 190 laps, which made Sneva's task just about impossible unless something dramatic were to occur. Bettenhausen and Johncock were now 20 seconds behind and Mears was a full lap plus six seconds to the bad. Carter and Ongais trailed Mears, while eighth-place Richmond was three seconds away from being lapped for the second time. Bigelow, Leffler, Engelhart, Vukovich and Whittington were the only others still running.

Lapping relentlessly as if it were the opening laps of the race rather than its waning moments, the yellow Chaparral was consistently four to five miles per hour faster than any car that remained. It was 17 seconds ahead at 193 laps, 18½ at 194 laps and 20 seconds at 195 laps.

Rutherford turned the 196th lap at 187.931 mph, one of the fastest laps of the race, and Sneva was buried by more than 22 seconds. Rutherford was down to

184 on the 197th lap as he lapped Vukovich for the eighth time, but back up to 185 on the 198th. A 180 mph lap by Sneva dropped Tom to 25 seconds, or half a lap, behind. John could lap at 125 mph for the final five miles, if he wished, and still come across the line in first. No such plan was on his mind as thousands of fans wrung their hands in the hopes that this late-race burst of speed would not exhaust his fuel supply.

Johncock was within half a second of Bettenhausen's third place as Rutherford took the white flag going even faster, 188.285 mph. Sneva faded to 28 seconds and was now only three seconds ahead of Bettenhausen and Johncock.

Meanwhile Rutherford had negotiated the second turn of his final lap while waving to the people in the V.I.P. suites. He continued waving down the back stretch, confident that victory was his. Through turn three, across the north chute and through turn four. Duane Sweeney raised the checkered flag high above his head as Tom Bigelow, like himself from Wisconsin, passed beneath. Down the straight with no one else even close came a wildly waving Johnny Rutherford, right elbow raised skyward and fist clenched behind his neck. Over the line he went, winner of the Indianapolis 500 Mile Race for the third time.

Greg Leffler came over, three laps down for 10th, followed by Billy Vukovich, eight laps behind after a three-and-a-half-hour struggle to claim 12th. Don Whittington came across at 30 mph off the pace but with enough laps to put him ahead of Foyt and Snider for 13th. Billy Engelhart, amazingly enough competing in the first Championship event of his long and illustrious career, got credit for his 193rd lap and 11th place. Rick Mears, falling way off the pace in the last couple of laps, salvaged 5th just two seconds ahead of a fast-closing Pancho Carter. One second later, almost half a minute after Rutherford had won the race, came Sneva, who held a near dead heat of Bettenhausen and Johncock at bay by three seconds. Johncock tried the inside route as the yellow flashed on. Bettenhausen, waving in much the same fashion and every bit as excitedly as Rutherford had done, protected 3rd place and completed 200 laps for the first time after a dozen years of competing here. Johncock, one fifth of a second later, took 4th in a race he was not even expected to start in. Right behind Johncock came Danny Ongais,

#35 SPIKE GEHLHAUSEN #26 DICK FERGUSON

Above and below: There's a conservative half a million dollars worth of rubble here. Luckily there were no injuries.

who, because of a lack of power, had driven a very Un-Ongais-like race to take 7th.

The yellow had flashed on as a car had slowed to a halt just north of the pit entrance. It was Tim Richmond, out of fuel just a couple of hundred yards from the finish line. Tom Bigelow was the last person to take the checker and beat Richmond out of a position, climbing from 9th to 8th in those closing yards.

Rutherford did not stop but raced by once more, still waving and demonstrating that the Chaparral had had more than enough fuel with which to complete its task.

John then slowed down as he finished the cool-off lap and finally braked to a halt within a few feet of Richmond's car. Was Rutherford out of fuel now? Would his car have to be pushed to Victory Lane?

It would not. Rutherford was merely beckoning Richmond to come over to his cockpit. Tim leaned over the winning driver and shook his hand. A brief

conversation ensued and Richmond climbed onto the side of the car. John then pulled slowly away and motored down the pit lane, the first winner ever to give a lift to another driver. Such a move

had been seen in some Grand Prix events in the past but no one could recall having seen it here. It was a delightful finishing touch to a thoroughly entertaining motor race, and something that the crowd

Pancho Carter looked like a sure second, but penalized a lap.

Gary Bettenhausen was challenged strongly at the finish line.

roared their approval at witnessing.

Everything had fallen into place for the personable Richmond during the month. He had captured the public's imagination with his fast practice laps and outgoing personality. He had made himself available to the press and public alike during the previous three weeks and was definitely an exciting new star in the making. He had seemed to always be in the right place at the right time, then make the most of an opportunity when it arose. Now this. He was getting a million dollars worth of publicity in riding down to Victory Circle on Johnny Rutherford's

winning car, reclined on the right side but taking care not to steal too much of the scene by consistently pointing at Rutherford and applauding his personal approval. The two had become good friends during the month while housed in garages next to each other on the north side of the Garage Area. Some observers reasoned that Rutherford, at 42, would not be expected to continue racing for many more years, and perhaps is already looking to his post-racing days when the public's attention to him might not be as great. By befriending Richmond, his name would still be mentioned in years to

come when Richmond, if he is successful, is asked to recall some of his early Speedway experiences, drivers who have helped him, etc. The theory is interesting, but whatever the motive, if any, it goes down as one of the "neat" things that have occurred at the track. It was a fine piece of showmanship and goodwill, something that will stick out in the minds of children and adults alike for years to come.

Rutherford braked to a halt at the foot of the checkered ramp to the winner's enclosure where Richmond shook the winning driver's hand once more and then hopped off into the crowd. The car was pushed up into the traditionally happy area of waiting crew, friends and relatives. John raised three fingers as the car was pushed up the ramp, symbolic of the third victory that ranks him with the immortals; Louis Meyer, Wilbur Shaw, Mauri Rose, and Al Unser. Only Foyt has won the race four times.

Photographers virtually own the space above Victory Lane as the flag is thrown.
Below: On his last lap, Rutherford waved to fans all around the track. Nice job.

After embracing members of his family and the 500 Festival Queen, John's quivering hands clutched an ice cold bottle of milk. He closed his eyes as he took a long, steady pull on the refreshing drink. It had been several hours since he had been able to relax and drink anything. A number of different caps were perched on his head for publicity photographs before he gratefully satisfied the hopes of another sponsor by popping the top on a can of Budweiser and taking a couple of lengthy draughts from that as well. Later on, while talking with the media in the press room, John accepted a Pepsi, which led Chris Economaki to speculate that the following morning might find John drinking Pepto Bismal.

An interesting thing happend this year. Nobody seemed to want to go home. Certainly mobility is difficult for an hour or two after the race, but usually one notes long faces on the throng as it

Fans mob the track immediately. *It's not a couch, but looks comfy.* *Some wait for the crowd to disperse.*

trudges away on the homeward journey. This year, with the race thirty minutes over, the stands still held a crowd that would make the promoter at any other event turn backward handsprings. Down behind the stands, all the little accessory buildings had broken open the food, beer and champagne. There was a decided party atmosphere all the way back to the Garage Area, where the feeling was happier than it had been in years. Even those participants who had not had a good day seemed to be serene in acceptance, for the most part.

Tom Sneva looked as fresh as a daisy and as easy-going as ever. You can never tell whether he has won or was the first one out. He is the same fellow whether he is shooting golf, basketball, racquetball or cards. He had just placed second in the Indianapolis 500 for the third time in four years, but there were no clues by looking at him. He was just grinning, thumping his fist into an open palm, and looking as if he was contemplating nine holes before sundown.

There were some long faces around the Penske camp. They had come to win, but had not. There were long faces around the Morales garage. Pancho Carter contended that the hand signal given him from the pace car had been misleading. Some drivers claimed he knew exactly what he was doing and got caught. The sad thing for him was that he might have placed second had it not been for the one-lap penalty. Or he might have tangled with another spinning car and finished much lower than the sixth position he was awarded. Who can know?

The two happiest garages were those of the Chaparral Team and the Sherman Armstrong "D" team of Gary Bettenhausen. Gary was slumped in an aluminum patio chair, red faced, spent, perspiring and grinning from ear to ear. He'd been crying. His mother had been crying. His brother, Merle, had been crying. The late Tony Bettenhausen had started the "500" for the first time in 1946. He had taken 2nd in 1955, but needed quite a number of laps' relief from his good friend Paul Russo. He finally went the distance alone in 1958. That's 12 years. Son Gary had made his

debut in 1968, just seven years after his father had died on the mainstraight at the Speedway. Now Gary had finally gone the full distance in 1980. That also is 12 years.

Three hours after Rutherford had won the race, there were still several hundred people on the grounds, mostly in the Garage Area. They could easily make their way out to West 16th street, which had now returned to normal traffic flows. Trash was ground in and piled up everywhere to be seen, but three enormous road sweepers were already on the job, rumbling up and down the streets and through the parking lots of the fast food outlets, returning things to order.

Local residents were relaxing on their front porches once more, the disappearance of the vast throng of the previous two nights allowing them to return to their otherwise quiet lives in this rural town of Speedway, Indiana.

The lightning bugs were out and the crickets chirping as the sun reached the horizon in a blaze of color.

It had been a good day.

Right and Below: Rutherford at his third victory dinner and posing for the official day after the race photo.

FASTEST RACE LAP

CAR NO.	DRIVER	LAP NO.	SPEED
1	Rick Mears	108	186.722
2	Bill Vukovich	156	174.081
4	Johnny Rutherford	149	190.074
5	Al Unser	26	177.971
7	Jerry Sneva	128	183.411
8	Dick Simon	26	182.076
9	Tom Sneva	78	184.087
10	Pancho Carter	27	186.916
11	Bobby Unser	109	189.793
12	Mario Andretti	8	186.104
14	A.J. Foyt	128	182.778
15	Johnny Parsons	8	183.225
16	George Snider	137	179.354
18	Dennis Firestone	126	181.598
20	Gordon Johncock	195	183.449
21	Tim Richmond	39	184.843
23	Jim McElreath	37	181.196
25	Danny Ongais	194	183.561
26	Dick Ferguson	7	176.609
29	Billy Engelhart	94	183.748
35	Spike Gehlhausen	8	185.147
38	Jerry Karl	51	179.784
40	Tom Bagley	2	179.892
43	Tom Bigelow	159	181.928
44	Greg Leffler	99	180.325
46	Gary Bettenhausen	161	184.124
48	Mike Mosley	4	187.071
66	Roger Rager	8	180.977
70	Gordon Smiley	41	181.050
94	Bill Whittington	7	181.269
95	Larry Cannon	1	147.083
96	Don Whittington	3	178.713
99	Hurley Haywood	104	178.218

PPG CHAMPIONSHIP RACING LEAGUE BOX SCORE -- INDIANAPOLIS, IND. -- MAY 25, 1980

Track: Indianapolis Motor Speedway	Avg. Speed: 142.862 mph	Basic Purse: $1,186,700
Type Track: 2.5-Mile Paved	Time: 3:29:59.56	Lap Prize: $ 50,000
Organizer: John R. Cooper	Distance: 500 Miles	Accessory: $ 265,725
Weather: Sunny	Event No.: 2	TOTAL: $1,502,425
"64th Indianapolis 500"		

FIN. POS.	ST. POS.	DRIVER	CAR NAME/ NUMBER	PTS. WON	MONEY WON	LAPS COMP.	RUNNING/ REASON OUT
1	1	Johnny Rutherford	Pennzoil Chaparral (4)	1000	$318,020	200	Running
2	33	Tom Sneva	Bon Jour Action Jeans (9)	800	$128,945	200	Running
3	32	Gary Bettenhausen	Armstrong Mould (46)	700	$ 86,945	200	Running
4	17	Gordon Johncock	N. American Van Lines (20)	600	$ 56,495	200	Running
5	6	Rick Mears	Gould Charge (1)	500	$ 45,505	199	Running
6	8	Pancho Carter	Alex XLNT Foods (10)	400	$ 39,175	199*	Running
7	16	Danny Ongais	Interscope/Panasonic (25)	300	$ 37,414	199	Running
8	31	Tom Bigelow	Armstrong/Jiffy Mix (43)	250	$ 44,707	198	Running
9	19	Tim Richmond	Uno Q95 Starcruiser (21)	200	$ 43,447	197	Out of fuel
10	23	Greg Leffler	Starcraft R.V. (44)	150	$ 39,047	197	Running
11	22	Bill Engelhart	Master Lock (29)	100	$ 32,303	193	Running
12	30	Bill Vukovich	Hubler Chevrolet/WFMS (2)	50	$ 31,087	192	Running
13	18	Don Whittington	Sun System (96)	25	$ 30,928	178	Running
14	12	A.J. Foyt	Gilmore Racing Team (14)	25	$ 29,512	173	Valve
15	21	George Snider	Gilmore Racing Team (16)	25	$ 30,351	169	Engine
16	24	Dennis Firestone	Scientific Drilling Cont.(18)	25	$ 28,776	137	Transmission
17	5	Jerry Sneva	Hugger's Beverage Holders (7)	20	$ 30,271	130	Accident
18	25	Hurley Haywood	Guarantee/Sta-On/Kiss 99 (99)	20	$ 28,273	127	Turbocharger
19	3	Bobby Unser	Norton Spirit (11)	20	$ 37,432	126	Ignition coil
20	2	Mario Andretti	Essex (12)	20	$ 33,611	71	Engine
21	28	Jerry Karl	Tonco Trailer (38)	15	$ 26,747	64	Clutch
22	29	Dick Simon	Vt.Amer./Silhouette/Regal 8(8)	15	$ 26,411	58	Lost wheel
23	10	Roger Rager	Advance/Carpenter (66)	15	$ 26,503	55	Accident
24	11	Jim McElreath	McElreath (23)	15	$ 26,323	54	Accident
25	20	Gordon Smiley	Valvoline/D'Head Ranch (70)	10	$ 26,771	47	Turbocharger
26	7	Johnny Parsons	Wynn's (15)	10	$ 25,597	44	Piston
27	9	Al Unser	Longhorn Racing (5)	10	$ 25,151	33	Cylinder
28	13	Tom Bagley	Kent Oil (40)	10	$ 25,983	29	Pump drive
29	4	Spike Gehlhausen	Winton Sales (35)	5	$ 26,143	20	Accident
30	27	Bill Whittington	Sun System (94)	5	$ 24,360	9	Accident
31	15	Dick Ferguson	AMS/OIL (26)	5	$ 26,647	9	Accident
32	26	Mike Mosley	Theodore Racing (48)	5	$ 24,591	5	Gasket
33	14	Larry Cannon	KRACO Car Stereos (95)	5	$ 25,063	2	Camshaft

FAST QUALIFIER: Johnny Rutherford (No. 4)–3:07.25–192.256 mph (4-lap average).

LAP LEADERS: Laps 1–15, Rutherford; Laps 16-17, Rager; Lap 18, Snider; Laps 19–24, Johncock; Laps 25–30, B.Unser; Laps 31–35, Johncock; Laps 36–39, Carter; Laps 40–46, Rutherford; Laps 47–56, Andretti; Lap 57, Carter; Laps 58–72, Rutherford; Laps 73, Richmond; Laps 74–84, T.Sneva; Laps 85–103, B.Unser; Laps 104–113, Rutherford; Laps 114–116, Mears; Lap 117, B.Unser; Laps 118–142, Rutherford; Laps 143–147, T.Sneva; Laps 148–171, Rutherford; Laps 172–178, Mears; Laps 179–200, Rutherford.

YELLOW FLAGS: Laps 4–6, Cannon stalled in turn 1; Laps 10–18, Ferguson-B.Whittington accident in turn 2; Laps 21–24, Gehlhausen accident in turn 1; Laps 30–33, Bagley stalled on backstretch; Laps 45–49, Parsons stalled in turn 1; Laps 57–62, Rager-McElreath accident in south chute; Laps 72–75, Andretti stalled on backstretch; Laps 85–90, D.Whittington spun in turn 4; Laps 118–124, Simon lost R.F. wheel; Laps 132–137, J.Sneva accident in turn 1; Laps 142–146, Firestone stalled on backstretch; Laps 157–159, debris on track in turn 4; Laps 177–179, Foyt stalled in turn 3.

* Car No. 10 penalized 1 lap for passing pace car during yellow flag period.

Spin & Wreck Report

Monday, May 5, 1980 — 2:24 p.m.
Tony Bettenhausen in the #32 Vita-Fresh Fruit Juice Eagle/Offy lost control coming off the short chute into the southeast (#2) turn. Describing a half spin, the car slid 240 feet, hit the outside wall with the left rear, then slid 380 feet to the inside. Car suffered extensive damage to left rear. Driver okay.

Wednesday, May 7, 1980 — 3:53 p.m.
Frank Weiss in the #68 Canadian II McLaren/Offy lost control coming through Turn 4 (Northwest), did one complete spin, sliding 540 feet, hit outside retaining wall with the left front, described a half spin off the wall, slid another 150 feet, got slightly airbourne, slid 300 feet across the track and stopped against the inside wall. The car was extensively damaged. The driver had to be freed with aid of the Hurst rescue tool and was taken to Methodist Hospital with a fractured left knee and fractured right ankle. He remained conscious throughout.

Wednesday, May 7, 1980 — 4:33 p.m.
Sheldon Kinser in the #24 Genesee Beer Wagon Watson/Cosworth lost control coming off Turn 1 (Southwest), slid 540 feet, executed a half spin, hit the wall with the left rear, slid another 420 feet to the center of the track. Car received moderate damage to left rear. Driver okay.

Wednesday, May 7, 1980 — 5:12 p.m.
Rookie Dennis Firestone in the #18 Scientific Drilling Controls Penske/Cosworth got into the edge of the infield grass in Turn 2 (Southeast), did a half spin, hit the wall with the left side, then slid an additional 65 feet. Car extensively damaged. Driver okay.

Thursday, May 8, 1980 — 5:34 p.m.
Gordon Johncock in the #20 North American Van Lines Wildcat/Cosworth lost control coming off the Southwest (#1) corner, did a half spin, hit the wall with the left side, got slightly airbourne, slid sideways 80 feet, then slid backwards along the wall for an additional 440 feet. Car was extensively damaged. Driver was taken to Methodist Hospital with slight fracture of the left ankle.

Friday, May 9, 1980 — 2:54 p.m.
Dana Carter in the #19 Scientific Drilling Controls McLaren/Offy lost control off Turn 1 (Southwest), slid sideways 500 feet. Got car gathered in and stopped 350 feet further down the track. No contact. Driver okay.

Saturday, May 10, 1980 — 10:07 a.m.
Tim Richmond in the #21 UNO-Q-95 Star Cruiser Penske/Cosworth lost control in Turn 1 (Southwest), spun once, slid 600 feet and hit the wall with the right side, slid another 375 feet and stopped in the middle of the track. Car extensively damaged. Driver okay.

Sunday, May 11, 1980 — 10:37 a.m.
Dana Carter in the #19 Scientific Drilling Controls McLaren/Offy got low in Turn 2 (Southeast), spun once and hit the wall, traveling 420 feet, with the right front striking the concrete, scraped along the wall 180 feet. Car extensively damaged. Driver okay.

Tuesday, May 13, 1980 — 11:53 a.m.
Jan Sneva in the #77 Walmotor Penske/Cosworth lost control and slid 120 feet into the grass in the Southeast (#2) turn. The car slid 100 feet in the grass and made a half spin, traveling another 180 feet and hitting the outside retaining wall with its left side, stopping 140 feet down the track. Car extensively damaged. Driver okay.

Wednesday, May 14, 1980 — 1:51 p.m.
Tom Sneva in the #9 O'Connell Phoenix/Cosworth right front tire lost air in Turn 1 (Southwest), driving car straight into the wall, 420 feet, slid along the wall 230 feet, then slid across the track 600 feet into the grass. Additional 300 foot slide in the grass. Stopped at entrance of No. 2 turn. Car totalled. Driver lacerations on left shin, stitches applied at track hospital.

Thursday, May 15, 1980 — 3:05 p.m.
Phil Caliva in the #47 Alsup McLaren/Offy got high in Turn 3 (Northeast), spun once, slid 570 feet into the wall with right front, coasted another 1,000 feet to the middle of the fourth turn. Car moderate damage to right front. Driver okay.

Sunday, May 18, 1980 — 1:48 p.m.
Rick Muther in the #82 Pacific Coast Racing Penske/Cosworth lost control in Turn 1 (Southwest), spun once 575 feet, no contact. Driver okay.

Sunday, May 18, 1980 — 3:35 p.m.
Howdy Holmes in the #43 Armstrong Mould/Jiffy Mix Orbiter/Cosworth brushed wall on back straightaway, spun once 650 feet to infield apron in Turn 3. Damage to right rear of car. Driver okay.

10 LAP RUN DOWN

LAP NO. 10

CAR NO.	POS. NO.	DRIVER
4	1	Johnny Rutherford
11	2	Bobby Unser
12	3	Mario Andretti
35	4	Spike Gehlhausen
1	5	Rick Mears
10	6	Pancho Carter
15	7	Johnny Parsons
7	8	Jerry Sneva
66	9	Roger Rager
14	10	A.J. Foyt
40	11	Tom Bagley
5	12	Al Unser
20	13	Gordon Johncock
21	14	Tim Richmond
96	15	Don Whittington
70	16	Gordon Smiley
25	17	Danny Ongais
46	18	Gary Bettenhausen
16	19	George Snider
9	20	Tom Sneva
44	21	Greg Leffler
23	22	Jimmy McElreath
8	23	Dick Simon
99	24	Hurley Haywood
38	25	Jerry Karl
18	26	Dennis Firestone
43	27	Tom Bigelow
29	28	Billy Engelhart
2	29	Bill Vukovich

LAP NO. 20

CAR NO.	POS. NO.	DRIVER
20	1	Gordon Johncock
11	2	Bobby Unser
16	3	George Snider
9	4	Tom Sneva
12	5	Mario Andretti
4	6	Johnny Rutherford
8	7	Dick Simon
25	8	Danny Ongais
1	9	Rick Mears
35	10	Spike Gehlhausen
10	11	Pancho Carter
7	12	Jerry Sneva
14	13	A.J. Foyt
70	14	Gordon Smiley
40	15	Tom Bagley
5	16	Al Unser
15	17	Johnny Parsons
21	18	Tim Richmond
46	19	Gary Bettenhausen
43	20	Tom Bigelow
66	21	Roger Rager
38	22	Jerry Karl
44	23	Greg Leffler
96	24	Don Whittington
2	25	Bill Vukovich
29	26	Billy Engelhart
23	27	Jimmy McElreath
18	28	Dennis Firestone
99	29	Hurley Haywood

LAP NO. 30

CAR NO.	POS. NO.	DRIVER
11	1	Bobby Unser
4	2	Johnny Rutherford
20	3	Gordon Johncock
12	4	Mario Andretti
9	5	Tom Sneva
10	6	Pancho Carter
7	7	Jerry Sneva
14	8	A.J. Foyt
1	9	Rick Mears
21	10	Tim Richmond
25	11	Danny Ongais
8	12	Dick Simon
5	13	Al Unser
46	14	Gary Bettenhausen
66	15	Roger Rager
43	16	Tom Bigelow
96	17	Don Whittington
38	18	Jerry Karl
70	19	Gordon Smiley
44	20	Greg Leffler
15	21	Johnny Parsons
2	22	Bill Vukovich
23	23	Jimmy McElreath
16	24	George Snider
29	25	Billy Engelhart
18	26	Dennis Firestone
99	27	Hurley Haywood

LAP NO. 40

CAR NO.	POS. NO.	DRIVER
4	1	Johnny Rutherford
10	2	Pancho Carter
21	3	Tim Richmond
11	4	Bobby Unser
20	5	Gordon Johncock
1	6	Rick Mears
12	7	Mario Andretti
25	8	Danny Ongais
70	9	Gordon Smiley
9	10	Tom Sneva
15	11	Johnny Parsons
66	12	Roger Rager
14	13	A.J. Foyt
7	14	Jerry Sneva
38	15	Jerry Karl
46	16	Gary Bettenhausen
44	17	Greg Leffler
96	18	Don Whittington
43	19	Tom Bigelow
8	20	Dick Simon
2	21	Bill Vukovich
23	22	Jimmy McElreath
16	23	George Snider
18	24	Dennis Firestone
29	25	Billy Engelhart
99	26	Hurley Haywood

LAP NO. 50

CAR NO.	POS. NO.	DRIVER
12	1	Mario Andretti
10	2	Pancho Carter
1	3	Rick Mears
20	4	Gordon Johncock
21	5	Tim Richmond
11	6	Bobby Unser
4	7	Johnny Rutherford
25	8	Danny Ongais
46	9	Gary Bettenhausen
9	10	Tom Sneva
96	11	Don Whittington
14	12	A.J. Foyt
7	13	Jerry Sneva
43	14	Tom Bigelow
38	15	Jerry Karl
44	16	Greg Leffler
66	17	Roger Rager
16	18	George Snider
29	19	Billy Engelhart
2	20	Bill Vukovich
23	21	Jimmy McElreath
18	22	Dennis Firestone
99	23	Hurley Haywood
8	24	Dick Simon

LAP NO. 60

CAR NO.	POS. NO.	DRIVER
4	1	Johnny Rutherford
1	2	Rick Mears
11	3	Bobby Unser
21	4	Tim Richmond
12	5	Mario Andretti
44	6	Greg Leffler
25	7	Danny Ongais
9	8	Tom Sneva
43	9	Tom Bigelow
20	10	Gordon Johncock
7	11	Jerry Sneva
46	12	Gary Bettenhausen
38	13	Jerry Karl
14	14	A.J. Foyt
96	15	Don Whittington
10	16	Pancho Carter
29	17	Billy Engelhart
2	18	Bill Vukovich
16	19	George Snider
18	20	Dennis Firestone
99	21	Hurley Haywood

LAP NO. 70

CAR NO.	POS. NO.	DRIVER
4	1	Johnny Rutherford
11	2	Bobby Unser
1	3	Rick Mears
12	4	Mario Andretti
21	5	Tim Richmond
9	6	Tom Sneva
20	7	Gordon Johncock
46	8	Gary Bettenhausen
7	9	Jerry Sneva
44	10	Greg Leffler
43	11	Tom Bigelow
14	12	A.J. Foyt
25	13	Danny Ongais
96	14	Don Whittington
10	15	Pancho Carter
16	16	George Snider
2	17	Bill Vukovich
29	18	Billy Engelhart
18	19	Dennis Firestone
99	20	Hurley Haywood

LAP NO. 80

CAR NO.	POS. NO.	DRIVER
9	1	Tom Sneva
4	2	Johnny Rutherford
11	3	Bobby Unser
7	4	Jerry Sneva
1	5	Rick Mears
46	6	Gary Bettenhausen
21	7	Tim Richmond
20	8	Gordon Johncock
44	9	Greg Leffler
43	10	Tom Bigelow
14	11	A.J. Foyt
96	12	Don Whittington
10	13	Pancho Carter
25	14	Danny Ongais
16	15	George Snider
29	16	Billy Engelhart
18	17	Dennis Firestone
2	18	Bill Vukovich
99	19	Hurley Haywood

LAP NO. 90

CAR NO.	POS. NO.	DRIVER
11	1	Bobby Unser
21	2	Tim Richmond
9	3	Tom Sneva
4	4	Johnny Rutherford
1	5	Rick Mears
46	6	Gary Bettenhausen

CAR NO.	POS. NO.	DRIVER
44	7	Greg Leffler
14	8	A.J. Foyt
7	9	Jerry Sneva
43	10	Tom Bigelow
20	11	Gordon Johncock
10	12	Pancho Carter
25	13	Danny Ongais
16	14	George Snider
29	15	Billy Engelhart
18	16	Dennis Firestone
2	17	Bill Vukovich
96	18	Don Whittington
99	19	Hurley Haywood

LAP NO. 100

CAR NO.	POS. NO.	DRIVER
11	1	Bobby Unser
4	2	Johnny Rutherford
1	3	Rick Mears
9	4	Tom Sneva
46	5	Gary Bettenhausen
21	6	Tim Richmond
14	7	A.J. Foyt
7	8	Jerry Sneva
44	9	Greg Leffler
20	10	Gordon Johncock
43	11	Tom Bigelow
10	12	Pancho Carter
25	13	Danny Ongais
16	14	George Snider
18	15	Dennis Firestone
2	16	Bill Vukovich
29	17	Billy Engelhart
96	18	Don Whittington
99	19	Hurley Haywood

LAP NO. 110

CAR NO.	POS. NO.	DRIVER
4	1	Johnny Rutherford
1	2	Rick Mears
11	3	Bobby Unser
9	4	Tom Sneva
14	5	A.J. Foyt
20	6	Gordon Johncock
46	7	Gary Bettenhausen
7	8	Jerry Sneva
21	9	Dennis Firestone
44	10	Greg Leffler
25	11	Danny Ongais
16	12	George Snider
10	13	Pancho Carter
18	14	Dennis Firestone
43	15	Tom Bigelow
29	16	Billy Engelhart
2	17	Bill Vukovich
96	18	Don Whittington
99	19	Hurley Haywood

LAP NO. 120

CAR NO.	POS. NO.	DRIVER
4	1	Johnny Rutherford
1	2	Rick Mears
11	3	Bobby Unser
9	4	Tom Sneva
20	5	Gordon Johncock
46	6	Gary Bettenhausen
14	7	A.J. Foyt
7	8	Jerry Sneva
21	9	Tim Richmond
25	10	Danny Ongais
10	11	Pancho Carter
44	12	Greg Leffler
16	13	George Snider
43	14	Tom Bigelow
18	15	Dennis Firestone
29	16	Billy Engelhart
2	17	Bill Vukovich
96	18	Don Whittington
99	19	Hurley Haywood

LAP NO. 130

CAR NO.	POS. NO.	DRIVER
4	1	Johnny Rutherford
1	2	Rick Mears
9	3	Tom Sneva
46	4	Gary Bettenhausen
20	5	Gordon Johncock
14	6	A.J. Foyt
21	7	Tim Richmond
7	8	Jerry Sneva
10	9	Pancho Carter
25	10	Danny Ongais
44	11	Greg Leffler
43	12	Tom Bigelow
16	13	George Snider
18	14	Dennis Firestone
29	15	Billy Engelhart
2	16	Bill Vukovich
96	17	Don Whittington

LAP NO. 140

CAR NO.	POS. NO.	DRIVER
4	1	Johnny Rutherford
9	2	Tom Sneva
1	3	Rick Mears
46	4	Gary Bettenhausen
20	5	Gordon Johncock
10	6	Pancho Carter
14	7	A.J. Foyt
25	8	Danny Ongais
21	9	Tim Richmond
44	10	Greg Leffler
43	11	Tom Bigelow
16	12	George Snider
29	13	Billy Engelhart
2	14	Bill Vukovich
96	15	Don Whittington

LAP NO. 150

CAR NO.	POS. NO.	DRIVER
4	1	Johnny Rutherford
9	2	Tom Sneva
1	3	Rick Mears
20	4	Gordon Johncock
46	5	Gary Bettenhausen
21	6	Tim Richmond
25	7	Danny Ongais
10	8	Pancho Carter
14	9	A.J. Foyt
44	10	Greg Leffler
43	11	Tom Bigelow
16	12	George Snider
29	13	Billy Engelhart
2	14	Bill Vukovich
96	15	Don Whittington

LAP NO. 160

CAR NO.	POS. NO.	DRIVER
4	1	Johnny Rutherford
46	2	Gary Bettenhausen
20	3	Gordon Johncock
1	4	Rick Mears
9	5	Tom Sneva
10	6	Pancho Carter
25	7	Danny Ongais
21	8	Tim Richmond
14	9	A.J. Foyt
44	10	Greg Leffler
16	11	George Snider
43	12	Tom Bigelow
29	13	Billy Engelhart
2	14	Bill Vukovich
96	15	Don Whittington

LAP NO. 170

CAR NO.	POS. NO.	DRIVER
4	1	Johnny Rutherford
1	2	Rick Mears
20	3	Gordon Johncock
9	4	Tom Sneva
46	5	Gary Bettenhausen
10	6	Pancho Carter
25	7	Danny Ongais
21	8	Tim Richmond
14	9	A.J. Foyt
44	10	Greg Leffler
43	11	Tom Bigelow
29	12	Billy Engelhart
2	13	Bill Vukovich
96	14	Don Whittington

LAP NO. 180

CAR NO.	POS. NO.	DRIVER
4	1	Johnny Rutherford
9	2	Tom Sneva
1	3	Rick Mears
46	4	Gary Bettenhausen
20	5	Gordon Johncock
21	6	Tim Richmond
10	7	Pancho Carter
25	8	Danny Ongais
43	9	Tom Bigelow
44	10	Greg Leffler
29	11	Billy Engelhart
2	12	Bill Vukovich

LAP NO. 190

CAR NO.	POS. NO.	DRIVER
4	1	Johnny Rutherford
9	2	Tom Sneva
46	3	Gary Bettenhausen
20	4	Gordon Johncock
1	5	Rick Mears
10	6	Pancho Carter
25	7	Danny Ongais
21	8	Tim Richmond
43	9	Tom Bigelow
44	10	Greg Leffler
29	11	Billy Engelhart
2	12	Bill Vukovich

LAP NO. 200

CAR NO.	POS. NO.	DRIVER
4	1	Johnny Rutherford
9	2	Tom Sneva
46	3	Gary Bettenhausen
20	4	Gordon Johncock

Pit Stop Report

<table>
<tr><th>CAR NO.</th><th>STOP NO.</th><th>LAP NO.</th><th>REASON</th><th>TIME IN SECONDS</th></tr>
<tr><td colspan="4">1st Place — JOHNNY RUTHERFORD</td><td>Pennzoil-Chaparral</td></tr>
<tr><td>4</td><td>1</td><td>16</td><td>Fuel only</td><td>13</td></tr>
<tr><td></td><td>2</td><td>31</td><td>Fuel only</td><td>10</td></tr>
<tr><td></td><td>3</td><td>47</td><td>Fuel, RF & LR Tires</td><td>20</td></tr>
<tr><td></td><td>4</td><td>73</td><td>Fuel only</td><td>17</td></tr>
<tr><td></td><td>5</td><td>86</td><td>Fuel only</td><td>10</td></tr>
<tr><td></td><td>6</td><td>114</td><td>Fuel, RR, LR and RF Tires</td><td>20</td></tr>
<tr><td></td><td>7</td><td>131</td><td>Fuel only</td><td>10</td></tr>
<tr><td></td><td>8</td><td>143</td><td>Fuel, RR, LR and RF Tires</td><td>16</td></tr>
<tr><td></td><td>9</td><td>172</td><td>Fuel only</td><td>19</td></tr>
<tr><td colspan="4" align="right">TOTAL TIME:</td><td>135</td></tr>
</table>

<table>
<tr><td colspan="4">2nd Place — TOM SNEVA</td><td>Bon Jour Action Jeans</td></tr>
<tr><td>9</td><td>1</td><td>11</td><td>Fuel, Adjusted Front Wing</td><td>9</td></tr>
<tr><td></td><td>2</td><td>13</td><td>Fuel, Adjusted Rear Suspension</td><td>37</td></tr>
<tr><td></td><td>3</td><td>30</td><td>Fuel, RF and RR Tires</td><td>13</td></tr>
<tr><td></td><td>4</td><td>45</td><td>Fuel, Adjusted RR Suspension</td><td>23</td></tr>
<tr><td></td><td>5</td><td>58</td><td>Fuel, RF and RR Tires, Adjust Front Wing</td><td>16</td></tr>
<tr><td></td><td>6</td><td>85</td><td>Fuel only</td><td>13</td></tr>
<tr><td></td><td>7</td><td>111</td><td>Fuel, RF and RR Tires</td><td>15</td></tr>
<tr><td></td><td>8</td><td>132</td><td>Fuel only</td><td>14</td></tr>
<tr><td></td><td>9</td><td>156</td><td>Fuel, RF and RR Tires</td><td>14</td></tr>
<tr><td></td><td>10</td><td>179</td><td>Fuel RF and RR Tires</td><td>14</td></tr>
<tr><td colspan="4" align="right">TOTAL TIME:</td><td>168</td></tr>
</table>

<table>
<tr><td colspan="4">3rd Place — GARY BETTENHAUSEN</td><td>Armstrong Mould</td></tr>
<tr><td>46</td><td>1</td><td>16</td><td>Fuel only</td><td>9</td></tr>
<tr><td></td><td>2</td><td>31</td><td>Fuel only</td><td>10</td></tr>
<tr><td></td><td>3</td><td>46</td><td>Fuel only</td><td>12</td></tr>
<tr><td></td><td>4</td><td>59</td><td>Fuel only</td><td>8</td></tr>
<tr><td></td><td>5</td><td>73</td><td>Fuel only</td><td>12</td></tr>
<tr><td></td><td>6</td><td>86</td><td>Fuel only</td><td>10</td></tr>
<tr><td></td><td>7</td><td>105</td><td>Fuel only</td><td>11</td></tr>
<tr><td></td><td>8</td><td>118</td><td>Fuel, RF and RR Tires</td><td>22</td></tr>
<tr><td></td><td>9</td><td>133</td><td>Fuel, RR Tire</td><td>25</td></tr>
<tr><td></td><td>10</td><td>143</td><td>Fuel only</td><td>23</td></tr>
<tr><td></td><td>11</td><td>168</td><td>Fuel only</td><td>15</td></tr>
<tr><td></td><td>12</td><td>178</td><td>Fuel only</td><td>10</td></tr>
<tr><td colspan="4" align="right">TOTAL TIME:</td><td>167</td></tr>
</table>

<table>
<tr><td colspan="4">4th Place — GORDON JOHNCOCK</td><td>No. Amer. Van Lines</td></tr>
<tr><td>20</td><td>1</td><td>13</td><td>Fuel only</td><td>9</td></tr>
<tr><td></td><td>2</td><td>44</td><td>Fuel only</td><td>13</td></tr>
<tr><td></td><td>3</td><td>51</td><td>Fuel, RF and RR Tires</td><td>36</td></tr>
<tr><td></td><td>4</td><td>73</td><td>Fuel only</td><td>8</td></tr>
<tr><td></td><td>5</td><td>88</td><td>Fuel, LF and LR Tires</td><td>17</td></tr>
<tr><td></td><td>6</td><td>118</td><td>Fuel, RF and RR Tires</td><td>16</td></tr>
<tr><td></td><td>7</td><td>133</td><td>Fuel, RF and RR Tires</td><td>17</td></tr>
<tr><td></td><td>8</td><td>143</td><td>Fuel, RR Tire, RF Wing Adj.</td><td>13</td></tr>
<tr><td></td><td>9</td><td>171</td><td>Fuel only</td><td>15</td></tr>
<tr><td></td><td>10</td><td>177</td><td>Fuel only</td><td>5</td></tr>
<tr><td colspan="4" align="right">TOTAL TIME:</td><td>149</td></tr>
</table>

<table>
<tr><td colspan="4">5th Place — RICK MEARS</td><td>The Gould Charge Penske PC-9</td></tr>
<tr><td>1</td><td>1</td><td>16</td><td>Fuel only</td><td>8</td></tr>
<tr><td></td><td>2</td><td>31</td><td>Fuel only</td><td>6</td></tr>
<tr><td></td><td>3</td><td>46</td><td>Fuel, RF and RR Tires</td><td>13</td></tr>
<tr><td></td><td>4</td><td>73</td><td>Fuel, RF and RR Tires</td><td>13</td></tr>
<tr><td></td><td>5</td><td>86</td><td>Fuel, Adj. Front Wing</td><td>6</td></tr>
<tr><td></td><td>6</td><td>117</td><td>Fuel only</td><td>13</td></tr>
<tr><td></td><td>7</td><td>133</td><td>Fuel, RF and RR Tires</td><td>21</td></tr>
<tr><td></td><td>8</td><td>143</td><td>Fuel, RF and RR Tires</td><td>13</td></tr>
<tr><td></td><td>9</td><td>158</td><td>Fuel, RF and RR Tires</td><td>13</td></tr>
<tr><td></td><td>10</td><td>179</td><td>Fuel only</td><td>10</td></tr>
<tr><td></td><td>11</td><td>183</td><td>Fuel, RF and RR Tires</td><td>20</td></tr>
<tr><td colspan="4" align="right">TOTAL TIME:</td><td>136</td></tr>
</table>

<table>
<tr><td colspan="4">6th Place — PANCHO CARTER</td><td>Alex XLNT Foods</td></tr>
<tr><td>10</td><td>1</td><td>14</td><td>Fuel only</td><td>12</td></tr>
<tr><td></td><td>2</td><td>42</td><td>Fuel only</td><td>14</td></tr>
<tr><td></td><td>3</td><td>58</td><td>Fuel, RF and RR Tires</td><td>18</td></tr>
<tr><td></td><td>4</td><td>85</td><td>Fuel only</td><td>16</td></tr>
<tr><td></td><td>5</td><td>106</td><td>Fuel, RF and RR Tires</td><td>19</td></tr>
<tr><td></td><td>6</td><td>118</td><td>Fuel, RF and RR Tires</td><td>13</td></tr>
<tr><td></td><td>7</td><td>131</td><td>Fuel only</td><td>12</td></tr>
<tr><td></td><td>8</td><td>142</td><td>Fuel only</td><td>10</td></tr>
<tr><td></td><td>9</td><td>171</td><td>Fuel only</td><td>16</td></tr>
<tr><td colspan="4" align="right">TOTAL TIME:</td><td>130</td></tr>
</table>

<table>
<tr><th>CAR NO.</th><th>STOP NO.</th><th>LAP NO.</th><th>REASON</th><th>TIME IN SECONDS</th></tr>
<tr><td colspan="4">7th Place — DANNY ONGAIS</td><td>Interscope/Panasonic</td></tr>
<tr><td>25</td><td>1</td><td>15</td><td>Fuel only</td><td>11</td></tr>
<tr><td></td><td>2</td><td>46</td><td>Fuel, RF and RR Tires</td><td>18</td></tr>
<tr><td></td><td>3</td><td>59</td><td>Fuel only</td><td>9</td></tr>
<tr><td></td><td>4</td><td>72</td><td>Fuel, RF and RR Tires</td><td>11</td></tr>
<tr><td></td><td>5</td><td>86</td><td>Fuel only</td><td>7</td></tr>
<tr><td></td><td>6</td><td>103</td><td>Fuel, RF and RR Tires</td><td>16</td></tr>
<tr><td></td><td>7</td><td>133</td><td>Fuel only</td><td>9</td></tr>
<tr><td></td><td>8</td><td>157</td><td>Fuel only</td><td>10</td></tr>
<tr><td></td><td>9</td><td>179</td><td>Fuel, RF and RR Tires</td><td>17</td></tr>
<tr><td colspan="4" align="right">TOTAL TIME:</td><td>108</td></tr>
</table>

<table>
<tr><td colspan="4">8th Place — TOM BIGELOW</td><td>Armstrong Mould, Inc./Jiffy Mix</td></tr>
<tr><td>43</td><td>1</td><td>15</td><td>Fuel only</td><td>12</td></tr>
<tr><td></td><td>2</td><td>32</td><td>Fuel only</td><td>10</td></tr>
<tr><td></td><td>3</td><td>46</td><td>Fuel only</td><td>11</td></tr>
<tr><td></td><td>4</td><td>58</td><td>Fuel only</td><td>9</td></tr>
<tr><td></td><td>5</td><td>72</td><td>Fuel, RF Tire</td><td>14</td></tr>
<tr><td></td><td>6</td><td>87</td><td>Fuel only</td><td>11</td></tr>
<tr><td></td><td>7</td><td>107</td><td>Fuel, RF and RR Tires, Rt. Skirt Torn</td><td>23</td></tr>
<tr><td></td><td>8</td><td>108</td><td>Tapes Rt. Skirt</td><td>26</td></tr>
<tr><td></td><td>9</td><td>117</td><td>Fuel, Taped Rt. Skirt</td><td>39</td></tr>
<tr><td></td><td>10</td><td>120</td><td>Adj. Wing</td><td>8</td></tr>
<tr><td></td><td>11</td><td>131</td><td>Fuel, Tapes Rt. Skirt</td><td>17</td></tr>
<tr><td></td><td>12</td><td>141</td><td>Fuel, Tapes Rt. Skirt</td><td>16</td></tr>
<tr><td></td><td>13</td><td>155</td><td>Fuel, Taped Rt. Skirt</td><td>17</td></tr>
<tr><td></td><td>14</td><td>178</td><td>Fuel, Taped Rt. Skirt</td><td>18</td></tr>
<tr><td colspan="4" align="right">TOTAL TIME:</td><td>231</td></tr>
</table>

<table>
<tr><td colspan="4">9th Place — TIM RICHMOND</td><td>UNO-Q95 Starcruiser</td></tr>
<tr><td>21</td><td>1</td><td>15</td><td>Fuel, LF and LR Tires</td><td>46</td></tr>
<tr><td></td><td>2</td><td>44</td><td>Fuel, RR Tire</td><td>22</td></tr>
<tr><td></td><td>3</td><td>73</td><td>Fuel, Adj. RR Toe In</td><td>24</td></tr>
<tr><td></td><td>4</td><td>103</td><td>Fuel, LF and LR Tires</td><td>22</td></tr>
<tr><td></td><td>5</td><td>132</td><td>Fuel, Adj. Frt. Wing</td><td>19</td></tr>
<tr><td></td><td>6</td><td>157</td><td>Fuel only</td><td>12</td></tr>
<tr><td></td><td>7</td><td>186</td><td>Fuel only</td><td>12</td></tr>
<tr><td colspan="4" align="right">TOTAL TIME:</td><td>157</td></tr>
</table>

<table>
<tr><td colspan="4">10th Place — GREG LEFFLER</td><td>Starcraft R.V.</td></tr>
<tr><td>44</td><td>1</td><td>15</td><td>Fuel only</td><td>23</td></tr>
<tr><td></td><td>2</td><td>46</td><td>Fuel, Adj. Boost</td><td>17</td></tr>
<tr><td></td><td>3</td><td>72</td><td>Fuel only</td><td>14</td></tr>
<tr><td></td><td>4</td><td>103</td><td>Fuel only</td><td>17</td></tr>
<tr><td></td><td>5</td><td>119</td><td>Fuel only</td><td>25</td></tr>
<tr><td></td><td>6</td><td>132</td><td>Fuel only</td><td>10</td></tr>
<tr><td></td><td>7</td><td>143</td><td>Fuel only</td><td>10</td></tr>
<tr><td></td><td>8</td><td>156</td><td>Fuel only</td><td>11</td></tr>
<tr><td></td><td>9</td><td>175</td><td>Fuel, RF and RR Tires</td><td>20</td></tr>
<tr><td colspan="4" align="right">TOTAL TIME:</td><td>147</td></tr>
</table>

<table>
<tr><td colspan="4">11th Place — BILLY ENGELHART</td><td>Master Lock Spl.</td></tr>
<tr><td>29</td><td>1</td><td>12</td><td>Fuel only, Stalled</td><td>12</td></tr>
<tr><td></td><td>2</td><td>12</td><td>Restarted</td><td>14</td></tr>
<tr><td></td><td>3</td><td>14</td><td>Fuel, LF Tire</td><td>41</td></tr>
<tr><td></td><td>4</td><td>16</td><td>Checked Car</td><td>14</td></tr>
<tr><td></td><td>5</td><td>22</td><td>Fuel, RF and RR Tires</td><td>38</td></tr>
<tr><td></td><td>6</td><td>26</td><td>Checked RR Tire</td><td>15</td></tr>
<tr><td></td><td>7</td><td>44</td><td>Fuel only</td><td>16</td></tr>
<tr><td></td><td>8</td><td>68</td><td>Fuel only</td><td>16</td></tr>
<tr><td></td><td>9</td><td>97</td><td>Fuel only</td><td>20</td></tr>
<tr><td></td><td>10</td><td>120</td><td>Fuel only</td><td>14</td></tr>
<tr><td></td><td>11</td><td>151</td><td>Fuel only</td><td>17</td></tr>
<tr><td></td><td>12</td><td>170</td><td>Fuel, RF Tire</td><td>30</td></tr>
<tr><td colspan="4" align="right">TOTAL TIME:</td><td>247</td></tr>
</table>

<table>
<tr><td colspan="4">12th Place — BILL VUKOVICH</td><td>Hubler Chev. WFMS Spl.</td></tr>
<tr><td>2</td><td>1</td><td>14</td><td>Fuel only</td><td>9</td></tr>
<tr><td></td><td>2</td><td>31</td><td>Fuel only</td><td>21</td></tr>
<tr><td></td><td>3</td><td>46</td><td>Fuel only</td><td>10</td></tr>
<tr><td></td><td>4</td><td>57</td><td>Fuel, Adjust Boost</td><td>18</td></tr>
<tr><td></td><td>5</td><td>71</td><td>Fuel, Adjust Boost</td><td>13</td></tr>
<tr><td></td><td>6</td><td>87</td><td>Fuel only</td><td>9</td></tr>
<tr><td></td><td>7</td><td>110</td><td>Fuel only</td><td>11</td></tr>
<tr><td></td><td>8</td><td>130</td><td>Fuel only</td><td>9</td></tr>
<tr><td></td><td>9</td><td>154</td><td>Fuel, RF and RR Tires</td><td>29</td></tr>
<tr><td></td><td>10</td><td>173</td><td>Fuel only</td><td>10</td></tr>
<tr><td colspan="4" align="right">TOTAL TIME:</td><td>139</td></tr>
</table>

CAR NO.	STOP NO.	LAP NO.	REASON	TIME IN SECONDS
13th Place — DON WHITTINGTON				**Sun System**
96	1	15	Fuel only	11
	2	16	Adj. Frt. Wing	13
	3	32	Fuel, Adj. Frt. Wing	16
	4	46	Fuel only	11
	5	60	Fuel only	13
	6	74	Fuel, RR Wheel Nut Loose in Pit Lane	30
	7	84	Car Spun, All Tires Changed, Stalled and Restarted	245
	8	89	RR and LR Tires	98
	9	92	Checked Rear of Car	24
	10	94	Fuel, RR Tire	24
	11	99	Fuel, Adj. Frt. Wing	39
	12	101	Fuel only	15
	13	103	Talked to Crew	28
	14	104	Talked to Crew	27
	15	107	RR and LR Tires	21
	16	120	Fuel, RR Tire, Adj. Front Wing	37
	17	130	Fuel, RR Tire, Six Men Over Wall	29
	18	142	Fuel, Six Men Over Wall	17
	19	150	Fuel only	16
	20	159	Fuel only	12
			TOTAL TIME:	726
14th Place — A.J. FOYT, JR.				**Gilmore Racing Team**
14	1	15	Fuel only, Wheel Unattended	9
	2	30	Fuel only	8
	3	44	Fuel, All Four Tires	18
	4	59	Fuel only	8
	5	72	Fuel, RF, RR and LR Tires	19
	6	85	Fuel only	8
	7	112	Fuel, Adj. Boost	11
	8	130	Fuel, Adj. Boost	13
	9	141	Fuel only	8
	10	156	Fuel, RF, RR and LR Tires	20
	11	172	Fuel, RR Tire	10
	12	173	Out of Race, Engine Problems	
			TOTAL TIME:	132
15th Place — GEORGE SNIDER				**Gilmore Racing Team**
16	1	11	Fuel, Nose Damaged	13
	2	22	Fuel, Changed Nose Cone	136
	3	45	Fuel only	12
	4	60	Fuel only	10
	5	85	Fuel, RF and RR Tires	21
	6	112	Fuel only	14
	7	132	Fuel only	9
	8	141	Fuel, LF and LR Tires	18
	9	170	Fuel only	16
	10	170	Engine stalled, Would Not Restart Out of Race	
			TOTAL TIME:	249
16th Place — DENNIS FIRESTONE				**Scientific Drilling Controls Spl.**
18	1	12	Fuel only	25
	2	17	Replaced Rt. Frt. Spoiler	74
	3	22	Adj. Rt. Frt. Nose Foil	32
	4	40	Fuel only	17
	5	56	Fuel, RF and RR Tires	26
	6	71	Fuel only	8
	7	85	Fuel only	8
	8	114	Fuel only	17
	9	131	Fuel, RF and RR Tires	30
	10	136	Ring & Piston Broke Out of Race	
			TOTAL TIME:	237
17th Place — JERRY SNEVA				**Hugger's Bev. Holders**
7	1	15	Fuel only	10
	2	31	Fuel only	12
	3	46	Fuel only	11
	4	57	Fuel, RF and RR Tires	32
	5	83	Fuel only	13
	6	107	Fuel only	14
			Out of Race — Crashed	
			TOTAL TIME:	92
18th Place — HURLEY HAYWOOD				**STA-ON/Guarantee Auto/ KISS Radio Spl.**
99	1	16	Fuel, Starter Problems	414
	2	40	Fuel only	17
	3	64	Fuel, Restarted Engine	29
	4	69	Fuel, Gear Box Worked on Second Gear Problem	1186
	5	88	Fuel, RF and RR Tires	57
	6	88	Fuel from vent spilled, Fire ignition wires	319

CAR NO.	STOP NO.	LAP NO.	REASON	TIME IN SECONDS
	7	101	Fuel, RR Tire, Engine dead, Gear box problems	712
	8	126	Fuel only, Fuel Fire, Electric wires burned up	53
			Out of Race	
			TOTAL TIME:	2787
19th Place — BOBBY UNSER				**Norton Spirit Penske PC-9**
11	1	15	Fuel only	10
	2	30	Fuel, RF and RR Tires	12
	3	46	Fuel only	8
	4	72	Fuel, RF and RR Tires	12
	5	104	Fuel only	8
	6	117	Fuel only	16
	7	126	Replaced ignition coil Out of Race	
			TOTAL TIME:	a6
20th Place — MARIO ANDRETTI				**Essex Penske PC-9**
12	1	16	Fuel only	11
	2	30	Fuel only	17
	3	45	Fuel only	8
	4	57	Fuel, RF and RR Tires	14
	5	70	Engine seized Out of Race	
			TOTAL TIME:	50
21st Place — JERRY KARL				**Tonco Trailer Co., Spl.**
38	1	17	Fuel only	13
	2	24	Fuel only	11
	3	32	Fuel only	9
	4	47	Fuel only	14
	5	59	Fuel only	11
	6	63	Out of Race — Clutch Failure	
			TOTAL TIME:	58
22nd Place — DICK SIMON				**VT Amer./Silhouette Health Spas/ Regal 8 Inn**
8	1	12	Fuel, LR Tire	57
	2	32	Fuel, Adj. Wing Lft. Side	15
	3	47	Fuel, Rear Stagger Changed	47
	4	49	Fuel, Lft. Lower 'A' Arm Broke, repaired	3228
	5	50	Fuel, Raised LF Wing, Air Press, LR Tire	75
	6	59	Broken Rt. Ft. Suspension Out of Race	
			TOTAL TIME:	3422
23rd Place — ROGER RAGER				**Adv. Clean Sweep/Carpenter School Bus Spl.**
66	1	17	Fuel only	15
	2	43	Fuel only	14
	3	55	Spun to miss a car Out of Race	
			TOTAL TIME:	29
24th Place — JIM McELREATH				**McElreath Spl.**
23	1	10	Fuel only	16
	2	11	RR Tire	40
	3	43	Fuel only	22
	4	55	Spun and wrecked car Out of Race	
			TOTAL TIME:	78
25th Place — GORDON SMILEY				**Valvoline-Patrick Racing**
70	1	15	Fuel only	9
	2	29	Fuel only	10
	3	44	Fuel, RF and RR Tires	17
	4	46	Fire from spilled fuel Out of Race	
			TOTAL TIME:	36
26th Place — JOHNNY PARSONS				**Wynn's Special**
15	1	15	Fuel, RF and RR Tires	30
	2	36	Fuel only	10
	3	43	Broken piston Out of Race	
			TOTAL TIME:	40
27th Place — AL UNSER				**Longhorn Racing**
5	1	15	Fuel only	15
	2	30	Fuel only	16
	3	31	Changed spark plugs	205
	4	32	Engine problems Out of Race	
			TOTAL TIME:	236

(Continued on Page 199)

Missed The Show

You couldn't tell that there was a recession going on in the United States as the Indy entries were as strong as ever. The rules this year seemed to put the field in a very competitive situation . . . so it's easy to say that a driver looked good, he just needed a couple more miles per hour.

Howdy Holmes looked like he had it made, then spun qualifying.

Successful Sprint car racer Ron Shuman needed more horses.

Roger Mears didn't get enough time in the Grant King car.

Janet had speed but crew wanted a bit faster than her run.

A capable Bob Harkey needed more horsepower than he had.

Billy Puterbaugh didn't get enough laps in to be competitive.

Pete Halsmer was close, but was bumped by Dennis Firestone.

Herm Johnson put in a good month, but needed a few more mph.

Rich Vogler looked very good but suffered car problems.

It was a surprise when Sheldon Kinser's speed didn't hold.

John Mahler's new car didn't arrive until the last day.

Tom Sneva made a pile of rubbish out of this new racer.

Hard working Tom Frantz had great looking car, no speed.

Tony Bettenhausen crashed, then didn't muster enough speed.

[93]

Mahoney

Frank Weiss looked good until the wall stopped his effort.

Mahoney

Rookie Phil Caliva did fine, but Engelhart bumped him.

Mount

Little Joe Saldana went through a frustrating month of May.

Mahoney

John Wood was capable, but he too needed more horsepower.

Mahoney

Al Loquasto was given a last minute ride, not enough time.

Mount

Jan Sneva put this Walther car into the unforgiving wall.

Mount

Bill Alsup again looked great and missed the show by inches.

Mahoney

Phil Threshie didn't have a chance, car arrived too late.

[94]

Lee Kunzman got a late start and didn't have enough ponies.

Veteran John Martin was close, but bumped by Greg Leffler.

Rick Muther looked teriffic, but suspension part let go.

Bill Tempero worked hard all month but didn't muster the speed.

Dana Carter looked like a shoe-in, then hit the fence.

Tom Sneva didn't make an attempt in the Woodward car.

Salt Walther kept a low profile in May . . . and speed too.

Joe Saldana's luck wasn't any better in his 69 car.

STARTING FIELD

#4 Johnny Rutherford — Pennzoil Chaparral
Qual: 5/10 @ 14:05
3:07.25 — 192.256
46.80 — 192.308
46.82 — 192.226
46.73 — 192.596
46.90 — 191.898

#35 Spike Gehlhausen — Winton Sales
Qual: 5/10 @ 11:53
3:11.14 — 188.344
47.65 — 188.877
47.34 — 190.114
47.78 — 188.363
48.37 — 186.066

#15 Johnny Parsons — Hopkins Special
Qual: 5/10 @ 13:17
3:12.09 — 187.412
47.90 — 187.891
48.03 — 187.383
48.14 — 186.955
48.02 — 187.422

#66 Roger Rager — Advance Clean Sweep/ Carpenter School Bus Spl.
Qual: 5/10 @ 14:39
3:13.16 — 186.374
47.91 — 187.852
48.35 — 186.143
48.30 — 186.335
48.60 — 185.185

#40* Tom Bagley — Kent Oil
Qual: 5/10 @ 13:39
3:14.17 — 185.405
48.50 — 185.567
48.45 — 185.759
48.51 — 185.529
48.71 — 184.767

#25 Danny Ongais — Interscope Panasonic
Qual: 5/11 @ 12:01
3:12.92 — 186.606
47.93 — 187.774
48.18 — 186.800
48.28 — 186.413
48.53 — 185.452

#21 Tim Richmond — The Uno-Q95 Starcruiser
Qual: 5/18 @ 14:08
3:11.15 — 188.334
47.75 — 188.482
47.64 — 188.917
47.92 — 187.813
47.84 — 188.127

#29 Billy Engelhart — Master Lock Spl.
Qual: 5/18 @ 14:57
3:15.40 — 184.237
49.00 — 183.673
48.86 — 184.200
48.82 — 184.351
48.72 — 184.729

#99 Hurley Haywood — Sta-On Glaze/Guar Auto/ Kiss 99
Qual: 5/18 @ 13:02
3:16.12 — 183.561
48.79 — 184.464
48.81 — 184.388
49.27 — 182.667
49.25 — 182.741

#38 Jerry Karl — Tonco Trailer Co., Spl.
Qual: 5/18 @ 13:10
3:16.71 — 183.011
49.10 — 183.299
48.96 — 183.824
49.05 — 183.486
49.60 — 181.452

#43$ Tom Bigelow — Armstrong Mould, Inc./ Jiffy Mix
Qual: 5/18 @ 12:00
3:17.21 — 182.547
49.08 — 183.374
49.30 — 182.556
49.42 — 182.113
49.41 — 182.149

#12 Mario Andretti — Essex Penske PC-9
Qual: 5/10 @ 12:41
3:08.47 — 191.012
46.93 — 191.775
47.17 — 190.799
47.23 — 190.557
47.14 — 190.921

#7 Jerry Sneva — Hugger's Beverage Holders Spl.
Qual: 5/10 @ 13:49
3:11.64 — 187.852
47.57 — 189.195
47.69 — 188.719
47.96 — 187.656
48.42 — 185.874

#10 Pancho Carter — Alex XLNT Foods Spl.
Qual: 5/10 @ 14:30
3:13.05 — 186.480
48.21 — 186.683
48.27 — 186.451
48.34 — 186.181
48.23 — 186.606

#23 Jimmy McElreath — McElreath Special
Qual: 5/10 @ 12:49
3:13.29 — 186.249
47.99 — 187.539
48.14 — 186.955
48.47 — 185.682
48.69 — 184.843

#95 Larry Cannon — KRACO Car Stereo
Qual: 5/10 @ 12:22
3:16.45 — 183.253
48.74 — 184.653
49.14 — 183.150
49.11 — 183.262
49.46 — 181.965

#20# Gordon Johncock — North American Van Lines Pacesetter
Qual: 5/11 @ 13:42
3:13.47 — 186.075
48.28 — 186.413
48.32 — 186.258
48.38 — 186.027
48.49 — 185.605

#70 Gordon Smiley — Valvoline-Patrick Racing Team
Qual: 5/18 @ 14:32
3:12.67 — 186.848
47.94 — 187.735
48.21 — 186.683
48.31 — 186.297
48.21 — 186.683

#44 Greg Leffler — Starcraft R.V.
Qual: 5/18 @ 15:51
3:15.92 — 183.748
49.04 — 183.524
48.94 — 183.899
49.05 — 183.486
48.89 — 184.087

#48 Mike Mosley — Theodore Racing Eagle
Qual: 5/18 @ 13:35
3:16.24 — 183.449
49.02 — 183.599
49.04 — 183.524
49.01 — 183.636
49.17 — 183.038

#8 Dick Simon — Vermont American/Silhouette Health Spas/Regal 8 Inn
Qual: 5/18 @ 12:07
3:16.95 — 182.788
40.08 — 183.374
49.00 — 183.673
49.23 — 182.815
49.64 — 181.305

#46 Gary Bettenhausen — Armstrong Mould, Inc.
Qual: 5/18 @ 15:24
3:17.30 — 182.463
49.15 — 183.113
49.25 — 182.741
49.27 — 182.667
49.63 — 181.342

#11 Bobby Unser — Norton Spirit Penske PC-9
Qual: 5/10 @ 14:07
3:09.48 — 189.994
47.15 — 190.880
47.38 — 189.954
47.39 — 189.913
47.56 — 189.235

#1 Rick Mears — The Gould Charge Penske PC-9
Qual: 5/10 @ 11:00
3:12.01 — 187.490
48.45 — 185.759
48.13 — 186.994
47.77 — 188.403
47.66 — 188.838

#5 Al Unser — Longhorn Racing
Qual: 5/10 @ 12:13
3:13.09 — 106.442
48.13 — 186.994
48.20 — 186.722
48.36 — 186.104
48.40 — 185.950

#14 A. J. Foyt, Jr. — Gilmore Racing Team
Qual: 5/10 @ 17:56
3:14.07 — 185.500
48.16 — 186.877
48.53 — 185.452
48.55 — 185.376
48.83 — 184.313

#26 Dick Ferguson — Amsoil Special
Qual: 5/10 @ 11:34
3:16.85 — 182.880
49.11 — 183.262
49.32 — 182.482
49.17 — 183.038
49.25 — 182.741

#96 Don Whittington — Sun System Special
Qual: 5/11 @ 16:58
3:15.73 — 183.927
48.71 — 184.767
48.85 — 184.237
49.25 — 182.741
48.92 — 183.974

#16 George Snider — Gilmore Racing Team
Qual: 5/18 @ 15:45
3:14.19 — 185.385
48.41 — 185.912
48.53 — 185.452
48.57 — 185.300
48.68 — 184.881

#18 Dennis Firestone — Scientific Drilling Controls Spl.
Qual: 5/18 @ 15:15
3:15.97 — 183.702
48.99 — 183.711
48.93 — 183.936
49.00 — 183.673
49.05 — 183.486

#94 Bill Whittington — Sun System Special
Qual: 5/18 @ 15:07
3:16.44 — 183.262
49.00 — 183.673
48.98 — 183.748
49.09 — 183.337
49.37 — 182.297

#2 Bill Vukovich — Hubler Chevrolet WFMS Spl.
Qual: 5/18 @ 12:35
3:17.00 — 182.741
49.16 — 183.076
49.10 — 183.299
49.31 — 182.519
49.43 — 182.076

#9@ Tom Sneva — Bonjour Action Jeans
Qual: 5/10 @ 12:32
3:14.29 — 185.290
48.21 — 186.683
48.37 — 186.066
48.86 — 184.200
48.85 — 184.237

---

* Qualified as car #20
# Qualified as car #40
@ Qualified for 14th position, but moved to 33rd position when car was substituted.
$ Qualified as car #3

The average speed of the 35 cars that started the race in 1979 was 186.737 MPH.

The average speed of the 33 cars that started the race in 1980 was 185.570 MPH.

(1.167 - MPH slower)

The Field

No. 4-1980 Chaparral/Cosworth. Driver Johnny Rutherford: Chief Mechanic Steve Roby. Rutherford started on the pole with this Jim Hall creation and won the race.

No. 9-1977 McLaren/Cosworth. Driver Tom Sneva: Chief Mechanic, Jud Phillips. 1978 Wally Dallenbach started 7th, finished 6th. 1980 started 33rd, finished 2nd!

No. 46-1976 Wildcat II/Sparks-Goosen-Drake. Driver Gary Bettenhausen: Chief Mechanic, Paul Leffler. 1976 Dallenbach started 7th, finished 4th. 1977 Dallenbach started 10th, finished 4th. 1978 Bigelow started 18th, finished 21st. 1979 Howdy Holmes started 13th, finished 7th. 1980 started 32nd finished 3rd!

No. 20-1979 Penske PC-6/Cosworth. Driver Gordon Johncock: Chief Mechanic George Bignotti. 1979 Wally Dallenbach started 7th, finished 27th. 1980 started 17th, finished 4th.

No. 1-1980 Penske PC-9/Cosworth. Driver Rick Mears: Chief Mechanic Darrell Soppe. 1980 Mears started 6th, finished 5th after 199 laps.

No. 10-1979 Penske PC-7/Cosworth. Driver Pancho Carter: Chief Mechanic, Johnny Capels. Started 9th, finished 6th, after 1 lap penalty.

No. 25-1977 Interscope-Parnelli/Cosworth. Driver, Danny Ongais; Chief Mechanic, Phil Casey. 1978 Ongais started 2nd, finished 18th. 1979 Ongais crashed in practice. 1980 started 16th, finished 7th.

No. 43-1979 Lola/Cosworth. Driver Tom Bigelow: Chief Mechanic, Paul Leffler. 1979 Tom Bigelow started 30th, finished 14th. 1980 started 31st, finished 8th.

No. 21-1979 Penske PC-7/Cosworth. Driver Tim Richmond; Chief Mechanic, John Barnes. 1979 Bobby Unser started 4th, finished 5th. 1980 Richmond crashed, replaced tub. Started 19th, finished 9th.

No. 44-1979 Lola/Cosworth. Driver Greg Leffler: Chief Mechanic, Paul Leffler. 1979 Janet Guthrie started 14th, finished 34th. 1980 started 23rd, finished 10th.

No. 29-1979 McLaren/Cosworth. Driver, Billy Engelhart: Chief Mechanic: Danny Jones. 1979 Tom Sneva ran on Championship Trail. 1980 started 22nd, finished 11th.

No. 2-1978 Watson/Offy. Driver Bill Vukovich: Chief Mechanic, A.J. Watson. 1978 Sheldon Kinser started 12th, finished 32nd: 1979 Sheldon Kinser started 10th, finished 28th. 1980 started 30th, finished 12th, 192 laps.

No. 96-1979 Penske PC-7-9/Cosworth. Driver Don Whittington: Chief Mechanic, Graeme Bartils. 1980 started 18th, finished 13th.

No. 14-1979 Parnelli/Cosworth. Driver A.J. Foyt, Jr. Chief Mechanic, Jack Starne. Not at track in 1979. 1980 started 12th, finished 14th.

No. 16-1978 Parnelli/Cosworth. Driver George Snider: Chief Mechanic, Jack Starne. This car won the Ontario 200 in 1979. 1980 Snider started 21st, finished 15th.

No. 18-1978 Penske PC-6/Cosworth. Driver Dennis Firestone: Chief Mechanic, Wilbur Bruce. 1978 Mike Hiss practiced. 1979 Tom Bagley started 15th, finished 9th. 1980 started 24th, finished 16th.

No. 7-1979 Lola/Cosworth. Driver Jerry Sneva: Chief Mechanic, Paul Leffler. 1979 Tom Bigelow was bumped. 1980 Sneva started 5th, finished 17th.

No. 99-1979 Lightning/Chevrolet V-6. Driver Hurley Haywood: Chief Mechanic, Mike Devin. 1979 Hurley Haywood, too slow. 1980 started 25th, finished 18th.

No. 11-1980 Penske PC-9/Cosworth. Driver Bobby Unser: Chief Mechanic, Laurie Gerrish. Started 3rd, finished 19th.

No. 12-1980 Penske PC-9/Cosworth. Driver Mario Andretti: Chief Mechanic, Bob Sprow. Started 2nd, finished 20th.

No. 38-1980 McLaren-Karl/Chevrolet V-8. Driver Jerry Karl: Chief Mechanic, Lew Parks. This is a car re-designed by Jerry Karl to be ground effects. Started 28th, finished 21st.

No. 8-1977 Vollstedt/Offy. Driver Dick Simon: Chief Mechanic, Chad Rogers. 1977 Simon started 30, finished 31st; 1978 Simon started 10th, finished 19th; 1979 Simon started 20th, finished 26th; 1980 Simon started 29th, finished 22nd.

No. 66-1979 Wildcat/Chevrolet V-8. Driver Roger Rager: Chief Mechanic, Bob Henderson. 1979 Spike Gehlhausen started 31st, finished 10th. 1980 started 10th, finished 23rd.

No. 23-1978 Penske PC-6/Cosworth. Driver Jim McElreath: Chief Mechanic, Shirley McElreath. 1978 Mike Hiss qualified for Andretti, started 33rd, finished 12th. 1979 McElreath started 19th finished 35th. 1980 started 11th, finished 24th.

No. 70-1980 Phoenix/Cosworth. Driver Gordon Smiley: Chief Mechanic, George Bignotti. 1980 started 20th, finished 25th.

No. 15-1977 Lightning/Offy. Driver Johnny Parsons: Chief Mechanic, Mike Devin. 1977, not on track. 1978, Parsons, no attempt made. 1979 Johnny Parsons started 9th finished 32nd. 1980 started 7th, finished 26th. Unique lay-down engine.

No. 5-1980 Longhorn LR-01/Cosworth. Driver Al Unser. Chief Mechanic, George Heuning. Started 9th, finished 27th after 33 laps.

No. 40-1980-PR-001 Wildcat/Cosworth. Driver Tom Bagley: Chief Mechanic, George Bignotti. Started 13th, finished 28th.

No. 35-1979 PC-7/Cosworth. Driver, Spike Gehlhausen; Chief Mechanic: Derek Mower. 1979 Bobby Unser ran at Phoenix. 1980 started 4th, finished 29th.

No. 94-1980 Parnelli/Cosworth. Driver Bill Whittington: Chief Mechanic, Graeme Bartils. 1980 started 27th, finished 30th.

No. 26-1979 PC6/Cosworth. Driver Dick Ferguson, Chief Mechanic: Jerry Eisert. This car made up from most parts of Mears' winning 1979 car. 1980 started 15th, finished 31st.

No. 48-1980 Eagle/Chevrolet V-8. Driver Mike Mosley: Chief Mechanic, Wayne Leary. Started 26th, finished 32nd.

No. 95-1975 Wildcat I/Offy, Driver Larry Cannon: Chief Mechanic, Phil Thrasher. 1975 Gordon Johncock started 2nd, finished 31st. 1976, not entered. 1977 Vern Schuppan, alternate. 1978 Larry Cannon hit wall on 2nd attempt. 1979 Cannon bumped. 1980 started 14th, finished 33rd.

The Rookies

Rookies-A-Plenty

When the rookies of the racing world heard that personable little Howdy Holmes was the only newcomer to make the 1979 starting field, they turned out in numbers like never seen before. A full two dozen were on the track this year and ten made the race, to prove there won't be any shortage of talent at the 500 in years to come.

by Jep Cadou

Whereas the 1979 rookie crop at the Speedway was "a class of one," the 1980 crop was "one of class."

It was definitely a whopper, with 10 drivers making the race, in marked contrast to last year when Howdy Holmes made up the entire rookie contingent in the 500.

Even before the Speedway opened for practice on May 3, it had set a record with 24 first-year drivers nominated for cars.

Seventeen neophytes passed drivers' tests for another record, and three more were excused from any testing because of previous experience in other 500-mile races.

The 10 drivers who made the race for the first time represented the largest Rookie group since the legendary Class of 1965, which included Mario Andretti,

Al Unser, Gordon Johncock, George Snider and the late Billy Foster.

Tim Richmond, a slender mustachioed bachelor from Ashland, OH., dominated the pre-race period like no rookie since Andretti.

Richmond's achievements started on the very first day of practice when he turned in the day's quickest lap of 185.491 in his Mach I Racing Enterprises Penske/Cosworth. They ended on race day when he drove to a ninth place finish and then became the first Rookie-of-the-Year to ride to Victory Lane as a passenger with the race winner.

In between was sandwiched a remarkable three weeks of highs and lows.

Richmond startled railbirds on the day before time trials opened. He waited until "Happy Hour" to get in his fast licks and, with barely a half-hour of practice left, got in the fastest unofficial lap of the whole month by any driver, veteran or rookie, with a 193.507

clocking in the Penske, which by that time had picked up sponsorship from UNO, a card game, and Q-95, a radio station.

At that point, Tim looked like a pretty good bet to be the first rookie in 30 years to sit on the pole. Not since Walt Faulkner's celebrated "stuck-throttle run" of 1950 had a driver won the pole on his first outing at Indy.

But that was not to be. The dream was ground out against the hard concrete of the wall in the southwest turn at 10:07 a.m. on Saturday morning when Richmond lost control and the car slid 600 feet to the barrier.

Tim's car owners, his father Al and Bob Schultz, made arrangements to buy a new Penske tub to replace the one the

Tim Richmond

Hurley Haywood

Greg Leffler

[115]

younger Richmond had crinkled. Richmond returned to the track the following Thursday and posted a quick time of 186.877, a good indication the accident had not slowed him very much, if at all.

Tim sweated as the second Saturday of time trials was rained out, but made the field handily at 188.334 in the fastest qualification run of the second Sunday, final day of qualifications.

Most of Richmond's colleagues in the Class of '80 were graduates of the road racing ranks, but the 24-year-old Tim came from a primarily oval-track background.

He raced go-karts when he was quite young but the racing bug didn't really bite Richmond until four years ago when he tried out a friend's Sprint car on the 1/3-mile Lakeville (Ohio) Speedway.

Airplanes had been Tim's thing up until then. He learned to fly at 14 and obtained his private license at 17, later adding multi-engine, instrument and helicopter ratings.

Tim raced modifieds in 1977 on the Sandusky (Ohio) International Speedway, a flat, paved half-mile, becoming one of the very few drivers to win a racing association championship in his first season. He won the Ohio Racing Association championship and also captured the Ohio State 500 title, a series of five 100-lap races at different tracks on consecutive days.

Richmond joined USAC in 1978 — with a bang. Driving a rear-engined car for the first time, Tim won the USAC Mini-Indy series opener at Phoenix, AZ., in the fiercest kind of competition.

In his first Sprint race with USAC, at

Indianapolis Raceway Park, Richmond won his heat race and moved up from 19th starting spot to finish ninth in the 40-lap feature.

He finished fourth in his next Sprint feature, a 50-lapper on the high banks of Salem (IN.) Speedway. Running 12 Sprint programs, Richmond finished 30th in the point standings and was named USAC Sprint Division Rookie-of-the-Year. He also placed ninth in the Mini-Indy series with four top-ten finishes in the six races in which he participated.

After driving in two Sprint races in 1979, Tim turned his attention to the Championship cars. He lasted only four laps in his debut at Michigan International Speedway before engine problems forced him out. In his next race at Watkins Glen, N.Y., Richmond finished eighth after starting 15th. It was only his third race on a road course.

Tim ran his first 500-mile race in the California 500 at Ontario in 1979. He turned in the fastest qualifying speed of all the four-cylinder cars at 191.477 and advanced to eighth place in the first 20 laps before a broken ring-and-pinion gear put him out after 39 laps. In the CART finale at Phoenix, Richmond was sidelined by an oil leak, finishing 15th.

Another oval-track graduate finished one spot behind Richmond. Greg Leffler, the son of veteran mechanic Paul Leffler, is the defending USAC National Sprint champion, so his 10th place finish was no surprise.

Also slim and mustachioed, Leffler is 28 and single. He began his racing career

Whittington Brothers

Frank Weiss

Bill Alsup

Dana Carter

Dick Ferguson

in 1972 in the USAC Sprints. He won one feature each in 1975, 1976, and 1977, finishing ninth in the point standings the latter year.

In 1978, he won three features and moved up to sixth in the standings and in 1979 climbed the mountain, recording four victories, five seconds, four thirds and five fourths en route to the title, which he won in a tight battle with Bubby Jones.

He made his Championship debut at Milwaukee in 1979 but crashed in practice. Leffler drove the Starcraft R.V. Lola/Cosworth in the 500 after qualifying at 183.748. He turned in a steady and consistent driving job, moving into the top ten at the 70-lap mark and getting as high as seventh at one 10-lap post.

Still another oval-track graduate, Billy Engelhart, brought his #29 Master Lock McLaren/Cosworth home in 11th place in another steady driving job.

Engelhart had a hard, uphill road in making the 500 field, so the finish was doubly sweet for him. He passed his driver's test in 1976 but was called in from a qualification attempt after completing only one lap. Rideless for Indy in 1977 and 1978, Billy did score his biggest career victory when he won the 1978 Hoosier Hundred Dirt Championship race.

In 1979, Engelhart hit the wall coming out of the southwest turn in a practice run, fracturing his left leg and damaging the car extensively. But he came back to finish second in the USAC Dirt Championship series with a second in the Hoosier Hundred and two fifth place finishes.

Don Whittington, who showed persistence by staying in the race after he spun and brushed the wall on the north-west turn, was the highest-finishing of the road-racer rookies with a 13th place in the #96 Sun System Penske/Cosworth.

Don became interested in racing in early 1978 and drove his first race at Sebring, FL. in a Porsche that March. By the end of the 1978 IMSA season, he had finished fourth in points and he and brother Bill Whittington had bought the Road Atlanta road racing plant.

In their first full season of racing in 1979, the Whittingtons attacked the World Challenge for Endurance Drivers and the Winston GT series with a vengeance. Don won the World Challenge, co-driving to victories at the 6-hour races at Watkins Glen, N.Y., Daytona Beach, FL. and Riverside, CA. and combining with brother Bill to win the biggest endurance race of them all, the Twenty-four Hours of LeMans in France.

Don started the 1980 IMSA season by setting a new qualifying record at the 24 Hours of Daytona in February. He, Bill and another brother, Dale Whittington, co-drove to a third-place finish in the 12 Hours of Sebring. He also got his feet wet in NASCAR racing with a 16th place finish in the Daytona 500, in preparation for a possible full season Winston Cup Grand National effort in 1981.

Dennis Firestone, the 1979 USAC Mini-Indy champion and another road racing raduate, finished 16th in the #18 Scientific Drilling Controls McLaren/Cosworth.

Recovering from an embarrassing moment which saw him get into the second turn grass and crash while going only about 90 miles an hour in practice, Firestone qualified at 183.702 and started 24th. Transmission problems eliminated him after 137 laps.

Born in Australia, Firestone began

Dennis Firestone

Gordon Smiley

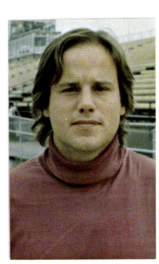

John Wood

Pete Halsmer

Herm Johnson

Tom Frantz

Bill Tempero   *Roger Mears*   *Phil Caliva*

Billy Engelhart

racing in Formula Fords at Riverside, CA. in 1971 and later moved into the Formula Atlantic series. He captured the 1974 and 1976 South Pacific Formula Ford titles and the 1976 Formula Ford national championship. He won 23 straight races in Formula Ford and

Formula Atlantic series in one stretch in 1976 and 1977.

Placing second in the Mini-Indy series in 1978, Dennis was named its Rookie-of-the-Year. When he moved up to the title the following year, Firestone won five of the eight races and was runner-up the other three.

Firestone is 35 and makes his home now in Gardena, CA.

Another top road racer who cracked the Indy field for the first time is Hurley Haywood, 32-year-old Jacksonville, FL. resident, who finished 18th in the Sta-On Car Glaze/Guarantee/Auto/KISS Radio Lightning/Chevy. Turbo-charger problems put him out after 126 laps. The car caught fire twice in the pits before that.

Only driver ever to sweep the LeMans and Daytona 24 Hours races and the Sebring 12 Hours, Haywood has been competing in endurance racing since early in this decade. He was IMSA champion in 1971 and 1972 and runner-up in that series in 1975 and 1977.

Haywood passed his rookie test at Indianapolis in 1979 and had a fine first qualifying lap of 190.638, but his speeds fell off due to engine problems and he missed the race.

Roger Rager, a 31-year-old driver from Mound, Minn., was the "people's choice." His Advance Clean Sweep/Carpenter School Bus Wildcat/Chevy was powered by a Chevy stock-block engine. The block came from a school bus with 70,000 miles on it.

Rager did a fine job in qualifications, putting the stock-blocker in 10th spot with a run at 186.374 mph. Staying out

on the track longer than the other front runners, Rager had the satisfaction of leading the 16th and 17th laps of the race and was running well when he was taken out in an accident touched off when veteran Jim McElreath lost control and hit the wall.

Rager finished 55 laps and placed 23rd.

A former all-state football player, Rager started racing in go-karts at 6 and was Nebraska State Champion in 1961 and 1962. He moved on to hobby stocks, drag racers and super-modifieds, then joined the IMCA Sprint circuit in 1968. Rager moved up to USAC Sprints in 1976, finishing 23rd in points and being chosen Rookie-of-the-Year. He drove his first Championship race at Trenton, N.J. in 1976, finishing 20th.

Rager passed his Speedway driver's test in 1978, but missed the race in both that year and in 1979.

One of the most impressive "hurry-up jobs" of the year was done by Gordon Smiley, another former road racing star, who didn't get his ride in the third Patrick Racing Team car until the first two were in the show. That put him a week behind everyone else, but Gordon responded beautifully.

He was the second-fastest rookie qualifier with a 186.848 run in the #70 Valvoline/Patrick Phoenix/Cosworth. He had moved up from his 25th starting spot to ninth in the first 100 miles, but was out with turbo-charger problems just seven laps later. That placed him 25th.

Bill Whittington, a 30-year-old Ft. Lauderdale (FL.) resident, has been

Jan Sneva

Tony Bettenhausen

Rich Vogler

Ronnie Shuman

Roger Rager

racing only two years but has a third place finish in the 1979 World Challenge for Endurance Drivers and victories in the 24 Hours of LeMans and the six-hour events at Riverside, CA., Watkins Glen, N.Y. and Daytona Beach, FL. to show for it.

His first Championship race was at Ontario, CA. in the 1979 California 500, where he finished 12th. He and brothers Don and Dale finished third in the 12 Hours of Sebring in the Spring of 1980.

Bill drove a Sun System Parnelli/Cosworth, which was eliminated after nine laps when he hit the wall on the southwest turn, placing 30th.

Dick Ferguson, a hard-luck guy at the Speedway, had the ill fortune to be in the wrong place at the right time when Whittington had his accident. Ferguson had no place to go but off the track and he slid into the inside guard rail, badly damaging his #26 AMSOIL Penske/Cosworth. That put him out of the race and placed him 31st.

Rookies who qualified but were "bumped" from the starting field were: Bill Alsup in the #41 Polaroid Time Zero Penske/Cosworth, 181.919; Pete Halsmer, #34 Wysard Motors Wildcat/SGD; 181.351; Phil Caliva, #37 Nicolosi's Italian Restaurant McLaren/Offy, 178. 873; and Tony Bettenhausen Jr., #32 Vita-Fresh Fruit Juice Eagle/Offy, 176. 410.

Rookies Frank Weiss, Dana Carter and Jan Sneva all crashed in practice runs. Weiss was the only one injured, suffering a fractured leg. Rookies Herm Johnson, Ron Shuman, Bill Tempero, Rich Vogler, John Wood, Roger Mears and Tom Frantz completed full driver's or refresher tests but did not complete qualifying runs.

Ed Finley and Buddie Boys were listed for cars but were told to get more experience and return later. Ross Davis was persuaded to hire another driver (John Martin) for his car and Bobby Fisher never surfaced.

Such was the Class of '80 at the Speedway.

Armstrong Mould

Sherman Armstrong comes to the Indianapolis Motor Speedway each year and obtains enough garage space to set up a small manufacturing facility. The Winchester, Indiana glass mould manufacturer had three cars finish in the top ten in 1980, a most impressive record especially when you consider many other teams are spending more money. Armstrong is one of the Speedway's more colorful car owners and can always be counted on to voice an opinion. His team is also deeply involved in Sprint and Dirt car racing where they are continual winners. Considering his consistency, we don't doubt that an Armstrong owned vehicle will be in victory lane at the "500" soon.

WFMS

HUBLER
CHEVROLET

Hubler

The Indianapolis based Chevrolet dealership owned by the father and son team of Frank and Howard Hubler are becoming familiar sponsors at the Speedway, having first had their name here in 1976. This year they joined forces with the progressive WFMS radio station and once again obtained the driving services of the humorous and always needling Billy Vukovich. Although they weren't in contention for the lead, it is nice to see a team having such a good time. We hope they're back for many years to come.

Genesee Beer

Dick Hammond, the upstate New York Genesee Beer distributor continued his involvement this year at Indianapolis but suffered the misfortune of having his car bumped from the field. He good-naturedly said, "We'll be back . . . that's the breaks sometimes," and trundled off to watch a USAC Sprint car race where he's also been involved in sponsorship for many years. The sport could use more like him.

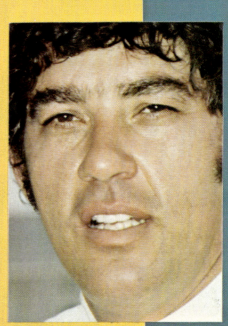

Rolla Vollstedt

Rolla Vollstedt is one of the most dedicated car owners ever to pass through the gates at the Indianapolis Motor Speedway. His involvement in auto racing dates back over three decades. Although his teams haven't always been blessed with an abundance of capitol, he's been one of the Speedway's most innovative individuals. He'll always be remembered as the man who brought the first woman to the 500 when he gave Janet Guthrie a ride and he was one of the first on the scene with a rear-engine Offy and a winged car as well. Rolla has long been trusted by fellow car owners and his tenure on the USAC Board of Directors speaks well for his diplomacy. He's currently teamed with amiable and talented Dick Simon. If they ever win the race, they'll have earned it.

INTERSCOPE

The Interscope team generated a tremendous amount of pre-race publicity this year as it was speculated they would arrive with a Porsche-powered mount. Rule changes kept the German car manufacturer from entering, a fact that saddened sports car fans world-wide. Nevertheless, the familiar #25 owned by Ted Field and driven by Danny Ongais gave a good accounting of themselves and were once again considered as candidates for victory lane.

KENT OIL

In just a few short seasons, Tom Bagley has risen from the ranks of amateur road racer to a full-fledged, capable Indianapolis 500 driver. He doesn't fit the mold of a swashbuckling, do-or-die racer, but is methodical in his approach which is paying dividends. Bagley has maintained a long association with his sponsor, Steve and Barbara Kent, two of the most enthusiastic participants seen at the Speedway in years. The amiable Bagley can be counted on to be a "500" front runner in years to come and it would indeed be a memorable victory lane celebration if the Kents are ever involved.

Tom Barrett

Thomas Barrett is one of the world's most respected antique and classic car dealers. For the past two years he's been involved in sponsorship at the 500 with talented Vern Schuppan. His love for cars of quality is evidenced by the 1941 Chrysler Le Baron shown here, the only non-production car ever to pace the 500. Barrett is also responsible for holding the world's largest antique car auction in Scottsdale, Arizona. He's one of those true sportsmen we'd like to see more of at Indy, and hope he comes back.

The 1941 Winner

IMS

Spoerle

Co-Winners -
Mauri Rose & Floyd Davis -
Indianapolis Motor Speedway -
1941.

Here's what the car looked like when it arrived in Indy.

Old Speedway Girl Comes Home From Carolina

There is something about the bending of metal that has always fascinated us. What was once a flat piece of aluminum becomes transformed into the graceful shape of a race car tail when given to the right craftsman. Jerry Weeks is such a man. His card reads: **"J. Weeks, Metalsmith"**.

In the old days, before fiberglass, race car bodies were hand-hammered out of aluminum and then later straightened when miles of running over rocky tracks made their smooth skins resemble a sack of walnuts. There are but a handful of men who practice the art of handforming aluminum, so it can become a real study when an old race car is located that needs to be restored.

Indianapolis 500 driver Bob Harkey, who is as close to a modern day soldier of fortune as you'll find (he still flies a World War II airplane) located the car that won the 1941 Indianapolis 500. Ironically, Harkey drove the car in the Fifties when it ran in the NASCAR promoted Speedway car races. Its engine had been replaced with a passenger car V-8 when Harkey drove it and the old girl hadn't seen a coat of polish in years. Harkey notified Speedway officials of the whereabouts of the car and a deal was subsequently made. The car was donated to the Museum by Mr. and Mrs. O.R. Corrhier of Landis, N.C.

After winning the 1941 race the car made a couple of Speedway appearances after the war. Its last Championship Trail appearance was believed to be at Williams Grove in 1951 when Walt Brown was killed in it during a warm-up lap. The story has it that NASCAR ace Buck Baker drove it successfully in their Speedway Division with a Cadillac V-8 and it was then garaged after the short-lived series ended.

It sat in the Museum basement for a time and then Speedway Museum men Barney Wimmer and Bill Spoerle started on its restoration. The frame and body were sent to Jerry Weeks' Brownsburg, Indiana shop where it was almost completely re-skinned. Weeks, who is a fine Midget and Sprint driver in his own right (with an eye toward running at Indy) learned his trade through years of work with California car builder Don Edmunds. Jerry moved to the Midwest several years ago to first work with Grant King and then hung out his own shingle.

We wish the **"Noc-Out Hose Clamp Spl."** could talk, for it would certainly provide hours of stories. For Mauri Rose and Floyd Davis it brought the pinnacle of auto racing. To Walt Brown it brought his last breath. To Jerry Weeks it gave a place to display his talents. Now, thousands of Speedway Museum visitors will glance at it and say, "My, what a pretty paint job."

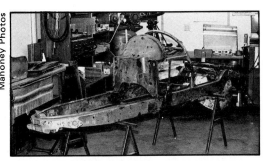

Weeks cut a section out of the tail and inserted a new one. Then he had to straighten out the whole thing.

Left Top: It would be easy to get discouraged when you see the car in this shape. Center: But with a few dozen hours' work it looks like this. Bottom: A new belly pan needed.

The Road To Indy

A rookie driver's road to Indy has changed over the years. In the early '50s, when the "Rookie of the Year" program was inaugurated, a solid background in Sprints and Midgets was your ticket to the Brickyard. Grand Prix champion Jack Brabham's success with his rear-engined Cooper Climax in the 1961 event opened the door to drivers with sports car and road racing experience, a trend very much in evidence today. The Speedway's publicity staff compiled the following statistics which graphically show the changes over the years.

*Denotes "Rookie of the Year"

Year	Name	Start	Finish	Background
1952	*Art Cross	20	5	Midgets
	Alberto Ascari	19	31	Formula I
	Eddie Johnson	24	16	Midgets, Champ cars
	Jimmy Reece	23	7	Modifieds
	Jim Rigsby	26	12	Sprints, Midgets
	Bob Scott	25	29	Sprints, Midgets
	Jimmy Bryan	21	6	Sprints, Midgets
	Bob Sweikert	32	26	Sprints
1953	*Jimmy Daywalt	21	6	Sprints
	Ernie McCoy	20	8	Sprints, Midgets
	Marshall Teague	22	18	Stocks
	Don Freeland	15	27	Sprints
	Cal Niday	30	30	Midgets
	Johnny Thomson	33	32	Sprints, Midgets
1954	*Larry Crockett	25	9	Sprints
	Ed Elisian	31	18	Sprints
	Frank Armi	33	19	Midgets
	Pat O'Connor	12	21	Sprints
	Bill Homeier	18	33	Midgets
1955	*Al Herman	16	7	Midgets, Sprints
	Chuck Weyant	25	12	Midgets
	Shorty Templeman	31	18	Midgets
	Keith Andrews	28	20	Hill Climb
	Eddie Russo	13	22	Midgets
	Ray Crawford	23	23	Stock & Road Race
	Al Keller	22	27	Sprints
	Johnny Boyd	26	29	Sprints, Midgets
1956	*Bob Veith	23	7	Sprints, Midgets
	Bob Christie	25	13	Stocks
	Billy Garrett	29	16	Midgets
	Johnnie Tolan	31	21	Midgets
	Jack Turner	24	25	Midgets

Year	Name	Start	Finish	Background
1957	*Don Edmunds	27	19	Midgets
	Eddie Sachs	2	23	Sprints, Midgets
	Mike Magill	18	24	Sprints
	Bill Cheesbourg	23	26	Modifieds, Stocks
	Elmer George	9	33	Sprints, Midgets
1958	*George Amick	25	2	Midgets
	Jud Larson	19	8	Sprints, Midgets
	Dempsey Wilson	32	15	Midgets
	A. J. Foyt	12	16	Sprints, Midgets
	Paul Goldsmith	16	30	Stocks, Motorcycles
	Jerry Unser	24	31	Stocks, Hill Climb
	Len Sutton	27	32	Modifieds, Sprints
	Art Bisch	28	33	Midgets
1959	*Bobby Grim	5	26	Sprints
	Chuck Arnold	21	15	Midgets
	Jim McWithey	33	16	Sprints
	Don Branson	10	24	Sprints, Midgets
	Red Amick	26	31	Sprints
1960	*Jim Hurtubise	23	18	Sprints
	Lloyd Ruby	12	7	Midgets, Sports Cars
	Bud Tingelstad	28	9	Sprints, Midgets
	Wayne Weiler	15	24	Sprints, Midgets
1961	*Parnelli Jones	5	12	Modifieds, Sprints, Midgets
	*Bob Marshman	33	7	Sprints, Midgets
	Jack Brabham	13	9	Formula I
	Norman Hall	32	10	Sprints
	Ebb Rose	19	23	Sports Cars
	A. J. Sheperd	14	26	Sprints
	Roger McCluskey	29	27	Sprints, Midgets
	Don Davis	27	29	Sprints, Midgets

*Denotes "Rookie of the Year"

Year	Name	Start	Finish	Background
1962	*Jim McElreath	7	6	Sprints, Midgets
	Dan Gurney	8	20	Stocks, Formula I
	Chuck Hulse	16	21	Sprints, Midgets
	Allen Crowe	22	31	Sprints, Midgets
	Chuck Rodee	21	32	Sprints, Midgets
1963	*Jim Clark	5	2	European Sports Cars
	Al Miller	31	9	Sprints
	Johnny Rutherford	26	29	Sprints
	Art Malone	23	31	Drags
	Bobby Unser	16	33	Pike's Peak, Sprints
1964	*Johnny White	21	4	Sprints
	Bob Harkey	27	8	Sprints, Midgets
	Bob Wente	32	9	Midgets
	Walt Hansgen	10	13	Sports Cars
	Bob Mathouser	28	22	Sprints, Midgets
	Dave MacDonald	14	29	Sports Cars
	Ronnie Duman	16	31	Midgets
1965	*Mario Andretti	4	3	Sprints, Midgets
	Bobby Johns	22	7	Stocks
	Bill Foster	6	17	Modifieds
	Al Unser	32	9	Pike's Peak, Sprints
	Masten Gregory	31	23	European Sports Cars
	Joe Leonard	27	29	Cycles, Stocks
	Arnie Knepper	19	18	Sprints, Midgets
	Jerry Grant	17	27	Sports Cars
	George Snider	16	21	Sprints
	Mickey Rupp	15	6	Go-carts, Sprints
	Gordon Johncock	14	5	Sprints, Modifieds
1966	*Jackie Stewart	11	6	European Sports Cars
	Graham Hill	15	1	European Sports Cars
	Gary Congdon	16	25	Sprints, Midgets
	Mel Kenyon	17	5	Midgets
	Cale Yarborough	24	28	Stocks
	Carl Williams	25	16	Sprints, Midgets
	Larry Dickson	32	32	Sprints
1967	*Denis Hulme	24	4	European Sports Cars
	Art Pollard	13	8	Modifieds
	Wally Dallenbach	15	29	Midgets
	Lee Roy Yarbrough	26	27	Stocks
	Jochen Rindt	32	24	European Sports Cars
1968	*Bill Vukovich	23	7	Midgets, Sprints
	Jim Malloy	14	22	Modifieds, Sprints
	Ronnie Bucknum	19	21	Sports Cars
	Gary Bettenhausen	22	24	Stocks, etc.
	Mike Mosley	27	8	Sprints, Midgets
	Sammy Sessions	31	9	Sprints, Midgets
1969	*Mark Donohue	4	7	Sports Cars
	Peter Revson	33	5	Sports Cars
	Bruce Walkup	28	33	Midgets, Sprints
	George Follmer	27	27	Sports Cars
	Sonny Ates	14	17	Midgets, Sprints
1970	*Donnie Allison	23	4	Stocks
	Rick Muther	15	8	Sports Cars
	Greg Weld	28	32	Sprints, Modifieds
	Dick Simon	31	14	Sports Cars
1971	*Denny Zimmerman	28	8	Modifieds
	Steve Krisiloff	27	31	Modifieds
	David Hobbs	16	20	European Sports Cars
	Bentley Warren	15	23	Modifieds, Sprints
1972	*Mike Hiss	25	7	Modifieds, Sports Cars
	Jimmy Caruthers	31	9	Midgets
	Lee Kunzman	30	17	Midgets, Sprints
	John Mahler	29	22	Sports Cars
	Salt Walther	27	33	Sprints
	John Martin	14	16	Sports Cars
	Swede Savage	9	32	Cycles, Stocks
	Sam Posey	7	5	Sports Cars
1973	*Graham McRae	13	16	Sports Cars
	Bobby Allison	12	32	Stocks
	Jerry Karl	28	26	Midgets, Sprints
1974	*Duane Carter, Jr.	21	7	¼ Midgets to Full, Sprints
	Bill Simpson	20	13	Sports Cars
	Tom Sneva	8	20	Super Modified Rear Engines
	Tom Bigelow	23	12	Midgets, Sprints
	Jan Opperman	32	21	Super Modifieds, Sprints
	Larry Cannon	33	24	Super Modifieds, Sprints
	Johnny Parsons	29	26	¼ Midgets to Full, Sprints
1975	*Bill Puterbaugh	15	7	Sprints
	Sheldon Kinser	26	12	Sprints
	Larry McCoy	28	30	Midgets, Sprints
	Eldon Rasmussen	32	24	Modifieds, Sprints
1976	*Vern Schuppan	17	18	Formula I & 5000
	Spike Gehlhausen	25	33	Midgets, Champ cars
	Al Loquasto	24	25	Sprints, Champ cars
	Billy Scott	21	23	Drags, Stocks, Sprints
1977	*Jerry Sneva	16	10	Modifieds
	Cliff Hucul	27	22	Stocks, Modifieds
	Bubby Jones	33	21	Dirt cars, Sprints
	Danny Ongais	7	20	Cycles, Drags, Sports Cars
	Clay Regazzoni	29	30	Formula I
	Janet Guthrie	26	29	Sports Cars
	Bobby Olivero	14	25	¼ Midgets to Full, Sprints
1978	*Larry Rice	30	11	Sprints, Midgets, Dirt
	*Rick Mears	3	23	Off-Road, Sprint Buggy
	Joe Saldana	24	15	Sprints, Midgets, Dirt
	Tom Bagley	14	27	Super Vees, Mini-Indy
	Phil Threshie	29	30	Sports Cars
1979	*Howdy Holmes	13	7	Super Vees, Formula Atlantic
1980	*Tim Richmond	19	9	Sprints, Mini-Indy
	Greg Leffler	23	10	Sprints, Champ. Dirt
	Billy Engelhart	22	11	Midgets, Sprints, Champ. Dirt
	Don Whittington	18	13	Endurance Racing
	Dennis Firestone	24	16	Mini-Indy
	Hurley Haywood	25	18	Endurance Racing, IMSA
	Roger Rager	10	23	Sprints, Champ. Dirt
	Gordon Smiley	20	25	SCCA, Aurora Formula I
	Bill Whittington	27	30	Endurance Racing
	Dick Ferguson	15	31	Formula Ford, Mini-Indy

[131]

THE GREATEST DEBACLE IN RACING

A Short Story by R.E. Smith
Illustrated by Don Cooper

After all the controversies, problems, hot tempers, and arguments of the 1979 Indianapolis 500, drivers, administrators, and fans alike prayed that the next Memorial Day Race would be simply good, clean, hard-driving racing.

They got plenty of competition and excitement, but they also received more than they asked for. They got the wildest Indy 500 in racing history, one that made the 1979 race look like an outing of the Baker Electric Car Club of America.

It began innocently enough when a secretary going through a stack of entry forms turned to the woman next to her.

"Here's a new one," she said. "Ever hear of an Ackroyd Special? It has a Ford engine and the chassis part says, 'Frame.' "

"Maybe it's one of those George Frame built originally," the woman said. "It sounds like one of those off-brand cars some of the little teams run. They buy an old racer, play around with it, and call it something brand new. Who's the team?''

"The Blue Creek Racing Team," the secretary said and looked at the postmark on the envelope. "That's funny," she said. "It's from Blue Creek, Wisconsin."

"Never heard of it," the other woman said. "Does the check look all right?"

"Yes."

"Send it on then."

The next sign was more obvious. Dark had just descended, and an early May thunderstorm was drenching the track. The guard at the gate was shivering from the wind and the water dripping inside his collar when a set of very high headlights came toward him and turned in. The vehicle was a high-wheeled and primitive-looking truck with a trailer behind it. On the trailer was something draped in canvas.

"We need some directions," the driver said. He was wearing rimless glasses and a red and black checked hunting cap over his silver hair.

"Sure," the guard said. "The Antique Car show is down at the Fairgrounds and to get there, you . . .''

"Not the Fairgrounds," the driver corrected him. "Gasoline Alley."

"But that's only for racing teams now," the guard said.

"What do you think we're here for?" the driver said. "We've come to go racing."

"You betcha!" a voice from the other side of the cab said.

The guard shone his flashlight in to see a wrinkled little man in a hugh Mackinaw with his hands resting on top of a cane.

"Where's your pass?" the guard asked.

"Right here," the driver said.

The pass was valid, and the guard had to wave them through. As he stepped back, he looked at the door where he saw "Blue Creek Racing Team" painted in bold letters.

For the rest of the stormy night a series of old cars went by him, each with "Blue Creek Racing Team" freshly painted on the door.

Mac Wilson, a first year driver, was the first to notice the odd thing about the Blue Creek Racing Team. Eating breakfast from a bag in the garage opposite Blue Creek's, he saw that everyone coming and going from Garage 47 was old. The youngest looked five years beyond retirement. One or two were bent, several moved slowly, and one was in a wheelchair.

The Assistant Track Steward checking the latest arrivals turned into Garage 47, looked at the crew, the car, and demanded angrily, "Who's in charge here?"

"Guess I am," one man said stepping forward. He was a small, wiry man wearing baggy jeans, a flannel shirt, and a cap with a Holstein cow pictured on the front. His face was tanned and wrinkled, but his blue eyes were clear.

"Look," the steward said, "you can't go on storing these museum cars over here. We've got a race on this month, in case you didn't know, and we have to have this place for a racing team due in today. Now get that blue monstrosity out of here." He pointed at the car.

"Would that be the Blue Creek Racing Team?" the man asked.

The steward flipped through the pages on his clipboard. "Yeah, it is."

"Then we're in the right place," the man said. He held out his right hand. "I'm Speedo Johanssen, the head of this outfit."

The steward looked at the name on his clipboard and shook hands warily. "Glad to meet you," he said. "Now where's your car?"

"That's it. Old Number 32," Johanssen said and jerked his thumb toward the machine in the center of the garage.

"That?" the steward asked in total disbelief.

"Yep," Speedo said. "That's it."

The steward moved toward the car and inspected it. The wheels were spoked and instead of being tucked behind airfoils, the skinny tires stuck out almost half their diameter in front of the nose of the car. Instead of ground clearance measured in fractions of inches, a mechanic could crawl under it without using jacks. Instead of being low and wide, it was high and narrow. The cockpit was scooped out two-thirds of the way back with deep openings cut into the body for entrance and exit. The boat-tail rear end was the only thing that looked vaguely aerodynamic.

Finished with his examination of the car, the steward turned back to Speedo, addressing him as if he were suffering from delusions, and said, "You honestly think you're going to race that thing?"

"Sure," Speedo said. "Why not?"

"What do you think we're here for? the driver said. "We've come to go racing."

"It's taken you a while, hasn't it?"
"Fifty Years exactly." Speedo said.

The steward shook his head. "It's your entry money down the drain," he said and left.

By noon an Indianapolis TV station had caught wind of the Blue Creek Racing Team, and eager for anything out of the ordinary, they sent a crew hustling down to the garage. When they first started shooting, they had problems with the men in the background waving at the camera and mouthing greetings to folks back home. Speedo finally told them to look busy working on the car. Then he stood ready for his interview next to the sleek reporter in his blazer with the station logo on the pocket.

Speedo didn't need much prompting. He quickly revealed that the Blue Creek Racing Team took its name from its hometown, Blue Creek, Wisconsin. Speedo identified himself and told why they were at Indy.

"You check the records," he said, "and you'll see that in 19 and 30 the Ackroyd Special was the first car out of the race. We'd worked and scrimped and saved to make it to Indy. Qualifying for the race was the biggest day in my life. But the car gave out, and I never was really in the race. I felt cheated."

"And that's why you came back?" the reporter popped in, feeling the need to say something.

"You better believe it, sonny," Speedo said. "Sitting there in the pits watching everybody else go by, I vowed I would come back someday. And here I am."

"It's taken you a while, hasn't it?" the reporter said.

"Fifty years exactly," Speedo said. "The owner of the car gave up after that race and went back to selling washing machines. I bought the car from him and held onto it. I didn't have any money to return the next year. Then I got married and had a family to raise. Been running a dairy farm all these years. Finally got ahead enough to come on back. So I rounded up the old crew and here we are. It's great to be back."

"Well," the reporter said with a big smile, "there you have the latest at the racetrack. A former driver who couldn't resist the lure of the Indy 500 and has returned to see it all again."

"See, nothing!" Speedo interrupted. "We're here to do it. We're going racing."

"Uh . . . well," the reporter stammered. "That's it for now from trackside."

That evening at the USAC offices a man rose from the conference table and switched off the TV set as Speedo's interview ended. Turning to the group of men at the table, he said, "That's our problem. The Blue Creek Racing Team is officially entered. What do we do with them?"

"Get rid of them," one man burst out. "I come here with two cars, two top drivers, crews, vans, the whole works. We're a million dollar effort, and these guys are nothing but a bunch of escapees from an old folk's home with an antique car making a mockery of everything."

"Don't worry," another said. "He'll never pass his rookie test."

"He's not a rookie. He's qualified before," the chairman reminded him.

"Let's look at the positive side," the Publicity Director said. "After all the hassles of last year, it'll be a big help to all of us to play up the fact that these guys see the Indy 500 as something magnificent, not just a bunch of people arguing. It's something you'd wait half a century just for the chance of rejoining it."

"I don't mind him being in a garage in Gasoline Alley," one of the drivers said, "but I sure don't want him out on the track doing ninety when I'm going 200."

The other drivers nodded agreement.

"No problem," the Chief Inspector said. "They'll never get past technical inspection."

"We're going to look bad, though," one said, "if they get a lot of coverage and then we drop them."

"That's another point," the Publicity Director said. "When we have to drop them, we do it because they don't measure up to the rules everyone has to follow. No matter how much fun they may be, the rules are the rules. It'll make us look a lot fairer."

"We can always let them run a lap or two just before the race," another suggested. "That ought to be a big enough thrill for them."

"All right," the Chairman said. "Then we're agreed? We let them stay but see to it they don't get in the way for practice."

"Or qualifying," a driver added. "I don't want to be denied a chance to get into the race because some old codger is throwing a temper tantrum just ahead of me in line."

"There's no way in the world they can make it to qualifying," the Inspector said. "Rest easy."

Other news teams and reporters picked up on the Blue Creek Racing Team. Moving around Gasoline Alley, Mac Wilson noticed that the crowd around the door of Garage 47 and the stream of people passing by and looking in was as big as those around the garages of the leading drivers.

The interviewers worked their way through the members of the Blue Creek Team, and each of them, it turned out, made for a great interview. Pop Wannamaker, the oldest of the bunch at 92, said he'd come back to listen to the cars and chase the girls. Everyone thought he was kidding until one of the Hurst girls in her tight shorts and halter posed for a publicity shot showing her giving Pop a big kiss. After the camera clicked, she squealed, grabbed her bottom, and ran out of the garage with Pop right after her. He chased her halfway down the row of garages before giving up. "Would have caught her, too, if I hadn't run out of breath," he was quoted as saying. "Have to cut back on my smoking and Jack Daniels."

Jesse Morgan had not one but two wheelchairs. One was a regular battery powered one. The other had a go-kart engine attached, and he delighted in doing wheelies for the camera.

"Reece the Grease" McCord, the chief mechanic, claimed to have kept a car going years ago when he was a riding mechanic by grabbing the two ends of a broken sparkplug wire. "That current surged right through my body as we went on to victory," he said. "That's why I don't hear today as well as I should."

"You don't?" the reporter asked.

"What?" said Reece the Grease.

Through it all Speedo and the crew insisted that they were at Indy to race.

The first morning of their rounds, the Chief Inspector turned to his assistant and said, "Looks like about time to shut down the carnival."

"Kind of hate to do it," the assistant said. "They're having so much fun."

"We're not stopping the fun," the Inspector said. "We're just seeing that it doesn't get out of hand."

A somewhat staggered Chief Inspector reported to the committee that night.

"What do you mean, they passed?" the chairman demanded.

"Just that," the Chief Inspector said. "I couldn't find anything to disqualify them."

"What about displacement?" one of the drivers asked. "That big old engine must be way over."

The Chief Inspector shook his head. "It's not supercharged. You can have an unsupercharged engine up to 355 cubic inches, only nobody runs them anymore. In 1930, the maximum was 366 cubic inches. That engine's at 352. They had the head off one bank and a set of micrometers waiting for me."

"There's nothing else?" another asked.

"Nothing," the Inspector said. "All the bodywork is between the wheels. They've added a roll cage. They don't have any airfoils to measure. Nothing." He shook his head in disbelief.

"You mean that old crock is going to be out on the track at the same time I am?" a driver demanded.

"It appears that way," the chairman said.

The driver swore.

"But only for practice," the chairman added. "We'll see to it that he doesn't get into the race."

"How?"

"I've been thinking about that, and I've come up with a solution," the chairman said. "We'll give him his qualifying slot and let him run because there's no way they can get that car to speed."

"Great," the Publicity Director said. "The fans will get a big kick out of that."

"Yes," the chairman said, "but he runs only if there's plenty of time for faster cars to qualify. If by some wild fluke like bad weather it even begins to look as if he might squeak into the field, we'll pull him out of line. We'll just tell him it's not fair to the faster cars to take up valuable qualifying time."

"You know what happened the last time you tried that," one of the drivers reminded him. "It was twenty minutes before a car could get out on the track."

"Trust me," the chairman said. "We'll be fully prepared this time."

Close on the heels of the cars competing for the privilege of being first on the track, Speedo was circulating too. He was booted and spurred in the regulation coveralls and crash helmet instead of the goggles and leather helmet he had worn for some of his television interviews, but he was still easily recognized. For one thing, the patches on his coveralls advertised "Ma's Cooper Kettle Cafe" and "Bill's Bait Shoppe." For another thing, his helmet was the only one with a picture of a Holstein cow on it.

"Them cows," he explained, "made the milk that was sold for the money that made it possible for a return to the brickyard. So I felt the livestock ought to get a little recognition."

The car itself made for instant identification in that besides looking different from everything else on the track, it sounded different. "Big Blue 32," as it was now being called, roared past the stands sounding as if it were on the verge of explosion.

Despite the drivers's misgivings, Speedo stayed out of their way. Somehow, when they were low, he'd be high, and when they were high, he'd be low.

"Drinking lots of milk and staying out of the way of mean bulls hones your reflexes," he was quoted as saying.

Speedo was obviously a hit with the fans. He'd roar past, waving. Off the track, he'd circulate, shake hands, talk, and pose endlessly for snapshots.

"How's the car running?" a reporter asked Reece the Grease as the first weekend of qualifying approached.

"Just fine," Reece Responded. "We've had her up to about a hundred and twenty-five."

"Think that'll make qualifying?" the reporter grinned.

"We're still experimenting," Reece said. "I've been setting up engines for tractor pulls for years, and I'm gradually putting some of what I've learned into that engine."

The run for the pole came. Speedo drew a number far back in line. As the expensive, big team cars reeled off close to record times, and the one car shoestring operations did their best and prayed it was enough to make the field and starting money, Big Blue 32 eased forward. Saturday ended with eleven cars in the field and big dark clouds on the horizon. It rained slowly but steadily all day Sunday so that nobody else got on the track.

The next Saturday, three more cars made the field before the rains came. Big Blue 32 sat at the head of the line most of the day.

The chairman checked the weather reports for Sunday and the next week — 80% chance of rain for the next three days. That evening, trailed by the Publicity Director and the Chief Inspector, the chairman paid a visit to Garage 47. If Speedo would pass up qualifying the next day, they offerred, he could do two laps as part of the pre-race ceremonies.

"We're here to race," Speedo responded, "and that's what we aim to do."

The clouds still threatened Sunday morning, but the track was dry enough for qualifying to begin. A few minutes before

Speedo was to take to the track, the chairman appeared once more, this time trailed by four police officers and a wrecker.

"Speedo," he said, "I hate to tell you this, but we have to pull you from the line. There's no way this car can qualify, and we need the time you'd take to get somebody else into the race."

"Nothing doing," Speedo said. "We're here fair and square and deserve a chance like anybody else."

"You'll have to leave," the chairman said, casting a significant look at the police. "The rains may start again any moment and we have to get cars qualified."

Speedo looked ready to protest again when one of his crew, a tall, straight man with a silver moustache, leaned over, said something to Speedo, and stood back up again. The man was wearing a pork pie hat with fishing flies stuck all in it.

"Think it'll work?" Speedo said.

"It's worth a try," the man said.

Speedo thought for a moment and then climbed out of the car. "Okay, boys," he said, "back to the garage."

Reporters followed them back, but Speedo closed the garage doors and for a change refused to give anyone an interview.

To the chairman's embarrassment and relief both, Sunday stayed dry. The day ended with a full field of cars and only a few questionables left waiting in line. Mac Wilson turned in a 183.997 average and secured a spot in the back row.

Monday and Tuesday were quiet or seemingly so. Little by little, though, what actually happened came out in the news during the days following.

Tuesday night the chairman looked down the long conference table at the lawyer at the other end who was saying, "Those guys did everything letter perfect. Legally, they deserved a qualifying run and we didn't give it to them."

"They're a bunch of old men," the chairman said apologetically. "I didn't think they'd do anything. And we had to get those other cars qualified."

The lawyer snorted. "You know who that 'old man' with the moustache and all the flies in his hat is? He's a retired justice of the Wisconsin Supreme Court. He moved to Blue Creek because he likes the fishing there. His petition to let Number 32 into the race was on the judge's desk bright and early yesterday morning."

"We've had these hassles before," the chairman said.

"The judge in this case is Harmon Killigrew," the lawyer said.

"So?"

"He and that retired justice are old fishing buddies going back to the time they were both law clerks," the lawyer said and slid a paper down the table. "Here's our copy of the injunction."

"Surely we can file a countersuit," the chairman said.

"We did," the lawyer said. "The judge is scheduled to hear it on the Monday following the race."

"You mean . . . "the chairman said, not wanting to believe what he knew.

The lawyer nodded his head. "I told you to let him run, but you wouldn't listen. Like it or not, Big Blue 32 is in the race."

A murky dawn signalled Race Day. The big boozers of Saturday night found their ways home under cloudy skies. Bumper to bumper lines of cars formed and snaked toward the gates. Interstates were full of out-of-county and out-of-state license plates and yellow school busses filled with bands, all headed for one spot, the Indianapolis oval.

The earlier arrivals saw the unwieldy Number 32 take its place in the pits between two streamlined beauties while the bands marched and the PA repeated again and again, "The Greatest Spectacle in Racing."

Speedo waved to the crowd as the crew pushed 32 into the 34th spot behind the regular field, but he wasn't smiling much, nor was the crew. Ordinarily, they joked and kidded each other almost unceasingly. Now they were tight-lipped and serious, like old soldiers going into what they knew was their last battle. For a change, there were almost as many photographers and reporters surrounding the last car as there were around the first.

The celebrities paraded and Purdue's band played the national anthem. Speedo removed his Holstein cow cap for the invocation and taps. He put on his helmet to "Back Home Again in Indiana," shook hands with each of the crew, and climbed *up* into his car while the others lowered themselves *down* into their machines.

". . . start your engines!" rang out. Starters whined and the track became a roar of shouts and revving engines. The crew retreated to the pits as the pace car eased onto the track. Speedo got a huge cheer as he came by on the parade lap. On the pace lap, Mac Wilson checked his mirror and saw Speedo hanging on gamely behind him, right in position.

The huge green flag dropped, and thirty-three drivers took up the last half-inch of throttle. The thirty-fourth made sure everyone was ahead of him into turn one.

By the second lap he was still the last car on the track but had moved up to thirty-third position. The earliest casualty was a car from the middle of the field — magneto failure.

The leaders caught Speedo and lapped him, but he seemed barely to notice. He moved to thirty-second position when the leader, Danny Ongais, blew his engine trying to develop a big early lead.

A three-way battle for the lead developed between Dallenbach, Mears, and Foyt. The three moved through the field like Scythes through grain. It was evident early that the race was going to be fast and hard fought. Speedo had not passed anybody by the time the leaders lapped him for the second time, but he was still close on the heels of the car just ahead of him. The racer would swoop through the turns, and Speedo would roll through them, the car leaning toward the outside, Speedo hanging onto the wheel and leaning toward the inside.

"Approaching lap fifty, one-fourth of this 1980 Indianapolis 500 now run," the tower announcer's voice echoed around the track, "and we have A.J. Foyt leading the race with Rick Mears right behind him. And here beside me is the man who was right up there with them. Tell me what happened, Wally."

In his calm engineer's voice Dallenbach described how his clutch had given out somewhere around the fortieth lap.

"That's a bad break, Wally. We wish you luck next year. Now here are the standings of the rest of the field . . . " He reeled off the cars's positions and finished with," . . . the last man in the field but now in twenty-ninth position is the person we all said would never make it, Speedo Johannsen."

Besides Dallenbach, Gary Bettenhausen and Pancho Carter had been forced out with mechanical problems. Mac Wilson had moved up to twenty-first place.

Speedo came down the straight hanging onto the big wheel with Tom Sneva right behind him. For a moment going into turn one it appeared that the low racer would run right under the higher, older car, and the crowd came to their feet with a gasp. At the last moment, Number 32 seemed to jump to the outside and Sneva slipped by without a break in his line.

Two more cars had retired with mechanical problems when the first accident of the day occurred. A rookie trying too hard smacked the wall and ricocheted across the track, right into a trio of top drivers maneuvering to pass him. When the dust and rubber smoke cleared, two cars were parked on the infield grass and two stopped at odd angles high on the track. Ambulances and wreckers swarmed toward the spot; the yellow flag came out; and drivers dove for the pits.

Most were out again in a matter of seconds. Three minutes and forty-seven seconds after entering, Speedo left with new tires and a filled tank.

None of the drivers were injured beyond the broken leg suffered by the rookie, but Andretti, Rutherford, and Bobby Unser were also out of the race.

The green flag dropped, and as it did, two drivers trying for the same opening locked wheels and brought out the yellow again.

"Now approaching the halfway mark," the tower announcer intoned, "we still have Foyt and Mears dueling for the lead. But keep your eyes on Tom Sneva. He's on the same lap with the leaders and only 28 seconds down and gaining. Right behind him is Al Unser, forty-five seconds behind the leaders." He ran down the standings of the others and finished with, "Finally, only 19 laps down from the leaders is Speedo Johannsen, number 21 in the field." He said it with a badly concealed chuckle.

The announcer may have chuckled, but some in the stands with money on Speedo were laughing out loud while those who

Five of the leaders and potential leaders were still on the track. Four of them were on the same lap, and the fifth, Johncock, was only one lap down. Circulating steadily, Speedo worked his way to sixteenth place and moved to fifteenth as the car ahead of him suddenly started billowing black smoke from the exhaust and nosed toward the grass.

"At the one hundred and fiftieth lap, three-fourths of this race run, we have four cars battling for the lead," the announcer called. "It's Foyt, Mears, Sneva, and Al Unser. Gordon Johncock is barely one lap behind them. Ladies and gentlemen, this is still anybody's race. Let's bring them down the straight with a big round of applause!"

The four cars shot by the stands, snarling and maneuvering and by milli-seconds of time and millimeters of space squeezed into turn one.

As Mac Wilson came past, the announcer called, "And how about a big hand for the only rookie left in the race!"

When Speedo's blue car appeared at the top of the straight, the announcer called, "He's only thirty-two laps down from the leaders. He'd better get on it if he means to win this race." The tone of amusement in his voice was evident.

Those with stopwatches noticed that Speedo had picked up

"Speedo came by him again, waving him on . . . horsepower versus footpower."

had taken the bets he would last halfway were reaching for another beer. Others broke out sandwiches or headed for the restrooms, the third quarter break when spectators, crews, and drivers begin to sort themselves out for the final fifty, the all-out efforts for the checkered flag.

Throughout the third quarter, Sneva kept gaining a second, a half-second on Foyt and Mears, and for every scrap of time he gained, Al Unser picked up the same. Mears's and Foyt's pit stops were frantic flurries of tires and hoses, neither one able by driving or pit stops to shake the other.

Some pit stops resulted in the car's not returning to the track. Janet Guthrie climbed out of her car when her pit chief told her a fin had broken in the turbocharger. A leaking transmission took another out while a knocking rod sidelined another. A fourth car went out with suspension failure, and a fifth lost his brakes due to a broken hydraulic line. The field was thinning faster than usual, but few noticed as there was plenty to hold their attention.

his pace several seconds per lap but at that speed he was almost sliding in the turns. Still, he drove on steadily and dependably.

In the countdown to the finish, people began checking the ever-darkening clouds that had hung over the entire race. The first burst from them might make a winner of whoever held the ever-changing lead.

On lap 161 the storm broke, but it was not rain that fell. It was disaster. One driver referred to it as "Forty laps of horror." The press picked up the term, and it became the label tied to that incredible race.

The first sprinkles were felt back of the leaders. A car pulled into the pits. The crew chief peered under the front, then stood up shaking his head. The driver climbed out and the crew began pushing the car back to the garage. Another came in leaking oil down the pit road.

The full brunt fell on the front runners as Foyt backed off the throttle for turn three and his hopes for a fifth victory went up in a cloud of black smoke. Two laps later it appeared that

Sneva and Unser's "wait and see" strategy was paying off. Mears came limping into the pits with a misfiring engine. The crew attacked the engine fratically but then slowed, backed off, and Mears climbed out of the cockpit.

Behind him two more cars came into the pits and didn't leave. On the back straight Mac Wilson noticed a car parked on the grass.

On his one hundred and seventieth lap, Sneva edged to the apron and continued around the track so slowly that the entire field passed him before he made it into the pits. A wheel bearing had given out and was slowly welding itself to a wheel spindle.

"Don't count your chickens before they're hatched, ladies and gentlemen," the announcer warned, "but Al Unser may be on his way to joining A.J. Foyt as a four-time winner!"

Three laps later, Al Unser joined A.J. Foyt but it was in the pits. Probably a burnt piston, his chief explained to the first reporters on the scene.

"It looks like this race may have passed to the hands of Gordon Johncock," the announcer called. "Let's bring him around with a big cheer!"

The people stood up to catch sight of the new leader and cheer him on. Most of them stood up, that is. Those on the back straight watching Johncock climb out of his car gave him a cheer but did it sitting down.

By lap 178 only five cars were left in the race. The others were in the pits, the garages or somewhere inbetween. The crowd was trying to put drivers's names with faces. Those who drew lower ranking drivers in pools were shouting with added zeal. The contingent from the little town of Linden, Indiana, were jumping up and down with excitement as Larry Rice, the local boy, was about to make good by winning the race. All he had to do was to hang onto the lead suddenly dropped into his lap.

Their high hopes disappeared shortly after high gear in Rice's car disappeared. He limped into the pits leaving only four cars in the race, one of those spluttering badly.

The splutterer came in two laps later.

The stands were boiling.

"What's going on?"

"Impossible! Only three cars!"

"Wildest race I've seen and I've been here every year since '32."

"This race is fixed."

"That old bastard may win this thing yet."

Speedo was a long way from winning though he had moved up considerably. As the lead changed so did the number of laps left to go and so did Speedo's position in regard to the leader. He was fourteen laps down and still had one pit stop to go.

He took the pit stop on lap 181. The crew put fourth a superhuman effort and sent him back onto the track in under three minutes.

"Incredible, ladies and gentlemen! Incredible!" the announcer said. "Never in the entire history of the Indianapolis 500 has the field been cut to this size. This is incredible." He continued for the next three minutes repeating how he could not believe what he was seeing.

The leader was an old vet whose highest finish to date had been eighth place three years before. He saw the years of watching others win. He saw the endorsements that had come to them. He saw himself backing off in earlier years to save the car for the owner when by pressing he could possibly have finished higher. He had worked hard and now it was finally falling into place. He saw the flowers of Victory Lane. All he had to do was hold off one rookie and one crazy old man. He was thinking what a boost the victory would be to his career when the needle indicating boost in his turbocharger suddenly did a nose dive.

"For the first time since . . . since Graham Hill won in 1968," the announcer said, "a rookie is going to take this race. Mac Wilson has only twelve laps to go to win this unbelieveable race."

Notified by helmet radio of his position, Wilson checked his guages. "Just drive,' he told himself. "Don't think. Just put the car where it belongs."

Still, he found himself counting laps to go. Each one down was like a huge weight removed from his shoulders.

". . . five, four, three, two," he counted. He looked at his fuel guage for reassurance. It was low but showed enough for at least three more laps. He saw the white flag and aimed for turn one.

In turn one, the engine balked. In turn two, it spluttered but caught again. In amazement, Wilson looked at his guages. He jabbed at the fuel guage with his index finger, and the needle collapsed against its pin. He swore as the tachometer went dead and the car coasted to a stop between turns three and four.

Speedo went by him and waved.

Wilson shouted "out of fuel!" into his radio and then slammed his helmet into the cockpit. Then he decided. He'd push that stupid car across the finish line. Speedo was down a number of laps and he might make it across the line before Speedo unlapped himself enough times. Wilson yanked his balaclava off, jerked open his collar, and started pushing.

The announcer's voice came back on the PA, but all he could say was, "I . . . I . . . I . . . uh . . . uh . . ." The speakers went dead. When they came to life again, the announcer was saying, "He's pushing his car. And Speedo Johanssen may catch him. Or he may not. I don't know. Come on, boy! Nobody touch that car. Help him and he's disqualified. Has to make it back on his own power. Here comes Speedo what's-his-name. What a finish! What a race! What a . . . a . . ." and his voice trailed off.

Wilson had to stop twice to warn people away from the car. Beery and eager to help, they climbed the fence until enough police came to keep them back while he sweated and panted to keep the car moving. He could hear the PA system from time to time and the sound of Speedo's car coming up behind him and diminishing in front of him. He could feel his calf muscles twitch as he caught his first sight of the finish line. Speedo came past him again, waving him on. Wilson had lost track of how many times Speedo had been by.

"Ladies and gentlemen," the announcer said, his voice barely restrained to intelligibility, "Speedo is only five laps from finishing his 200! Mac Wilson is only a quarter of a mile away from finishing his 200! It's between these two. Horsepower versus footpower or something like that . . ."

Speedo came by again. Wilson was moving in slow motion through a wall of noise. Crews lined the pit wall screaming at him. Spectators were cheering. Everytime Speedo went by the noise level went up. Wilson could feel the perspiration squishing in his racing shoes. He thought that he would never again be able to get enough air. He thought that he was going to faint.

"Ladies and gentlemen," the PA rang out, "Speedo is now on his last lap and entering turn two.

Wilson tried to find new energy. The line was so close.

"He's moving down the back straight."

"He's entering turn three."

Wilson closed his eyes and pushed more. The gap between him and the finish line was so small and yet so hard to cross.

All around the track was pandemonium-frenzied shouts and hysterical cheering, fighting over binoculars, pounding on backs, and waving arms.

Behind him, coming through the other noise, Wilson heard Number 32 and Speedo.

"Where's the car now?" Wilson asked. "In the shed. Want to have a look?"

The noise of the car bored louder and louder into Wilson's head.

"He's going to do it!" the announcer shouted. Then, "No, he's not! Yes, he is! Wait! Wait! I . . . I . . . aaaargh . . . " The announcer's voice dissolved into an incoherent primitive noise.

Number 32 seemed to lunge forward.

With his airfoil three feet from the finish line, Wilson saw something blue flash by. Then he collapsed. The car rolled on with its scant momentum until the airfoil was over the line by a few inches.

When Speedo was halfway down the back straight on his victory lap, the overshadowing clouds finally burst, drenching the whole chaotic scene in a blinding deluge of rain.

Pictures in the papers showed a very weary looking Speedo surrounded by his jubilant crew accepting the first place trophy. They showed Speedo and Wilson with their arms around each other's shoulders. They showed the other drivers shaking hands with Speedo.

TV sports showed clip after clip of the soaked Speedo, a glass of milk in his hand, recounting the race for them, always ending with, "We came here to race and by gum, that's what we did," The clips of other drivers showed them shaking their heads in disbelief. The clips of crew chiefs showed them saying that the mechanical problems were real problems, that they liked Speedo but they weren't about to play dead so that he could win the race.

Number 32 went through its post-race inspection, found with no flaws, and sent back to its garage. By morning it was gone and so were the old cars belonging to the Blue Creek Racing Team, all the tools in the garage, and even the calendar that had extolled the benefits of trading with Sam Evan's Grocery Store.

Nobody came forward at the awards banquet to accept the check and make a speech, much to the disappointment of the reporters. The check was mailed via registered mail to the address listed on the entry form. The signed form came back.

The television networks and wire services all sent stringers to find Blue Creek and Speedo. None of them made it to Blue Creek. A washed-out bridge, a minor car accident, a car breaking down or some other perfectly explainable occurrence stopped each one. One did get as far as Simon's Crossing, the town closest to Blue Creek, but nobody there claimed to have ever heard of Speedo Johanssen. As the teams pulled out of Indianapolis, news bureaus let the story drop.

Mac Wilson kept looking at the closed doors of Garage 47 all

the while his crew was packing up for the haul to Milwaukee and the Rex Mays 150. With a few days to spare in Milwaukee, Wilson found the tiny dot of Blue Creek on the map and set out. The roads got worse and worse the closer he got, and he had to drive across a rickety temporary bridge to find the little town, but he did.

"The Johanssen place? the man at the general store said. "Three miles out on the main road, turn right, and it's the second place on the left.

Wilson found the farm, a two-story white house with gingerbread trim, a huge barn, and sheds scattered behind. A herd of Holsteins were picturesquely grouped under a tree placidly chewing their cuds. As Wilson stopped his car, a young man came out of the house and introduced himself as Rolfe Johanssen.

"Speedo Johanssen?" Rolfe said and looked puzzled but brightened. "Almost forgot," he said. "That's what some of the old timers used to call my grandfather. He was always messing around with that old race car out back."

"Where's the car now?" Wilson asked.

"In the shed. Want to have a look?"

Wilson followed Rolfe to one of the larger buildings behind the barn where Rolfe pulled back a tarpaulin to reveal Number 32 looking just as it had when Wilson saw it after the race.

"Is your grandfather around?" Wilson asked. "I'd like to talk to him."

Rolfe shook his head and gave Wilson a funny grin. "I'm afraid he's not here."

Wilson felt a chill. No, he thought, you're not going to tell me he's dead and I've been racing a ghost.

"He left yesterday," Rolfe went on.

Wilson was surprised to find himself so relieved.

"Said he'd always wanted to fly around the world, retrace Amelia Earhart's route. I'm not sure where he went. He's always been kind of secretive. I do know he'll be gone a good long while."

"Why's that?"

"He had a stack of traveler's checks with him that thick."

Rolfe indicated an inch between his thumb and index finger. He chuckled. "I like the old man, you know, but sometimes I can't help thinking he's plain, downright crazy."

Wilson explained just how crazy Speedo had been. At the end of his visit, walking back to his car, Wilson hoped that a long while down the road he'd be crazy too. And not just crazy. If Speedo was crazy, being a raving lunatic sounded just fine.

TIRE TESTS
(and Other Oddities)

by David Scoggan

IMS Photos

"Laying in wait for May . . . the eleven-month lull . . . used only once a year . . . " To many people, the Indianapolis Motor Speedway is thought to be devoid of any activities except guided tours during the off-season. But at least twice a year (and much more often in previous years), the tents go up in the pit area and the track is once again open for business.

Tire testing basically consists of selected racing teams running closely supervised, high-speed trials on various compounds, constructions, and/or designs of tires. Usually it's strictly business — drivers get a paid opportunity to polish their styles and mechanics try to keep their machines dialed in, while the Rubber Barons decide which particular weenies will become "this year's model."

This story will deal with how these underpublicized practice sessions helped make the drastic changes in Championship Racing over the last two decades (and some of the unusual on-track occurences during that span).

Off-season running is certainly nothing new at the Speedway. Barney Oldfield, Tommy Milton, and Pete DePaolo were among the earlier participants, while a government-approved, wartime tire test led to Wilbur Shaw convincing Tony Hulman to purchase and rebuild the decrepit Brickyard into the showcase of today. The first turbine powered race car appeared in early 1955 at the hands of Henry Banks, the chassis of which originally belonged to one Anthony Granatelli.

Jack Brabham gave a hint of things to come when, in October of 1960, he buzzed his underpowered Cooper-Climax F1 racer around the oval at over 144 MPH. Suitably encouraged, Black Jack brought over a slightly modified sister car for the '61 race, effectively beginning both the rear-engine revolution and foreign invasion.

On November 21/22 of 1961, one of the largest non-tire testing programs took place. Pontiac Motor Division decided to run two Ray Nichels prepared '62 Catalina stock cars in a 24-hour endurance test. The drivers were: Paul Goldsmith, Marvin Panch, Fireball Roberts, Len Sutton, Rodger Ward, and Joe Weatherly. Goldsmith set a one lap

Pontiac Motor Division ran a pair of '62 cars in a 24 hour endurance test. We don't doubt that there will be more stock car testing for a possible Indy race.

record of 122.432 and assisted in marks of 113.292 for 500 miles and 107.787 for 24 hours.

The great Jim Clark made his first IMS appearance in October, 1962, testing the handling of his F1 Lotus 25-Climax for application with the next year's Ford Fairlane V-8 Indy entry. Clark ran in excess of 143 with the Climax, giving roadsterites cause for concern when the stock blocks would be ready. The original Lotus-Ford first tested in March, 63 at the control of America's premier road racer, Dan Gurney. Gurney, who had a major hand in the Ford/Colin Chapman marriage, ran almost 151 MPH in the "Mule" test Lotus. The Mule's individual, upswept exhaust pipes were replaced with

horizontal collector headers on the May Day models.

The Great Tire Debate of 1963 centered around the 15" diameter Firestones ran in early May by some of the faster cars, particularly Parnelli Jones and the Lotus. Cries of favoritism abounded, since the coveted sizes were not yet plentiful enough for all the teams to use them. Then, A.J. Foyt showed up with a set of Goodyear stock car specials mounted on his roadster. Resulting tests were inconclusive, but the Goodyear people vowed to start a full-scale study on championship car tires for the '64 season.

Andy Granatelli ran his Novis on both Goodyears and Firestones after the '63 race, then had a Ferguson P-99 road

The late Jim Clark and Colin Chapman caused concern to the roadster contingent.

Dan Gurney was instrumental in convincing Ford Motor Company to become involved in the 500. He tested this stock-blocker with great sounding exhausts in 1963.

racing car shipped over from England to observe its four-wheel drive system. Jack Fairman and Bobby Marshman wheeled the P-99 to a flat-out 141 MPH average in August evaluations, inducing Granatelli into an all-out 4WD Novi effort for the upcoming "500".

"Miss STP" Paula Murphy took five moderate speed laps in the Novi on November 7, becoming the first woman to: (a) drive a USAC champ car at the Speedway, and (b) give Clarence Cagle heart failure.

The day after Miss Murphy's jaunt, A.J. Foyt set an unofficial track record of 154½ in his Goodyear-shod Sheraton Thompson roadster. Len Sutton tested the new Rolla Vollstedt built rear-engine Offy, clocking better than 152 in the first-of-a-kind creation.

More bad news for the roadster boys came in the form of a double overhead cam Ford engine, built specifically for rear-engine racers. A successful fall test saw Jim Clark run just under 150 with the new powerplant; as before, the vertical exhaust stacks were replaced by the so-called "bundle of snakes" by May.

Four different tire companies braved the elements in March of 1964. King Firestone and Pretender Goodyear were joined by Mickey Thompson's Sears Allstate team and Dunlop, chosen by Colin Chapman for the Team Lotus effort.

Len Sutton upped the top numbers to 154.9 in the RE Vollstedt and A.J. Foyt was right behind at 154.7 in his new

Liquid Suspension RE Huffaker-Offy, both using Goodyears. Foyt also took a ride in the #28 rear-drive Novi, reaching 151 on only his third hot lap. Andy Granatelli himself shook down the just-completed Ferguson 4WD Novi, then turned it over to Bobby Unser. A March 31 garage fire only slightly damaged both Novis but wiped out much of the team's equipment.

Don Branson crashed his new RE Watson-Offy while testing Firestones in 36-MPH wind and Masten Gregory spun the M/T-Harvey Aluminum Ford when he mistook the brake pedal for the clutch.

The super-quick combination of Bobby Marshman and Pure Firebird Lotus-Ford blistered the IMS oval to the tune of 162.3 on October 30, 1964 (faster than any lap ran in May of '65). Less than one month later, Marshman was killed in a fiery test crash in Phoenix.

Jim McElreath made history on two different fronts while testing at the Speedway; he set a new straightaway speed record of 199.93 in the #3 Novi, and smacked the wall with the John Zink RE Brabham-Offy, burning his arm in the process.

Big money hit the Championship Trail in 1965, courtesy of Goodyear's open-wallet policy. Their previous year's "500" effort was an exercise in futility, as all potential Wingfoot drivers temporarily switched back to Firestone. For the '65 race, Goodyear had signed such drivers as A.J. Foyt, Dan Gurney, and Roger McCluskey to lucrative contracts. A.J.

won the pole and Gurney was outside front row, but Firestone again dominated on Race Day.

Another side benefit of the mounting tire battle was free rubber; teams which were previously running up large bills suddenly started getting their tires on the house.

"Rookie of the Year" Mario Andretti set an unofficial lap record of 164.1 driving his Dean Van Lines Hawk-Ford in December Firestone tests. On the same day, Al Unser crunched the fourth turn cement in the Harrison Chevy while straining to reach 152.

Jackie Stewart got his first shot at the Indy asphalt during the same session, wheeling the John Mecom #97 Lola-Ford up to 155 MPH. Another first-timer was NASCAR golden boy Fred Lorenzen. Freddy drove some laps in one of George Bryant's BRP-Fords, but declined an offer to drive in the '66 race and never returned.

One notable experiment was that of Jim Hall and his Chaparral sports-racing Group 7 car in the summer of 1965. Hall ran as fast as 144+ with the Chevy-powered creation and rumors of an Indy car program began to surface. Reportedly, the Chevrolet "non-racing division" was interested in challenging Ford on what had then become Ford's personal playground, but the project was shelved due to internal meddling. The supposed Indy chassis appeared in 1971 as a Formula A racer briefly campaigned by Hall's motor man, Franz Weiss.

The majority of the Offenhauser supporters had turned to either turbochargers or superchargers for help in combatting the Fords in 1966. Parnelli Jones brought his new Shrike-S/Offy to town for some March testing, as did Bobby Unser with the Vita-Fresh Huf-

Paula Murphy drove the Novi.

This Ferguson road racer convinced Andy Granatelli to pursue four-wheel drive.

faker-T/Offy. Also, Dan Gurney shook down his newly finished Eagle-Ford, the first of its marque to run at Indy.

One of the occasional oddities of tire testing occurred in the summer of '66, when A.J. Foyt took some laps in his #31 Ford Galaxie stock car. The stocker wasn't particularly set up for the 2½ mile oval, so no times of note were recorded.

More recruits for the "Foreign Invasion" appeared in late fall — Denis Hulme, Jochen Rindt, and John Surtees. Hulme and Rindt tested the Goodyear-backed Eagles of Roger McCluskey and Lloyd Ruby respectively, both finding enough to their liking to return for the '67 "500". Surtees, however, ran into contractual problems with his European contacts, so his laps in the Mecom/Bignotti Lola went for naught. (Ironically, Big John again tested a Bignotti Lola the following fall, but was forced to withdraw his name from the 1968 entry list.)

All-American Racers' improved 67-model Eagle made a mid-December debut in the hands of Head Hatcher Dan Gurney and Indy novice Richie Ginther; Dan circled at over 167 MPH.

The "Sound of Tomorrow" became a reality in March of 1967, thanks to the Granatelli brothers and designer Ken Wallis. Car #40, the soon-to-be-legend STP Turbine, made its first Speedway bow with potential permanent driver Parnelli Jones at the wheel. PJ hit 162 MPH with the monster, then turned the controls over to Jim Clark and left for Sebring. Clark upped the speed level to 163.2, having nothing but praise for the machine. Parnelli officially signed to drive #40 in the May classic soon afterward.

March, '67 also saw numerous first (and last) time chauffeurs take to the track Aldo Andretti, twin brother of Mario, cruised a Jim Robbins Vollstedt-

Ford at around 135 MPH in his only Indy try. John Hollansworth, veteran Colorado midgeteer, ran his antique lay-down FE Offy with Goodyear's approval, thus achieving his lifelong dream of driving at the Speedway. NASCAR rising star Sam McQuagg test-hopped a Johncock Gerhardt-Ford and suggested a "500" attempt, one that never materialized. Other first-timers who did stick around until May were: Lucien Bianchi (Robbins Ford), Chris Amon (BRP Ford), and Norm Brown (Weinberger Ford).

The Gurney-Weslake stock block Ford

powerplant made a 162+ premiere in March, but Dan was forced to relegate the unit to back-up status because of potential embarrassment to Ford's high-dollar DOHC squadron.

Jackie Stewart's Lola-Ford lightly scraped the fourth turn wall in March tests; the summer sessions, however were not as kind to Jim McElreath and Art Pollard. Pollard's Thermo-King Offy broke its LR suspension and hit the turn 2 concrete, giving Art slight posterior burns. McElreath's John Zink Ford snapped a throttle spring in the same turn, with the same result as Pollard — minus the injury.

Two unique "rookies" took Speedway drives in post-race 1967. Astronaut Gordon Cooper reached 134 in the #76 Mongoose-Ford that he co-owned with Jim Rathmann. "Tonight Show" host Johnny Carson accepted an offer to pilot the STP Turbocar in a September publicity session, hitting 133 MPH and calling it "easier than driving the Camaro pace car." (Mario Andretti also took his initial turbine trip during this promo gig.)

To protest the 1968 turbine specifications (15.99 inch annulus area), Andy Granatelli brought Car 40 back to Indy for a December test. Deliberately cutting the original 23.99 annulus down to the

Undoubtedly Bobby Marshman would have starred at Indy, but was killed.

Mr. STP, Andy Granatelli himself, took a rapid test spin.

Stock car racer Freddie Lorenzen practiced in this Ford.

new limit resulted in a 161 top mark for driver Jim Clark. Andy chided USAC to allow all entered turbines guaranteed placement into the '68 race, claiming they could not possibly qualify.

On hand to steal some of the turbine spotlight from STP in March, '68 was the Goodyear-Shelby-Wallis creation co-driven by Denis Hulme and Bruce McLaren. Hulme reached 158 MPH, while McLaren was limited to 150 in his Speedway debut.

But the boys from Des Plaines weren't giving up without a fight. Jim Clark had a new wedge Lotus-Turbine at his disposal and Parnelli Jones was back with old #40, considerably lightened to compensate for the horsepower loss. Speeds were not impressive for either car, causing Jones to withdraw in anger from the effort. Jim McElreath also tried car 40, but ran no faster than Parnelli — around 161 MPH. Sadly, this was to be Jim Clark's last visit to Indianapolis; he was killed racing in Hockenheim, Germany on April 7.

The first IMS appearance of the turbo-charged DOHC Ford also occurred in March, after numerous late '67 post-ponements. Race rookie Jim Malloy (who took his first Indy run the July previous) and Mario Andretti shared the honors in the Jim Robbins Vollstedt, with Malloy setting a straightaway speed record of 214 MPH, then tapping the turn 1 wall. A.J. Foyt tested his similarly equipped Coyote the following week.

Al Unser's Lola also made March wall contact, smacking the turn 3 barrier thanks to a malfunctioning differential. Arnie Knepper spun his Bryant Heating Vollstedt, but luckily avoided the hard stuff.

Immediately after the '68 "500", film crews from Universal Studios set up camp on the Speedway grounds to shoot six weeks worth of footage for the movie "WINNING", starring Paul Newman and Robert Wagner. Newman, in an Eagle-Offy painted to resemble Bobby Unser's winning edition and Wagner, placed in a Denny Hulme #42 Eagle replica, performed many of their own driving scenes — supposedly averaging near 150 MPH.

The "Unfair Advantage" boys, Mark Donohue and Roger Penske, had their introduction to Indy in October of 1968. Donohue drove the Sunoco Eagle-Chevy intended primarily for the few USAC road races and easily reached the 150 limit placed on all so-called "rookies."

A new "track record" for piston-engined cars was set in July, '68 by Bobby Unser's Rislone Eagle-Offy — 172.413. Bobby's speed fell slightly short of Joe Leonard's 173+ qualification warm-up lap in the wedge turbine.

From the land of the Rising Sun came the last Formula One car to test the Speedway asphalt; the winged Honda V-12 3-liter was driven by Ronnie Bucknam to a best of 156.5 during the late November experiment. (Bucknam's speed is the current IMS standard for F1 autos, although Ronnie Peterson's March-711-Cosworth exceeded 170 MPH at Ontario in 1971.)

Two of Ford's biggest customers switched camps in late 1968, but to varying degrees. Mario Andretti decided he needed the extra power of the Turbo Offy to combat Bobby Unser for the USAC points showdown. Andretti tested his converted ONA Hawk at Indy prior to the fall Trenton race, topping 167 MPH. A.J. Foyt, however, decided against racing his Coyote-Offy after a reported October IMS check-out.

Professor Glen Bryant took some terse shakedown laps in the Jack Adams "soapbox Derby" turnbine which he designed and built. The fall excursion did little more than end the questions of when the car would "go public".

Bobby Unser shook down the new four-wheel drive Lola-Offy owned by Roger Penske in March of 1969. Unser was to receive a similar car for the "500", so the testing was a co-operative effort. The new Lotus-4WD-Ford of Mario Andretti failed to show for March IMS tests due to numerous design flaws discovered in earlier runs.

Al Unser established a piston-engine track record of 172.8 in October Firestone testing. Al's Vels-Parnelli Lola-Ford barely missed the Leonard turbine mark.

A stock car race at the Indianapolis Motor Speedway? That question arose following Pete Hamilton's amazing 147.4 lap in the Gene White Camaro NASCAR Grand Touring car. Hamilton's speed came during a USAC-sponsored evaluation of the smaller-engined (305 CI) "pony cars" such as the Camaro versus the larger 429" USAC stockers. To place Pete's tire smoking effort into perspective, his 147 would have won him the "500" pole position only ten years prior.

Art Pollard again experienced problems with turn #2, his STP Gerhardt-Offy hitting the wall on the same day of Hamilton and Unser's achievements.

The Kiwis are Coming! That message was made clear in November of '69 when Can-Am king Bruce McLaren unveiled his first USAC racer, an Offy powered machine clearly patterned after his domineering Group 7 cars. Veteran Denny Hulme topped 162 with the creation, which featured a temporarily illegal rear wing.

By March of 1970, the Indy oval was being used by fewer teams and, later in the season, at fewer times. Attributing to the slowdown in IMS tire testing were: (a) Tight money within the two tire companies; (b) the increase in Champion-

Astronaut Gordon Cooper, left, was coached by Jim Rathmann.

Left: We haven't seen publicity that matches the STP quality since Granatelli left Indy. Here, he's working with Johnny Carson of "Tonight Show" fame. The wiry Carson really got a leg in the turbine and thoroughly enjoyed himself.

ship Trail races and territory; and (c) the opening of Ontario Motor Speedway in mid-70, offering year-round testing weather.

March test news at Indy amounted basically to Donnie Allison's first ride in A.J. Foyt's Coyote, Denis Hulme's spin in his McLaren, and Denny Zimmerman smacking the wall with Barney Navarro's turbo Rambler.

Johnny Rutherford "won" a seven-car exhibition race staged for the Shriners convention in July of '70. The "race" was a 10-lap affair, complete with pace car and mandatory pit stop.

Temporary car-hopping in November included Gary Bettenhausen driving the #67 Robbins Eagle-Ford, Mike Mosley (on loan from the Wilkie camp) in Clint Brawner's Scorpion-Ford, and A.J. Foyt taking a ride in Jack Brabham's Offy.

Mark Donohue gave a hint of May expectations when he set an unofficial lap record of 173+ in Roger Penske's new McLaren M16-Offy during March '71 Goodyear tests. Again the question of an illegal wing arose, because the airfoil was not an integral part of the bodywork. Penske assured the press that the offending piece would be legalized for competition.

Three rookies made Speedway debuts in off-season 1971. David "Salt" Walther reached 155 in his father's Morris-Ford during March; David "Swede" Savage took Dan Gurney's Olsonite Eagle-Offy near 174 MPH in fall runs; and

Canadian road racer George Eaton practiced his Colt-Ford in both August and November. (Eaton's #116 Colt is the last three-digit number car to appear at IMS.)

Lloyd Ruby and Steve Krisiloff both experimented with stock-block engines in August Firestone sessions. Rube topped 168 in Gene White's Laycock powered by a turbocharged Chevy, and Krisiloff struggled at 160 with the underpowered STP McNamara-Weslake/Plymouth.

Mel Kenyon emerged "victor" in the October exhibition race staged for the Indiana Sesquicentennial Salute. Over 15,000 fans watched the show, which also featured antique race- and passenger cars. Mike Mosley made his return to racing in this event, following his horrendous 500 crash.

A new era of speed was ushered in by the flying Goodyear Eagles of Bobby Unser and Jim Malloy in March of 1972. B.U. hit an astounding 190.8 lap in Dan Gurney's latest factory model and Malloy was right behind at 188.6 in the Thermo-King twin. (Malloy's run, incidentally, came amid light snow flurries.) Billy Vukovich's Sugaripe '72 Eagle hit 184+ and Gordon Johncock easily ran 181 in his 71-model Team McLaren.

Designer Maurice Phillipe's first effort in conjunction with employer Parnelli Jones also made test news in March. The Firestone-shod Parnelli, featuring dihedral side "V-wings" (which were later

discarded), ran a best of 182.3 with Al Unser at the controls. Unser had a thrill in turn #3 when the recently-added conventional rear wing came loose, causing him to spin.

Salt Walther was not so lucky as Al, hitting the fourth turn wall after the LF shock on his Morris-Ford collapsed.

Blazing Bobby Unser really broke in the new paving over the just-completed south chute tunnel, setting a new track record of 197.522 in November Goodyear tests. Right behind Bobby's Olsonite Eagle-Offy was Johnny Rutherford, topping 192 in the newest Thermo-King Eagle.

Everyone predicted a 200 MPH lap for 1973, and Gordon Johncock just missed with a 199.4 during Goodyear's March installment. Other big numbers by Wingfoot boys were: Swede Savage at 198 in an identical-to-Johncock's Patrick Eagle-Offy; Billy Vukovich at 195+ in the Sugaripe Eagle; A.J. Foyt and his new low-CG Coyote at 194; and Mark Donohue's 193.3 in the McLaren destined for teammate Gary Bettenhausen. One super shoe who missed the two-week session was Bobby Unser, nursing slight injuries sustained in a 201 MPH crash while testing at Ontario in February.

Firestone's March program was marred by bad weather and mechanical troubles. Mario Andretti and Al Unser debuted their new wide-nose Parnellis, with Andretti hitting 195 before brushing the turn 3 wall. Unser later burned a piston, rendering both PJs ineffective. Mike Mosley carried the bulk of the testing in his Leader Card Eagle-Offy.

There was no fall testing at the Speedway in 1973, due to the safety modifications being made on the front straightaway.

Both tire companies conducted brief sessions in March of 1974, brief because of the rescheduling of the Ontario "500" to the earlier part of the month. A.J. Foyt's 190+ was the fastest time recorded during Goodyear tests, while Al Unser had the quick Firestone lap at over 185; speeds were down significantly from 1973 due to the slowdown measures being enforced by USAC. Mario Andretti unveiled the newest generation Parnelli-Offy, which went virtually unused throughout the year, and Bill Simpson grazed the wall with the American Kids Eagle.

Bad news for many of the championship teams came in August of 1974, when Firestone decided the high cost of racing did not justify their participation. This left Goodyear as the sole manufacturer/supplier of Indianapolis car rubber.

One Firestone car which did test on a 2½ mile oval, however, was Mario Andretti's Formula 5000 Viceroy Lola-Chevy. The August experiment was originally planned for Indy, but schedule conflicts forced a switch to Ontario. Andretti reached 171 MPH before burning a piston, ending the chance to evaluate a possible stock-block-only formula for champ cars.

World Champion Emerson Fittipaldi made a blazing Speedway bow in October, '74. Driving Johnny Rutherford's Team McLaren-Offy, Fittipaldi topped 183 MPH, a speed which would have put him high into the '74 starting field. Strong talk of Emerson entering the 1975 "500" followed, but he reportedly told his F1 sponsor, Texaco, that Indy really didn't appeal to him.

Left without competition, Goodyear cancelled the traditional March test session at Indianapolis to concentrate on supplying all the teams for the '75 Ontario race. The roster for an uneventful October, '75 program listed A.J. Foyt, Johnny Rutherford, and Wally Dallenbach (driving a Patrick Eagle, rather than his usual Wildcat).

Goodyear decided to give the "little guys" some early practice time with a two-day "open house" in March of 1976. It was like the good old days again as eight teams took advantage of the opportunity. Johnny Rutherford's McLaren-Offy had the fastest lap of 189 MPH; his attempt with the new

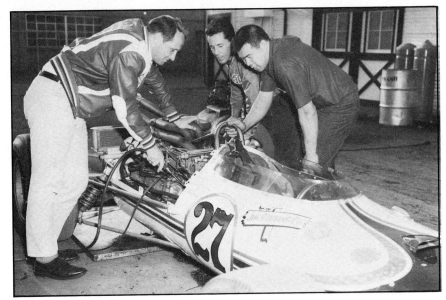

Famed racing artist Ron Burton, left, stooged for Aldo Andretti and Grant King.

Formula I standout Jackie Stewart braved some chilly weather in his first Indy car ride.

Cosworth powered car ended very early due to loss of oil pressure. Gordie Johncock shook down the newest of the Bignotti Wildcats, while Larry Dickson, Spike Gelhausen, Larry McCoy, Eldon Rasmussen, and George Snider tried out their "500" rides. Supermod standout Gary Allbritain made his only IMS appearance in the Routh #75 Eagle-Offy; he later crashed the car at Trenton and was turned down in his "500" bid by USAC officials.

The Brickyard received the first entire, 2½-mile paving job in its history immediately following the '76 "500". Five drivers made the initial runs on the new surface in a 10-lap "race" for the Governors Conference crowd on July 26. Lee Kunzman, John Martin, Roger McCluskey, Dick Simon, and George Snider participated in the show, which was diplomatically judged a tie by

Indiana Governor Otis Bowen.

Rookie Danny Ongais eased his Vel's-Parnelli/Cosworth at 175 MPH in his maiden Indy voyage, a prelude to competing in the upcoming Ontario "500".

Mike Mosley and Gordon Johncock tested in late September and discovered that the new asphalt caused the tires to run hotter than the old surface. Speeds were in the 187-MPH range, running under the 75" pop-off valve restriction.

But the last session of 1976, with a cured track, cool weather, trick tires, and 80" of boost, saw speeds shoot up dramatically. Roger McCluskey blistered a 198.6 in his rebuilt Hopkins Lightning-Offy, Johnny Rutherford got 195+ out of his still-unraced McLaren-Cosworth using only 74" of boost, and Wally Dallenbach ran 193 in his Wildcat before losing a wheel bearing. Also, Wayne

The Shelby Turbine was withdrawn before it had a chance. Parnelli and Jim Clark silently whooshed around in 1968 tests.

Rutherford, Lone Star JR's younger brother, took a slow ride in the ShurFine Atlanta-Offy, his only Indy run to date. (All the cars reportedly tested radial racing tires during this session, which were rumored to be 10 MPH slower than the usual rubber. Goodyear denied the accusations, but also discontinued any further radial experiments.)

So as in 1973, all eyes looked for a possible 200 MPH lap in March of 1977. And just like '73, it was Gordon Johncock coming out on top with an amazing track record of 200.4 set on Saturday, March 19. Perfect weather and track conditions encouraged Johncock to run "flat out all the way around", a feat he was not able to duplicate in the heat of May. Gordo also experienced a major mechanical malfunction when the RF wheel vacated the bi-winged Wildcat in turn 1 earlier in the week, but no damage was incurred.

Mario Andretti hit 194 in his new Penske-owned McLaren-Cosworth before blowing the engine and Roger McCluskey struggled at 192 in his new Lightning-Offy during the same session.

The "Second Annual Open House" occurred in the lousy weather of April 6, and Johnny Rutherford led the slim turnout with a 198+ clocking in his Cosworth. Wally Dallenbach shook down the new, narrow-nose Wildcat (later to become the 1978 "Texaco Star"), and Todd Gibson and Eldon Rasmussen tested their respective mounts.

September, '77 track time saw Tom Sneva in the Norton McLaren-Coswroth, A.J. Foyt's Gilmore Coyote, and Wally Dallenbach's Wildcat all obtaining now-mundane mid-190's.

The March (now April) session of 1978 was, for the most part, disappointing. Scheduled no-shows included: Tom Sneva and the new Penske PC-6 (suspension work), A.J. Foyt and his unfinished '78 Coyote, and the Drake

V-8 of the Patrick/Bignotti team (drive belt troubles). Al Unser made up for the lack of "competition" with a mysterious 202.2 lap in the Citicorp/Chaparral Lola-Cosworth (mysterious because it went unreported by the Indianapolis media for over three days). Unser's previous best throughout the period was in the mid-198 range, comparable to fellow testers Johnny Rutherford and Gordon Johncock (resorting to the tried-and-true 4-cylinder Wildcat).

Another exhibition race was staged on August 9, '78 — this one for the Rural Letter Carriers Convention (?). Sheldon Kinser crossed the line first, ahead of Gary Bettenhausen, Dick Simon, and Johnny Parsons.

Ominous rumblings pervaded the October '78 trials; while Danny Ongais was tying the track record of 203.6 in his Parnelli-Cosworth, the initial incantation of CART was taking shape at the Speedway Motel. Johnny Rutherford experimented with a smaller, 36"-wide wing which was supposed to become the new USAC standard, and National Champion Tom Sneva performed his last rounds as a Penske employee.

So with the CART/USAC split in full gear, the April 1979 runners were perplexed about the new USAC 50" boost restrictions. The best any of the invited CART hot dogs (Rutherford, Ongais, Rick Mears, Johncock, Bobby Unser, etc.) could manage was 185 MPH, and remarks like "drone" (DO) and "flat to the floor" (JR) were hard to ignore.

A special, one-day USAC program was implemented one week after the '79 race to check the effectiveness of the pop-off valve (which obviously failed miserably during qualifications). George Snider did the driving on the A.J. Watson-Offy, and from this research came the use of two pop-off valves for remaining USAC races.

October of '79 saw the end of the Jim Hall-Al Unser two-year marriage. Al's fall Chaparral rides at IMS were his last before joining the Longhorn team. Danny Ongais' aging Parnelli-Cosworth was not what the curious observers wanted; rumors of the Porsche project had now been confirmed, but the car remained on the west coast.

This spring's gathering again featured the Pennzoil ground-effects machine, now controlled by Johnny Rutherford. JR and Danny Ongais both circled at over 194 MPH, albeit with Goodyear-encouraged high boost levels (USAC-legal, 48" settings were closer to 187 MPH). Ongais remained Cosworth propelled, as Porsche guaranteed an Indy boycott if forced to compete at the same turbocharger limitations of the 8-cylinder motor. Also, Pat Patrick's new "wing car" debuted with Gordon Johncock at the helm.

These tests were concluded just before the long-discussed USAC/CART peace plan became a welcome reality.

So what can we look for in future off-season Speedway developments? Goodyear will most certainly continue their traditional schedule, but don't be surprised if Michelin makes inroads on Indianapolis. One of Michelin's top Formula One teams — Renault — has designs on an Indy effort if all goes well. An IMS NASCAR stock car race looks like a certainty for '81 or '82, so obviously some pre-event testing would be needed. In the driver ranks, such diverse talents as Dale Earnhardt, Doug Wolfgang, and Don Prudhomme have voiced desires to participate in the "500", as have third-generation shoes Louis Meyer III and Kyle Petty, and the Junior cousins — Al and Bobby Unser.

Whatever the occasion, whatever the reason, just remember that the old Brickyard doesn't sleep *all* those eleven months!

[146]

Oil Burner

at Indy

For Freddie Agabashian the adventure began the day after the 1951 Indianapolis 500-Mile Race when representatives of the Cummins Engine Company approached the California race driver and tendered him an offer to drive a diesel powered racer that the firm planned to build for the next "500" — a full year away. The company officials informed Freddie that the car would be of a revolutionary design. As a part of their presentation they walked Freddie out onto the Speedway track and had him sit down on a wooden Coke case. Then they informed him that the proposed car would have it's driver sitting that distance off of the track's surface — a mere four inches. Agabashian readily agreed to take the assignment which called for him to work with the company's engineers in the construction of the new racing machine.

The Columbus, Indiana diesel engine firm had run cars in the race on several previous occasions, and now it was again interested in undertaking such a research and promotional program.

The Cummins Company had been formed in 1919 to manufacture marine diesel engines. When the depression hit the country in 1929 the firm decided to go into the automotive and industrial fields to supplement the declining marine market.

In an attempt to alert the public to the practical value of the diesel powered car, a Packard sedan was outfitted with a four-cylinder diesel engine for a run from Indiana to the 1930 New York Automobile Show. The Company asserted that this was "the first practical" use of an "automotive diesel," and that it "made the nation diesel conscious overnight." The company informed the price conscious public that the fuel cost for the trip was $138.

This publicity performance was followed by an appearance of a Cummins Diesel powered entry in the 1931 Indianapolis 500. The car weighed 2,800

The oil shortage of the Eighties is making the Diesel engine familiar to Americans, but old line Indy fans will tell you, "Shucks, those things aren't new . . ."

by George Peters

[147]

The Great Depression of the Thirties was just getting underway when Dave Evans ran the entire 500 in this Cummins entry on only 31 gallons of fuel. The car made the distance without a stop.

pounds, of which 1,500 was attributable to the massive powerplant. The engine was a four-cylinder Cummins capable of 85 horsepower at 1,800 rpm's. The 360 cubic inch engine averaged 86.107 mph to finish the event in 13th place. Driver Dave Evans (assisted by riding mechanic Thane Houser) ran the entire 500 miles non-stop, and in doing so used 31 gallons of fuel. The oil burner estalbished two records. It was the first diesel to compete in the Indy race and it was the first car to run the entire event without a pit stop.

The unprecedented non-stop run was a novel and shrewd performance as it gained a tremendous amount of newsprint regarding the capabilities of the diesel engine.

The company's greatest desire was to demonstrate the dependability of the diesel to the young trucking industry. In an effort to do this the firm undertook some long distance non-stop runs. One of them called for a run from New York to Los Angeles. A Cummins diesel covered the 3,214 miles in a bit over 97 hours with a fuel cost of $11.22

In 1934 the company entered two diesels in the "500." One car carried a four-cylinder, two-cycle engine while the other had a four-cylinder, four-cycle model. As with the 1931 entry the intention was not to focus entirely on winning, but to "use the Speedway as a proving ground" to test the adaptability and durability of diesel power.

Driver H.W. "Stubby" Stubblefield brought his No. 5 Cummins Diesel in for a 12th place finish while Dave Evans' No. 6 diesel racer was forced out of the race on the 81st lap due to the stripping of the transmission gear.

Sixteen years lapsed before the company returned to the Speedway. At this time the entry rules permitted diesels up to 402 cubic inches while the

conventional engine was allowed only 274 cubic inches of displacement. This 1950 entry driven by Jimmy Jackson was a conventionally designed race car with the engine set to develop 340 horses at 4,000 rpm's using a Rootes-type blower. While the engine performed up to par, the car was sidelined on the 52nd lap due to a faulty supercharger. The car wound up finishing 29th in a field of 33 cars.

Unwilling to be easily deterred, the company, under the guiding hand of founder Clessie Cummins, persisted in its determination to stay in racing. Thus it was that Freddie Agabashian was contacted regarding a ride for the 1952 Memorial Day racing classic.

The 1952 Cummins mill was essentially a modified truck engine. The six cylinders contained 401 cubes capable of 430 horses at 4,100 rpm. In order to reduce the tremendous weight of the engine an aluminum head, block and pistons were used, while the crankcase was made of a magnesium alloy. In spite of these lighter components the engine hit the scale at 800 pounds.

On one point the engine was radically different from the 1950 Cummins engine. The supercharger was now replaced by a turbocharger. The turbo unit was considered to be a step up as it did not require direct power from the engine to operate. The turbo was propelled or driven by the exhaust heat and pressure exerted against the fins located within the turbo unit. Such a procedure thus eliminated any "drag" on the engine. It's disadvantage was the lag in acceleration as the Cummins personnel discovered that it would take approximately fifteen seconds for the turbo to build to its maximum power.

The company's timetable called for them to iron out such wrinkles as they tried to produce a lighter, but more powerful diesel. While the firm's engineers were too busy themselves with the powerplant, the chassis design work was contracted out. The creative genius of famed California race car designer Frank Kurtis was tapped. With the large engine and it's profile to overcome, Kurtis built a low riding chassis that would accommodate a lay-down engine in order to reduce the frontal area, with the underslung car gaining a low gravity line (in a few years a lay-over engine would win the Indy classic). The only real alteration required by the lay-over engine was the oil pump. A dry sump unit was added to the car to insure the proper flow of oil throughout the engine.

In its final form the Cummins car design was low, flat, and heavy with a profile that was wider than it was high.

Not only was the acceleration to offer a problem, but the tremendous weight of the car presented various difficulties. While most of the race cars tipped the scale at about 1,700 pounds the diesel weighed 2,400 pounds. The car's suspension and tires were to be particularly affected by such weight.

The cockpit was designed for the 138-pound frame of the veteran driver while it was offset to the right to accommodate the driveshaft in its linkup with the lay-down engine.

During the winter the car was flown from Kurtis' Glendale, California workshop to the University of Wichita wind tunnel for a check of the air flow patterns about the car. The car was then returned to California for some modifications as the builders wanted a design that would offer the least possible resistance as it was moved around the track. With the stress placed on body design the Cummins racer was to become the first Indy car to be fully aerodynamically designed for competition at the famed track. While some other cars of the period did show some streamlining, the emphasis tended to still be with horsepower. Handling and chassis were usually downgraded as a strong and direct correlation between these elements and horsepower was still a few years off. Late in the winter the Cummins car was flown east for some shakedown activities. More modifications followed, including work with the sidebars as the car was equipped with torsion bars all the way around. When the Indy track opened in May the car underwent some more testing after which it returned to Columbus for some last minute adjustments.

Although Agabashian had assisted the car's builders while on a monthly retainer since the 1951 Indy race, his real challenge was to come when the car was trackside, attempting to make the 1952 show.

It was easy to see why the company had selected Freddie Agabashian to pilot their new creation. He was a veteran racing chauffeur who had been active in the sport since 1931. Freddie was an outstanding driver on the West Coast where he gained a reputation as an exceptionally fine Midget race car driver. He first raced in the "500" in 1947, finishing ninth. Freddie was to drive in the next ten Speedway races until his retirement following the 1958 speed contest.

Around the race tracks Freddie was regarded as a driver with tremendous mechanical skills who was able to get the most out of any car he drove. Quite often he was approached by car owners or chief mechanics who had malfunctioning or poor handling cars and who requested Freddie's help in diagnosing the causes. As a result of this one could come to the track any time the cars were in practice sessions and find "Fast Freddie" testing most any car. Some dubbed him "Dr. Agabashian" because of the extraordinary expertise he possessed whenever troublesome racing cars were being worked on. Having

Freddie with all of his mechanical knowledge and driving experience on the Cummins team certainly provided the diesel manufacturer with a real asset.

The crew included Neville Reiners, the head of research at Cummins laboratories, as chief mechanic; Don Cummins, the company's vice-president; and Thane Houser, who had been the riding mechanic in the 1931 non-stop diesel racer.

The arrival of the Cummins entry at Indianapolis quite naturally caused a good deal of conversation and rubber necking as one and all seemed to talk and look at the race car powered by a truck engine. Freddie has said that the Cummins crew received a great deal of ribbing from other racing personnel. But then this is always the case around the racing circuit whenever anything different from the norm comes along. Few took the car seriously as it was not considered to be truly competitive. After all, when the diesel entry qualified for the 1950 race it registered the slowest time for the entire 33-car field. While it was conceded that the Kurtis-prepared chassis was very attractive and most certainly a contrast from the usual body design, the motor's large displacement was not judged to be a threat. In the minds of many, any advantages provided by the piston displacement were more than offset by the car's weight.

In discussing the cars at the Speedway the Chicago *Tribune* asserted that "from a pre-race angle, the most intriguing new car will be driven by Agabashian." No doubt about it the very mod looking low-slung creation caught much attention.

The car garnered much attention irrespective of the fact that it housed a diesel powerplant and the body represented the latest in streamlining. Sitting a mere four inches off of the ground was cause enough for the car to be in the limelight. It was certainly a contrast to the other entries. The contrast to the earliest diesels was also extensive and provides visual proof of the changes that had occurred in race car designing. The official photograph of the 1931 Cummins car shows Clessie Cummins standing behind the car with only the upper portion of his body in view.

The Indianapolis *Star* said that "it would be a feather for the oil-burner to qualify high up the list in the starting field, and Freddie Agabashian will drive it as fast as possible without taking a chance of messing up an investment of close to $100,000 for the Columbus firm." (As it turned out the entire operation was to cost the company $500,000.)

As the first day of qualifications opened on Saturday, May 17, trackside discussion centered on which car would gain the pole position. The drivers mentioned most often were Jack McGrath, Chet Miller and Duke Nalon. Miller and Nalon were driving the famous V-8 Novis. These cars had been at the track for several years and they had won the pole position on three occasions. They were powerful machines with much promise, yet they always failed to live up to the high expectations. While they may have been the fastest cars at the track, when the checkered flag fell they were always out of contention.

During the first hours of qualifying that Saturday, driver Andy Linden secured the pole spot with a time of 137.003 mph in his Miracle Power Special. This speed broke the record of 136.672 which had been set a year earlier by Walt Faulkner.

Freddie felt very confident about the competitive nature of the beautifully prepared No. 28 red and gold racer as he waited to go out for his qualification attempt. In practice he had been able to reach speeds greater than those being recorded by other entries.

The car was parked in the pits during the afternoon while driver George Connor attempted to qualify his ride. As George came down the front chute at approximately 165 mph the crankshaft broke, tearing the engine into chunks of metal. The car's wheels locked up causing it to go into a spectacular spin. The car careened backwards down the front stretch for over 1,700 feet before George could stop it. In the sensational "brush with death" the Connors' machine came through the pit area causing crews to scurry for cover. The parked Cummins car was missed by only inches during the wild ride.

When Freddie's time came for an attempt he put the car through some torrid laps. While the speed for each lap was off that of the previous lap, he established a new qualifying mark of 138.010. The first lap was 139.104, the second 138.206, the third 137.931 and the last lap 136.820. Tongues were really wagging now as a truck engine was on the pole with the fastest time ever recorded at the Indianapolis Motor Speedway!

However, the run was not without its problems for as Freddie came down the front straightaway on his fourth and last lap the right front Firestone began to shred. As he crossed the start/finish line a chunk of the tire flew off. In the face of this frightening situation, Freddie was able to hold the car the last 100 yards or so due to the excellent stability of the car and the fact that the tire did not blow despite the extraordinary weight of the car.

In addition to the overall four lap record, Freddie also established a new speed for one lap with his 139.104. Andy Linden had to relinquish the pole spot after having it for five hours. Freddie surely was able to have some sympathy for Andy as he had gone through a similar situation in 1950. After gaining the pole position on the first day of qualifications, Walt Faulkner came along with a faster record breaking speed to knock Freddie out of the enviable pole spot.

The publicity that resulted from the new record speeds was priceless and most certainly something of a coup for the car's builders.

The Cummins crew was exhuberant over Freddie's sterling performance. The smiles and congratulations exchanged among the driver, crew, and race officials provided a scene of considerable excitement and happiness. Later, three-time Indy winner and then Speedway president, Wilbur Shaw, drove the car for a few laps. Coming in he referred to it as a "sweetheart of a car." Shaw further noted that the car possessed "so much power we unquestionably will reduce the displacement advantage conceded diesel engines since 1950."

Members of some of the other crews who had laughed off the oil burner were also now concerned. The pole sitting performance had caused them to have a quick change of heart from their rather casual consideration of the Cummins car prior to the qualification run.

As far as the Cummins camp was concerned the satisfaction of having secured the pole was temporary. After all the tires were good for barely four laps while the race would consist of 200 trips around the oval.

It was determined that the diesel would be able to retain its rubber if Freddie maintained lap speeds of not more than 135.5 mph. Moving in traffic would certainly assure speeds below the level where the diesel's tires would shred. At that time the race tires were not made for any specific type car as they are today through the use of various compounds and sizes. The diesel simply used the biggest race tire available.

The following weekend two cars broke "Fast Freddie's" qualification record. Veteran driver Chet Miller averaged 139.034 in his Novi Pure Oil Special while Bill Vukovich hit a 138.212 in his Fuel Injection Special, but the history making record of the diesel with all the resultant publicity had already secured a large share of the public's attention.

The race got off to a ragged start with Freddie, as anticipated, falling back as the field of cars moved into the first turn. The slow acceleration simply would not offer him any chance of running off from the other front runners. By the time the cars hit the backstretch Freddie was back to 12th spot. However, as he gathered speed Freddie was able to assert himself and by the end of the lap he was up to ninth. By the third lap he was in seventh place and a lap later he had moved into sixth spot. Freddie remained in strong contention as the race progressed. On the 44th lap the diesel pitted for new rubber on the right side. Then as Freddie passed the 70th lap misfortune struck. He pitted again with smoke billowing out from under the hood. It was discovered that the intake duct for the turbocharger was clogging. In choking off the air, the enriched fuel mixture was causing the emission of black smoke. The clogging had caused the oil and water temperature to soar as Freddie parked the car.

While the track had been slippery in 1951 due to the oil loss from the racers, the track now remained relatively dry. As a result the track surface was grinding the tires down like sawdust. Some of the cars were to use up to 16 tires during the race. The turbo had then acted like a vacuum cleaner as it sucked up the floating particles of debris.

The decision was made to withdraw from the race. It was predicted on the notion that the company offered its product to the prospective buyer as a smokeless engine. If a smoking Cummins remained in the race (at a reduced rate of speed) the image left with the public would be most deterimental. In addition there was the possibility that the track officials might black flag the car for traveling too slow. Such an event was too humiliating to even seriously ponder.

In reflecting back on this episode years later, car designer Kurtis suggested that the diesel's demise might have been avoided if he had been allowed to put the air scoop "on the outside and upper part of the radiator shell. . .the reason for this being that it would have taken in a lot less of the sand and rubber off the track. . .and for better ducting to the turbo" but he says that Cummins insisted on having it hidden behind the grill where it would not hinder the car's general appearance.

Freddie's withdrawal at the 71st lap caused him to finish the race in 27th place. The record-setting Novi was out earlier to finish 30th, while Vukovich was to come in seventh. He had the lead with eight laps to go when the car's steering broke. Troy Ruttman then moved on up to win the race.

The Cummins creation had averaged 131.5 mph for its run of 71 laps while it consumed 18 gallons of No. 2 diesel fuel for the 180 miles of racing. Ruttman's winning speed was 128.92 mph.

Trucks and transporters are nothing new at Indy as evidenced by this clean-looking flatbed rig.

The Cummins plant immediately went to work to solve the problem of clogged-up turbochargers and by December of that year the firm had perfected a turbo that could digest rubber and other airborne particles with ease. This enabled them to then integrate the turbocharger into their regular line of engines. Yet turbochargers were not to become standard equipment at Indy for years to come, so the Cummins outfit was certainly ahead of the times in this respect.

In 1953 Cummins was to enter an 'ad' in the "500" racing program stating that "every car we ever entered in the race served as a laboratory on wheels...Our engineers are still working on things we learned in last year's race." Ultimately the data collected helped the company to come up with a truck engine that was more efficient in regard to weight ratio to power as well as in the use of lightweight alloys. Additionally, the research allowed Cummins to fully integrate the turbocharger into their line of truck engines.

As a result of the body contour presented by the diesel racer more streamlined race cars soon appeared at the Speedway. Body lines became straighter and smoother as the roadster model became the fad. Such a body style remained in vogue until Jack Brabham arrived in Indianapolis in 1961 with his rear engine racer. This represented the beginning of the end for the low-slung roadsters that had started at the time of the diesel race car.

While the roadster era was to end the basic concept of aerodynamic gody designing remained. The stress on air flowing over the car's configuration eventually led to air foilers and wings. In time, the turbocharger was to become standard equipment on the Indy Champ car circuit, though today's model is considerably smaller and lighter than what Agabashian used.

On the day following the 1952 race, No. 28 was outfitted with a new turbocharger and sent back out onto the Speedway where the car performed in a flawless fashion as it put several smooth laps at 137 mph. For Freddie the experience had now come full circle as he was again on the track the day after a "500." However, the Coke box seat had now been replaced by the desired object—a diesel race car and one that epitomized the latest in race designing.

"Dr. Agabashian" went on to finish fourth in the next "500" in a more conventional car. Before his retirement from race driving in 1958 he also had a sixth place finish (1954) in the racing classic.

Even with his driver retirement Freddie was to remain a part of the racing fraternity. For years he has worked with the Champion Spark Plug Company as coordinator of its driver safety program which features various Indianapolis racing veterans. Freddie has also been back at the Speedway for some years to provide technical information for the worldwide radio broadcast of the "500." Thus, his racing knowledge is still being called upon.

In 1955 Speedway rules reduced the piston displacement for any oil burner down to 335 inches in what may have been the death knell for any further diesel activity. To make a huge diesel engine competitive at Indianapolis was an extraordinary challenge, and one that Freddie Agabashian, the Cummins people and Frank Kurtis were willing to accept. The new restriction on the diesel powerplant was mute testimony to the success of their undertaking.

The pole-sitting car was preserved and it is on display from time to time at the Museum of Speed which is located in the infield of the Indianapolis Motor Speedway.

Winning The Indy 500 – JINX OR JEWEL?

Pete DePaolo left, and George Souders lived long lives.

Slim Corum finally wound up committing suicide in 1949.

by Jack C. Fox

"Boy! A quarter of a million bucks . . . and that's only the top of the iceberg . . . that guy sure must have it made!"

Maybe so but you couldn't prove it by the careers of some . . . in fact a majority . . . of "500" winners. Of the 49 men who have received the checkered flag emblematic of victory in the world's richest auto race perhaps only a dozen (not counting active drivers) could be said to have had long, successful, happy lives afterwards. Six were dead within a year, four more died within three years. On the other hand some winners became multi-millionaires and/or respected members of the automotive, accessory or engineering industries. A few were, and still are, fine spokesmen for auto racing and one, more than any other man was responsible for making the Speedway the great institution it is today.

Back in 1911 Ray Harroun came out of retirement to win the first "500" in a car which he designed for Howard Marmon. With his prize money in his pocket he immediately retired again and never drove another race although he continued to design for, and manage, racing teams, most notably the Maxwells of 1914 which featured kerosene-burning engines. Eddie Rickenbacker and Billy Carlson were his drivers, two of the best of the pre-WWI chauffeurs. Ray held a number of other positions in the automotive industry and went through several comfortable fortunes although he died at the age of 88 in greatly reduced circumstances living with his attentive (and much younger) wife in an Anderson, Indiana mobile home park.

Young Joe Dawson inherited the 1912 race when Ralph DePalma broke down with less than two laps to go. Two years later he was badly injured when he crashed his Mercer in the 1914 "500." This was his last Speedway race although he was only in his mid-twenties. Joe became an AAA official and died in Philadelphia just after World War II. Although his driving career was a disaster after his win, he continued his contribution to racing as an official for the American Automobile Association.

If there was a jinx associated with winning the race as some of the oldtimers would tell you, it must have started with Joe Dawson although it apparently skipped the next few. Jules Goux and Rene Thomas returned to Europe with their winnings and lived to ripe old ages. Both competed at Indianapolis after the Kaiser War with Thomas taking a second in 1920. Goux was 4th in 1914 and third in 1919. The next two years he failed to finish.

Ralph DePalma might have been known in racing circles as "Hard Luck Ralph" but much of that was of his own making as his intense dislike for Barney Oldfield made him refuse to use Firestone tires. Oldfield's slogan, painted on his cars was "My only life insurance . . . Firestone tires" was just too much for the haughty Italian, but since Firestone was the only company building competitive racing skins, the inferior products he was forced to use put him at a serious disadvantage. If DePalma lost a number of big races when sidelined with tire

---

There Have Been 49 '500' Winners To Date . . . Some Became Millionaires and Others Wish They Had Never Seen The Place.

trouble, his overall career must still be considered one of the most successful in the history of auto racing. Almost every man who has driven a race car would be happy to trade his career for that of "Hard Luck Ralph." He won on dirt with astounding regularity and was a threat on board and paved tracks and was still active behind the wheel into the 1930's. From his retirement to his death in 1956 Ralph DePalma was a respected spokesman for auto racing and a valued automotive consultant.

Dario Resta, the British-Italian, was the most consistent winner of big American racing events just before WWI. His Peugeot was the hottest machine in the AAA and he not only won the 1916 "500" but also the 1915 and '16 Vanderbilt Cup races and the 1915 Grand prize which was run in a driving rainstorm around San Francisco's Panama-Pacific International Exposition grounds. He came back to finish out of the money in the 1923 "500" and died on the high concrete banks of England's Brooklands track the following year.

Howdy Wilcox was the post WWI winner in a Speedway-owned Peugeot but he failed to finish the following four years and was killed at Altoona on September 4, 1924.

Gaston Chevrolet, like Joe Dawson, inherited the 1920 race from DePalma in the final laps. This celebration was short-lived as less than six months later he died in a crash at the Beverly Hills board speedway which also claimed the life of Eddie O'Donnell.

Tommy Milton won in 1921 and '23 and remained active as a driver finishing 5th in 1925 and 8th in 1927. He was often closely associated with the Speedway after his retirement from driving in '27 and served as chief steward for several years after the second World War. Much of the remainder of his life was spent in ill health and he committed suicide in 1962.

Kelly Petillo wound up in the penitentiary.

Jimmy Murphy won the 1920 French Grand Prix in a Duesenberg (and was snubbed and insulted by the French for his efforts), then with a Miller Engine under the hood of his Duesey won the 1922 "500." He had a revolutionary new front-drive Miller under construction when he crashed to his death through a wooden guard rail in a dirt track race at Syracuse on September 15, 1924, His career as a driver was only five years long, but he is still remembered as one of the finest and most likable drivers to ever don a helmet. Even Milton, who had first secured a driving assignment for Murphy on the Duesenberg team and then fought bitterly with him in later years, asked for the honor of accompanying Murphy's body to his California home.

Little Peter DePaolo overcame his nickname "Wall Smacker" to win in 1925 and he is still very much in evidence every Memorial Day. Like his "Uncle Ralph" DePalma he has always been a great ambassador for both the Speedway and for auto racing in general. He and Sally, his wife of over 55 years, live in a southern California retirement community although to racing people he seems to be anything but retired. Several years ago his fine Italian tenor voice sang the traditional "Back Home Again In Indiana" before the "500" a lot better than many "crooners" of half his age had done in previous years. It was truly a thrilling experience.

Frank Lockhart was a young driver-engineer bred on the dirt tracks of California and believed by many to be the greatest race driver of all time. His engineering knowledge was gained through experimentation rather than by formal education but he had such natural ability for the field that he was soon making valuable modifications to Harry Miller's already fast engines. His particular concentration was on the engine's supercharging and he was able to squeeze extra horsepower out of the allotted 91 cubic inches.

Lockhart came to the 1926 "500" looking for a ride. His reputation on the shorter tracks was good but not so good as to get him a spot on one of the big teams. He was helping out in the Miller garages when Pete Kreis became ill and he was allowed to prove his ability in Kreis's white car. Starting back in 20th position, Lockhart was way out in front when the race was halted at 400 miles by a rainstorm. He set a new qualifying record to win the pole the following year and was again in command when a broken rod sidelined his Miller at 300 miles.

The blond Californian was not content holding the Indianapolis record. He had even higher aims and with the financial backing of the Stutz Company he, Riley Brett and Myron Stevens constructed a 16-cylindered streamliner to go for the world's land speed record. He was well on the way to setting the record when a blown tire caused the car to crash end-over-end down the Daytona sands. Lockhart was killed instantly.

Louie Meyer has lived a long and prosperous life.

Wilbur Shaw became one of racing's most respected men.

Floyd Roberts died in an attempt to avoid a driver lying prone in his path.

George Souders won the 1927 race when Lockhart dropped out and he came back the following year to take second behind Louis Meyer and Lou Moore. A few months later he was badly injured on the dirt at Detroit and his hand was so crippled that he never drove again. Nine years later he sold shares in a battered Duesenberg to friends in Lafayette, Indiana as a way of reentering the sport as a car owner, but officials ruled the ancient car off the track after a smiliar Duesey had crashed into the pits causing a number of injuries and two fatalities. After this Souders held minor official positions, did a little promoting and stayed on the fringes of racing. His later life wasn't particularly happy and he died two years ago in a mobile home across Georgetown Road from the starting line. He had alienated many of those who had tried to help him and despite his proximity to the Speedway his visits, even during the month of May, were infrequent. The statement "the worst thing that ever happened to him was winning the '500'" could have easily been coined for George Souders although it could have just as easily been applied to Kelly Petillo, Lou Schneider and several others.

Ray Keech won the 1929 race and died two weeks later in a multi-car crash on the Altoona broads. Little Billy Arnold led all but two laps of the 1930 "500" in the most impressive win in Speedway history, but he crashed badly the following two years and gave up racing. He rose to the rank of General during WWII but after the War, he was rarely seen at the track. He died a few months ago in Oklahoma.

Lou Schneider was an odd kid from a wealthy Indianapolis family. He had been educated in private schools and given many advantages, but he was hooked on fast cars and motorcycles. Before he became a AAA driver, he was arrested for riding his cycle around the Speedway with track guards giving chase. In 1927 he entered his own Miller in the "500" and by 1931 he had a two-car team. He won the '31 race, finished 23rd in '32 and ran only one lap to finish 42nd in 1933. This was his final race. He switched to Midgets the following year and eventually moved to California where he regularly competed in the small cars at Gilmore and Atlantic Stadiums. He had been drinking rather heavily most of his career and for several years he had been considered an "outlaw" by the AAA for competing in unsanctioned events. Early in 1938 Schneider crashed his Midget through a pile of track hurdles at San Diego's Balboa Stadium and his arm was badly broken. It ended his racing career since it never healed correctly. A year or so later tuberculosis of the bone developed and Lou died in a sanitarium in 1942.

"Wild Bill" Cummings didn't fare much better than Schneider. After he won the big race in 1934 and took third in '35, he failed to get away from the starting line in '36 when his clutch failed. On a freezing February night in 1939 Cummings crashed his passenger car into a bridge abutment on the outskirts of Indianapolis and was killed.

Colorful little Kelly Petillo, one of the hardest Speedway drivers of all time was perhaps the most tragic winners in the history of the race. The tragedy didn't come from Speedway injuries as was the case with most of the other "jinxed" drivers. Kelly's came from just not being mentally able to handle the instant fame and fortune which was thrust upon him. Ignoring such friends as Peter DePaolo who advised him to stay home with his family and invest his winnings, it wasn't too long before his marriage was over and he was beginning to drink and get involved with the law. He built a nice new one-man car in 1939, but he never again finished a "500." The aging Petillo drove Sprint cars in California a few times after the War and built a speedway near San Diego in the late 1940s which held only a handful of races before it failed. He had been involved in the shooting of a Marine in a saloon he was running in Los Angeles and later served a number of years in the Michigan State prison for rape and assault. He would write pathetic letters from his cell to Speedway owners telling them his strategy for the race and asking for rides when he was released. The Speedway finally barred him from the grounds after he started an abortive lawsuit to allow him to drive (he claimed to have located a ride although he was, by then, in poor health and almost blind). Possibly the track could have humored him as a harmless eccentric but they took the direct route. Track guards occasionally looked the other way when Kelly would sneak into Gasoline Alley in the early evening and the garage personnel generally treated him with the respect usually accorded to a former winner, but it was sad to see a once-great driver so far down on his luck. He died in California in 1970 a broken man cared for by his dentist son.

Troy Ruttman suffered the anguish of having a son killed.

Bill Vukovich died in a gruesome accident while leading.

Auto racing took big Jim Bryan's life.

Popular Englishman Graham Hill met his demise in a light aircraft crash.

Louis Meyer and Wilbur Shaw, the track's first three time winners not only defied the jinx they apparently totally ignored it. Meyer is still most active in racing associated with his son-in-law, George Bignotti. For many years he and the late Dale Drake manufactured the Meyer-Drake engine (successor to the Miller and Offenhauser . . . undoubtedly the most successful power plants in the history of auto racing).

Wilbur Shaw won three out of four races (1937, '39 and '40) and was leading his fourth when, with victory within sight, a rear wheel collapsed and his Maserati crashed into the first turn wall. Wilbur's back was broken but he recovered rapidly to take over the Aviation Division of Firestone and some of his suggestions culled from his Speedway lessons greatly helped the country's War effort. When the War was nearing its conclusion Wilbur interested Tony Hulman in buying the Speedway from the Rickenbacker interests and served as President and General Manager until his death in a plane crash on October 30, 1954.

Floyd Roberts, like Petillo, was a California Sprint car driver. He was portly and balding and had a fine family in Van Nuys. His Speedway career had been unspectacular but consistent and Lou Moore, a fine judge of race drivers, had seen promise in his ability. Roberts broke Shaw's 1937 record by almost four miles an hour while winning the 1938 race. In 1939 he was in the same car and, naturally, one of the favorites. Just after the halfway mark he was coming out of the second turn when Bob Swanson's car spun and exploded directly in his path. Swanson was thrown to the track and Roberts drove his No. 1 over the outside crash wall to miss Bob's prostrate form. Swanson wasn't badly injured although

friendly Floyd Roberts died instantly of a broken neck.

Little Mauri Rose, the lead-footed Jewish driver from Ohio shared the 1941 win with Floyd Davis, like Rose, a Midwestern Sprint driver of some fame. Rose went on to win two more races after the War for Lou Moore but Davis didn't make another "500" start and held a grudge against Moore for the rest of their lives, feeling that he hadn't been fairly treated by the car owner. His case seems to parallel that of Lora "Slim" Corum of the other co-winning team (1924). Corum, like Davis, started the race in his maroon Duesenberg but running well back from the leaders when Joe Boyer, like Rose, took over as relief driver. Both Boyer and Rose overcame their car's deficit to win and their spectacular performances pushed Davis and Corum into the background. Unlike Davis, Corum did keep driving for another ten years although he only made the starting field three times. He committed suicide in 1949. Davis died the day following last year's race after suffering a heart attack just after the "500" Festival Parade.

World War II did little to dissipate the jinx. Just over three months after George Robson won the 1946 revival of the classic he died in a multi-car accident in the dust at Atlanta's Lakewood Speedway. Also killed in the crash was veteran driver George Barringer.

Mauri Rose won the next two races in Lou Moore's front drive Blue Crown and his teammate, Bill Holland, finally saw the checker in 1949 after finishing second to Rose the previous two years. He was second again in the rain-shortened 1950 event but then ran afoul of the AAA for competing in "outlaw" races. He came back to drive a race for Ray Crawford in 1953 and then dropped from the Speedway scene.

Johnnie Parsons was the rain-shortened 1950 race victor and completed through 1958 although 4th was the best he could finish. He is still on the racing scene in southern California and often drives the pace car for USAC events at J.C. Agajanian's Ascot Speedway. For a time he was USAC's West Coast supervisor. His son is now a regular "500" competitor.

Lee Wallard won the 1951 race in Murrell Belanger's pretty blue and gold No. 99 dirt track car but the ink was hardly dry on his prize check when he was critically burned in a Sprint event at Altamont, N.Y. He recovered after months in the hospital, but although he took some practice laps at the Speedway several years later, he was never physically able to resume racing and died of a heart ailment in 1963.

Troy Ruttman, the youngest driver (22) to ever win the "500," like Petillo, ignored those who could have made him a millionaire and was virtually broke in a year or so. J.C. Agajanian, his car owner, had tried to help him but his advice fell on deaf ears. Troy was a big, good-looking, polite kid from Oklahoma who had started driving jalopy races in the Los Angeles area at just about the time he entered puberty. With a forged birth certificate he ran the Speedway at 19. Not long after his 1952 victory Troy was injured in a Sprint car accident that left an arm almost useless for over a year. He still came back to lead almost every "500" in which he competed until his retirement at the age of 34. Although his marriage had broken up he had great hopes of making a winner out of his strapping son, Troy, Jr. These hopes were dashed when his son was killed in a Pennsylvania super modified race several years ago. Troy, Jr. ironically was driving a car Troy had raced at the Speedway.

Talented Jim Clark died in an insignificant Formula II race. Mark Donohue wanted to be a Formula I star and died trying.

The still youthful-looking Ruttman lives in Michigan but rarely attends the "500."

Perhaps no driver so completely dominated the Speedway during his career as did Bill Vukovich. One of the many drivers to get his start in Midget racing, "Vukie" literally blew the other drivers off the track. He came within seven laps of winning the 1952 race, easily won in 1953 and '54 and was well on his way to an unprecedented third straight win when he, like Floyd Roberts before him, crashed to his death off the backstretch after tangling with Al Keller and Johnny Boyd in one of the most horrifying accidents in Speedway history.

After Vukovich crashed Bob Sweikert guided Jack Zink's Kurtis roadster to the checker and went on to win the 1955 National Championship. His next appearance at the Speedway brought him a sixth place finish after a brush with the backstretch wall when a tire popped. Two weeks later the handsome blond Californian died in a Sprint car crash over the first turn fence at Salem, Indiana.

Pat Flaherty's fate was similar to Ruttman's. After winning the 1956 race handily, he suffered serious arm injuries in a championship race later that season and didn't return to an Indianapolis starting lineup until 1959 when he crashed his Zink roadster on the front stretch temporarily blocking the entrance to the pits. This was Flaherty's last race. He now lives in Chicago and has rarely returned to the scene of his fleeting glory.

Sam Hanks tried for seventeen years to win the big one and once he did in 1957, he tearfully announced his retirement in Victory Lane. Sam later returned to the Speedway with the title of Director of Racing. In this capacity he has been on hand every May to make speeches, guide VIPs around the Speedway and do promotional work for the Hulman forces. On occasion he has driven the pace car and the rest of the year he has represented various automotive accessory firms including Monroe and Champion. Racing has been good to Sam Hanks; the only time he ever turned a car over was in practice for the 1941 "500" when the crank broke in his 7-Up Special and he flipped through the infield fence in the first turn. Sam Hanks has always been good for racing, promoting the sport all over the country with literally thousands of speaking engagements. Looking much younger than his 64 years, he makes his home in Pacific Palisades, California.

Jimmy Bryan, the big crew-cut Arizona cowboy, may have been one of the eight or ten best drivers in American racing history . . . some will say he rates in the top three. His talent, however, was no match for the jinx. The year after he threaded his yellow lay-down Offy through the first lap tangle in 1958 which reduced a score of fine race cars to rubble in a matter of seconds and which cost the life of popular Pat O'Connor, Bryan was left at the starting line with a broken cam housing. After that he cut back his non-Speedway appearances . . . shunning the dirt tracks which he had formerly driven with so much skill. His friends were dismayed the following year when he announced that he would attempt a dirt track comeback in the June 19th race at treacherous Langhorne. You had to be brave to drive the yellow, sandy surface of the circular mile and Bryan wanted to show that a year's layoff had not diminished that bravery. He qualified for the outside of the front row but lost control as the field reached "puke hollow" on the first lap and started a series of flips. When help arrived it was too late and racing had lost one of its best and most popular drivers.

Rodger Ward won the "500" in 1959 and '62 and you would think that this would have made him a wealthy man, but several businesses he entered failed to work out. He tried his hand at race promoting a couple of years ago and has more recently become aligned with the Circus-Circus casino in Las Vegas as a good-will ambassador, a job that seems to suit him well. A couple of years ago Ward temporarily returned to competition in jalopies (or the equivalent) . . . rather degrading for a former Indianapolis winner. Jim Rathman, whose 1960 victory was sandwiched between Ward's pair, retired in 1963 and moved to Florida where he has a successful Cadillac agency. He occasionally makes an appearance at the wheel of the Speedway pace car.

Unlike Ruttman, Parnelli Jones listened to his mentor Agajanian and invested his money wisely. He has interests in various auto-related businesses including a lucrative Firestone dealership in southern California and considerable real estate holdings. He has also headed a top notch racing team which scored two Speedway wins and a trio of USAC National Championships.

Both Jim Clark and Graham Hill felt the full brunt of the jinx. Clark died in a practice accident at Hockenheim, Germany less than three years after his 1965 win and Hill was badly injured a year or so after his unspectacular, inherited win in 1966. Of all the long string of Speedway winners Hill was perhaps the best competitive but certainly the luckiest. Most of the hot cars were eliminated on the first lap and others fell by the wayside in droves. Although Hill was the first rookie driver to win the event since George Souders did it in 1927, his feat was not considered good enough to gain him Rookie-of-the-Year honors. This was reserved for the talented Jackie Stewart. Hill didn't drive much after the accident which crippled his legs rather badly, but he was a Speedway spectator. His last Speedway appearance as a driver was in 1969 when his STP Lotus had to be withdrawn as being unsafe for competition. Two years ago Hill was killed in an airplane crash.

Fifteen months after Mark Donohue won the 1972 "500" he was fatally injured while practicing for the Austrian Grand Prix, much as Jim Clark had five years before.

It seems prudent to omit active drivers from this exposition. Mario Andretti, the brothers Unser, Gordon Johncock, Johnny Rutherford, Rick Mears, and the Speedway's first four-time winner, A.J. Foyt are still very much in action. Despite some automotive and personal problems, none of them seem to be following in the footsteps of past ill-starred winners. Hopefully Clark, Hill and Donohue took the jinx, if there ever was one, across the Atlantic forever and ever.

GEORGE THE T-SHIRT MAN INC.

The standard driving uniform for yesterday's Indianapolis 500 driver consisted of a pair of baggy slacks, a crash helmet and a MOBIL OIL T-shirt emblazoned with the familiar flying red horse. That was back in the days when drivers stepped up to get into their cars and the crowds could see bare elbows and huge steering wheels. About the only positive thing we can say about the driving attire was that MOBIL sure received a lot of advertising value out of their T-shirts.

Driving uniforms today sometimes look like grandma's patchwork quilt work with accessory company patches sewn front and back. You can be sure that for every mini-billboard you see sewn on a driving uniform, the company has also invested in thousands of T-shirts displaying their trademark. And if they haven't, then one George Thornton, known around Gasoline Alley as George The T-shirt Man, is going to give them the opportunity to do so.

Over the years, Gasoline Alley has attracted everyone from mobsters to millionaires, scientists to fools. Without any prior knowledge, one look at George The T-shirt Man tells you that he likes flash, pzazz . . . and here is a character that definitely came out of a different mold than a horn-rimmed book-keeper. He has enough 14 carat gold hung on his fingers and around his neck to satisfy most any normal ransom note.

Since George is always selling advertising, he himself is his own best form of publicity. He hands out business cards die-cut in the shape of a T-shirt. Around his neck hangs a 14 carat gold T-shirt medallion, and his overall appearance makes you think he's just unplugged himself from a nearby electrical socket. And when he starts talking you're sure he's wound up tighter than an eight-day watch.

"Listen my friend," he says in a raspy voice that tells you he's definitely from the East coast (probably Boston), "I'll make you a shirt that is classy. No junk you understand. You follow what I'm sayin'? Now you don't want your business on some piece of trash do you?"

And his beat goes on. George plays all customers the same. There's a definite hustler air about him, and he talks no

Mahoney

differently to A.J. Foyt (who bought from George in 1980) than he does to a corporation president. As soon as you get used to the fact that he thinks on his feet and doesn't stop the talking while he does, you find it not only entertaining to talk to him, but his product is competitively priced and he delivers what he says.

"I'm a hustler," he admits. "I was born naked and always told myself that I'm gonna be rich. I like to wheel and deal with people and always deliver the goods. Some people may not take real kindly to my quick-talking ways, but I'm in a hurry. I got a lot of things to get done. I can't spend a lot of time just jawin', you know. Unless, of course, it's just talking about race cars . . . I sure do love these Indy 500 cars."

George has been coming to Indianapolis for the past few years and first became friends with the father and son team of Gus and Dick Hoffman. He's

come to know more and more of the Gasoline Alley residents each May and the bug to finally sponsor a car bit him this year. Late in the month he struck a deal with the Hoffmans and their second car proudly displayed "George-The-T-Shirt-Man Spl." on its side. Lee Kunzman was the driver, but the weather washed out any serious attempt for the car to qualify.

"Actually, I want to own an Indy car," the former country club golf pro says. "I've never had anything like this racin' get into my blood like this before. These are the greatest people I've ever met. I know there was a lot of arguin' and fighting going on around here last year due to the CART-USAC thing, but there was always that one underlying thing . . . they all want to race . . . and they all want to help each other. I think I'll always want to be a part of it. I'm just sorry I didn't get here years ago."

In previous years before he was involved in T-shirts, he was George The Meat Man. He drove around in a truck with a giant hamburger on top and sold filet mignon. As a kid he peddled newspapers, then joined the Marines and was naturally the base loan shark. Nowadays he employs a couple of dozen people in St. Louis and turns out thousands of shirts monthly. How's business? That's a question you never ask a hustler. Business was never better they'll tell you, even if they are in town on a shoestring. When George drives into town he does it in style. His gas guzzling Lincoln is equipped with a telephone, CB and all the ammenities of someone who is in a hurry to get the job done.

It won't be too many years before we see a race car at Indianapolis with a body, or maybe the wing, or something that is shaped like a T-shirt. Along side it will be this electric looking character with a 32 tooth smile who'll say, "Hiya podnuh, great day isn't it . . . man I'm glad to be here."

Next time you see him, walk up and introduce yourself. Chances are he won't be able to resist the chance to send you home with a T-shirt for you and your lady. After all, somebody in your town just might want to buy some worthwhile advertising and George wants to give everyone the same opportunity.

OFFICIAL INTERVIEW

Our thanks to the Syndicated Sports Network for assistance in compiling this interview.

Popular and articulate Johnny Rutherford made his third trip into the Official's Winner's Interview only moments after winning the 1980 Indianapolis 500. "Lone Star J.R." as he has been termed by the racing press was once again modest in victory and credited the Jim Hall-Chaparral Team with providing a great car. Following is a word-by-word transcription of the official interview.

Q. Why weren't you able to pass Tom Sneva mid-way in the race?

RUTHERFORD: The reason for that was my car was not handling properly. I'd move up to challenge him and the turbulence off his car would just absolutely turn mine loose and I didn't want to take a chance. So I backed off and waited until we could get into the pits and make a change. Then the car handled from then on, very good.

Q. What did you change?

RUTHERFORD: We raised one of the front wings.

Q. Johnny, now it seems like you raced at Ontario with the articulating skirts and 60 inches and here with the 48 inches, and it seems to work both ways for that car. Is that car that much better than the competition?

RUTHERFORD: Well, I guess we have to toot our own horn a little bit. I guess it must be, because the car is phenomenal. It does the job I ask for it to do. It's not black magic. The thing is just like any other race car I've driven, I take it to the limit when I can. And when something's wrong with it, and it doesn't let me, then I can't and you have to drive it accordingly. Any race car's the same, I don't care what it is, a go-kart or an Indianapolis car. So, we're always taking them to the brink, or to the edge and it's no different. That car is probably just a little bit better and the design, I think, is unique and it's probably two or three years ahead of its time. Or at least I hope so.

Q. Was there any time today when you felt threatened by any other car? You talk about tires and the various spins and things. Were you threatened at any time?

RUTHERFORD: It got close a couple of times, but it wasn't a situation where it meant getting knocked out of the race or staying in. It was a good clean race for me I think.

Q. Why was the race so sloppy for so many other drivers?

RUTHERFORD: I don't know. I really don't know.

Q. Turn one seems to be the trouble spot all month. If there was trouble it would have been there, right?

RUTHERFORD: It seems that way. The shadows in turn one from the grandstands and other things play tricks on you sometimes. Like I say, I don't know any of the circumstances of the crashes. Rager and McElreath looked like they came together. I don't know if one of them hit the wall first and then got the other one or what happened, but the track got a little slippery today. It wasn't bad for me, but I'm sure you'll find

"It's not black magic. The thing is just like any other race car I've driven, I take it to the limit when I can."

Whitlow

somebody else who'll say 'Oh, Boy!' It was slippery, but my race car responded to the changes we made to it, I could make to it in the cockpit with the anti-sway bar adjusters and it stayed the same all day.

Q. Were you concerned about fuel at the end of the race? You stopped with about 30 laps to go.

RUTHERFORD: No. No., in fact I talked to Jim (Hall) on the radio after we made our pit stop and asked him if we could make it to the end and he said 'Yes' and I asked him if he was sure and he said 'Yes.' Of course that yellow light that came on during that late period helped. That saved us a lot of fuel. So I

think probably that, with the fact we were going to try to go to the end anyway helped . . . there was really no problem.

Q. What was the projected distance you could go on a tank of fuel?

RUTHERFORD: We could go 31 or 32 laps.

Q. That was cutting it pretty close.

RUTHERFORD: Yeah, Unser did the same thing.

Q. You said over TV that you were sorry Bobby Unser went out. What'd you mean . . . was he going to be the guy to beat for you?

RUTHERFORD: Well, you always like a race. If he's strong enough to beat us, then that's the way it goes. You hate to sit out there and putter around . . . but I guess I'll take it any way I can get it.

Q. Tell us about the hitch-hiker you picked up.

RUTHERFORD: Oh, that was Tim Richmond. His car, something had happened to it and he was stalled down in the pit entrance and I was coming in. And I thought, what the heck, don't want to have to walk all the way back. So I stopped and picked him up and gave him a ride down to the victory circle anyway.

Q. Did you expect a sprint to the end with Mears?

RUTHERFORD: Quite honestly not, because Mears had not been a factor all day.

Q. How difficult is it to live with the new yellow flag rule, when you've built up a lead?

RUTHERFORD: Well, it's exasperating to sit out there with a lead like we had on two or three occassions and have it snatched away by somebody smacking into the wall or running out of fuel or breaking his car and stopping on the race track. You know, I like the Pacer Lights, but I know that there's a lot of guys who couldn't figure out how to cheat them so they wanted them thrown out.

Q. Did you figure out how?

RUTHERFORD: (Laughter) I honestly didn't do any more than anyone else. (More laughter)

Q. Johnny, All month you had the tag of being favorite. Does that put any extra pressure on you, or just how conscious are you of being called the favorite all month?

RUTHERFORD: Oh, it was. Lot of pressure all month. Deke Houlgate and Bill Dredge (Pennzoil publicity men) were able to keep me busier than I wanted to be most of the time. Between the two of them they had me hopping and of course being the favorite and having the pole position and doing everything the right way, I guess you could say here at Indianapolis, made us newsworthy. It got exasperating at times, because I'd try to keep my mind on the car or what we were doing and there'd be three or four of you fellows from the press that would just have to get your story right then . . . or you'd fall over dead (laughter). So it is . . . it is exasperating, but now that it's all come to this . . . Thank You.

Q. A lot of people before the race said the winner would come from either you or the Penske team. At any point did you stop and think to yourself, 'there's three guys on that team and just you by yourself on Jim Hall's team?

RUTHERFORD: No, no I never do at Indianapolis. I was surprised that A.J. wasn't more of a factor. There were several surprises. Tom Sneva being up there, going for it. Who did finish second by the way?

ANSWER: Tom.

RUTHERFORD: Who finished 3rd?

ANSWER: Gary . . . Bettenhausen

RUTHERFORD: Really! Now see, there you go . . . a guy started in the last row and finished third. By golly . . . what happened to . . . Pancho?

ANSWER: Pancho was sixth . . . he got a penalty though. He passed the pace car.

RUTHERFORD: Ohhhhh.

Q. You came from 24th didn't you, before.

RUTHERFORD: Twenty-fifth.

Q. I was intrigued by a statement you made. You wouldn't come flat out and say you're gonna win. You said you'd be satisfied with a finish in the top three.

RUTHERFORD: No . . . no I said if the car would finish without any

just right. I was able to get in on the mark.

Q. Two cars were coming down pit road when you were leaving . . . I didn't know if you knew you almost got hit?

RUTHERFORD: No . . . no, I'm glad I didn't know it.

Q. Would it have been close at the end if there had not been that yellow?

RUTHERFORD: Probably, but we felt like we could do it.

Q. If McLaren had not dropped out of racing, and this car had become available, would Johnny have quit McLaren and gone after this ride?

RUTHERFORD: (Laughing) We'll never know that for sure, will we? It's very hard to say. I had a tremendous relationship with McLaren for seven years. It would have depended on a lot of things at the time. Whether or not they would have come with a new car. How emphatic Jim Hall would have been to secure my services. There are a lot of variables . . . a lot of things. I'm sure glad it happened the way that it did.

"I was surprised that A.J. wasn't more of a factor."

---

problems, I would be in the top three. I guess I could look like a hero now and say I knew we were gonna win it. But, that's never the case here . . . as soon as you get boastful and start making great statements, this place will land right in the middle of your head.

Q. How close did you come to getting hit on that first pit stop?

RUTHERFORD: Not very . . . I came close to eliminating a few of my guys on the first pit stop. It was crowded and I very nearly over-shot, or was a little hot when I made my turn in. But it happened

Q. Who is your crew chief?

RUTHERFORD: Steve Roby is my chief. He's an Australian from Sydney Australia.

Q. Is he the guy you talk to on the radio?

RUTHERFORD: Actually, no. I talked to Jim Hall on the radio today. Steve had a headset and was able to listen to me and tell the guys anything that was happening. And, I'd tell them when I was coming through turn four, coming in on the pit stop.

Q. How about tire wear?

Tippy

RUTHERFORD: We made four tire changes, I think. We had hoped in the beginning we could go all the way on one set. But the tires changed characteristics after probably 30 . . . 40 . . . 50 laps . . . and we had to change tires, and it came right every time.

Q. *Was it due to debris on the track?*

RUTHERFORD: No ... debris would cut a tire.

Q. *John, you said it's been sort of an exasperating month. There's been a lot of people after you and you've been asked to do a lot of things. Is it better this way than last year when there were times when maybe you did more chasing and maybe people were talking to people other than Johnny Rutherford?*

RUTHERFORD: (Laughing) Sometimes I wonder. No . . . really, this is always great. If I ever get short with anybody, just try to realize that there are times when we are thinking about a whole lot of different things about those race cars, because there's a whole lot to think about. And if I ever turn anybody off, or turn my back or run in the garage or anything, it's just because I'm trying to do my job. I know you guys are trying to do your job . . . and if you'll go to the Speedway staff they'll send somebody down and say, "Hey Jerk, get out there and talk to these guys," and I will, it's just that simple.

Q. *Do you think your car can go 500 miles on one set of tires?*

RUTHERFORD: Al Unser did it when he won for Jim Hall . . . they never changed tires.

Q. *Do you expect to see copies of the Chaparral coming out?*

RUTHERFORD: I hope not. I'm sure there will be. It's a fantastic race car. And I think the car by itself is very good, but I think the car with Jim Hall and the crew I've got working it, is a heck of a lot better. Jim is unique in that he was a driver of note himself. One of the top

drivers in the country and I can come in and tell him problems with the car and he can relate because he's been there. So with a situation like that, it makes the test driving a pleasure, because you're really able to get some things sorted out and get things done.

Q. *With about 50 laps to go you passed Mears on the front straight and raised your hand. What did that mean?*

RUTHERFORD: When things are going right, I always acknowledge everybody I pass. I just stick my fingers up and give a little wave as I go by. It's not a defiant gesture or "Ha, I'm passing you," or anything like that. I'm just saying thanks for not getting in the way . . . or . . . see you in a lap (laughter).

Q. *Do you expect Al Unser to ask you for his percentage?* [laughter]

RUTHERFORD: He did for Ontario (laughter) . . . so I don't see why there's any difference for here.

Q. *What are you going to do tonight?*

RUTHERFORD: I'm going to go to sleep.

Q. *Johnny, we all said you were going to win it . . . what did you think?*

RUTHERFORD: Well, I had a pretty good deep-down feeling, but I've been in this business long enough to realize that when you start getting boastful about the position you're in, then it can bite you. So I just didn't want to say "Hey, we're gonna win this thing," but we all had a pretty good feeling about the car and we knew if it didn't break we'd stand a pretty good chance.

"When things are going right, I always acknowledge everybody I pass."

Car Builder Grant King

Hard Work and Heartaches

by Fritz Frommeyer

All Photos from Grant King Collection

Mahoney

Life in auto racing often resembles a ride on an emotional roller coaster. In 30 years of racing, car-builder Grant King has reached the exhilarating peaks of success and descended into deep valleys when plans went astray.

His career began at a youthful age 18 when he built his first race car. This was an all-oriental affair. Grant built the car for a Chinese owner and a Chinese driver. Since then, he has known the security of a generous sponsor, joining the brigade that wore the famous Granatelli/STP logo-ladened "pajama" team uniforms. In sharp contrast, he has

seen sponsors leave town, leaving him with $100,000 in bills they ran up before departing. Early in his career he believed the small racing operation like his had a chance to be competitive at Indianapolis. He feels differently today. He has had the satisfaction of bringing quick rookies to the Speedway and the disappointment of having agreed to sign a driver only to learn later that the driver went to another team without telling him.

The roller coaster made a plunge with Grant King aboard in 1980. His car missed the 500 for the first time since his first year at Indy in 1964. Grant's new ground-effects car was not completed in time. As the final qualifying weekend approached, he wheeled out his four-year-old Chevy-powered car that made the race a year ago. Rick Mears' older brother, Roger, was hired to drive the car. Engine problems interrupted practice along with the weather. Three engines were gone in a like number of days. Mears' final-day qualifying run fell short of the needed speed.

"Roger is a super candidate," Grant King says. "On that last qualifying day I changed the cylinder heads in the qualifying line, but the engine was down by about 500 rpm. I know Roger would

have put the car in the race if we didn't have all that engine trouble. I watched the race from the stands and the pits. I was kind of lost. Missing the race means I've lost a lot of money, too. I just don't know how to accurately describe my feelings about not making the race."

Grant likely deserved better treatment from his engines because he does have a good reputation as an engine-builder. In fact, he was dubbed "Chinahauser" by some of his competitors in the Northwest because his engines were so good. "At that time, the Offy was the mark of excellence in racing," Grant says. "I've always considered 'Chinahauser' to be a highly complimentary nick name."

Grant has built almost every type of race car. He began by building Sprint cars, then moved to jalopies (or "stockers"), modifieds, champ dirt cars, Indy cars, Midgets (full-sized and TQ), and a road-racing Chevy Monza.

His early activities were centered in his native Canadian province of British Columbia and the neighboring states of Washington, Oregon, and Idaho. It was on the West Coast that he also had his first glimpse of USAC racing during a 100-mile race at Sacramento. "J.C. Agajanian gave me a pit pass for that

Here's an old, old copy of a photo of Grant's first open cockpit car and it sports some mighty fine lines. A Chinese fella by the memorable name of Bung Eng drove it.

As a tyke, Grant attented both Chinese and American schools.

A little nostalgia here: A goateed Grant King adjusts the injectors on his GMC-powered Sprinter. Driver Bob Simpson assists.

race he was promoting," Grant relates. "I had high esteem for the USAC mechanics and never even thought they'd use the same kind of tools I did. I thought everything was special. I just couldn't believe the money or the equipment. They were all running Offys and the cars were super-looking. 'I could never compete with them' I thought."

His big chance with USAC came a few years later when Rolla Vollstedt asked him to be part of his first effort at Indianapolis. Grant accompanied the team to tire-testing in the fall of 1963. Bob Sowle was on the crew and taught Grant how to build an Offy. This came during an overnight engine re-build during the testing. The next day Len Sutton, Vollstedt's driver, ran 154.5 mph with ease. "He was so happy he jumped for joy," Grant recalls. "A.J. Foyt, Clint Brawner, and everyone else who was there wanted to see our car."

This was obviously an exciting experience for Grant, but he used it to learn more about his occupation. "I owe a lot to Rolla Vollstedt and to Bob Sowle. They introduced me around and showed me the ropes. Rolla races the same way I have always raced . . . by working out of his own pocket."

Grant's life has been singularly dedicated to expending a lot of desire, energy, and talent in racing. "I thought about racing a lot back then and used to live and breathe it," Grant says. "When I was eating, sleeping, watching a movie, or whatever, I was constantly thinking about race cars and how they should be built."

The energy Grant King has devoted to racing for so many years is now being re-directed, but not entirely. Today, when his phone is answered, "Grant King Racing," this designation is somewhat of a misnomer. He has been "winding down" his racing activities for the last few years and has now reached his goal of quitting the customer car building business. Instead, he is fabricating metal industrial equipment used in the roofing business.

His extensive shops that were once filled with race cars (there were 18 cars in a photo published in *National Speed Sport News* several years ago) now are devoted to the production of items like clam buckets, hoppers, and two-man lifts. He also is renting huge cranes to customers. Both interests are in connection with a Milwaukee firm. "I have five or sometimes six full-time people working for me and I am collaborating with Guiffre Brothers of Milwaukee to improve their ideas and to work on some of my own," says Grant of his new venture.

Today, his only racing activities are participation at Indianapolis, the championship trail, and the champ dirt series with his own cars. He will make race car parts for others but not complete cars for anyone but himself. "This way, I can keep my desire to race going and keep the cash flow going," says Grant.

Board fences and telephone poles provide about as dangerous a setting as you could wish for, but they were a familiar sight to King for years. Above, his V-8 Sprinter driven by Bob Simpson leads a race.

Once upon a time it was accepted practice to find an old wrecked coupe, or even a running one and turn it into a stocker. In 1940 the Ford Motor Company introduced a new brand of automobile, the Mercury. The one above ultimately became a Grant King racer long before the days he began building Speedway cars. The track is Duncan, British Columbia and today King would pay a bundle to get the coupe back ... he'd restore it to new condition.

King has spent most of his adult life tucked away in a garage, bending metal. Here he and driver Bill Crow check over a 1960 suspension part.

The neighborhood kids always turn out in force when a new race car is rolled out. King wanted to go to the Speedway in 1963, so he churned out three spiffy looking Sprinters to pay expenses.

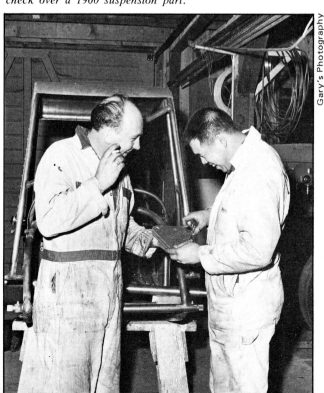

Grant was assisted by ace fabricator (and fine race driver) Jerry Weeks, right, in the construction of this Monza for Tom Neal, left.

"The Speedway is just an ego thing. I know I won't do any better than I have in the past because all the big money goes to those who already have it."

The decision to significantly curtail his racing activities was undoubtedly a difficult one, but one that was likely pushed to its culmination by today's inflationary economy. Building race cars ". . . is a zero business, unless you can build one or two rear-engine cars for a very big price," Grant comments. "It's hard to hire good people that you can work with. It's not a profitable business because you spend so many hours working on a car if you detail it properly.

"A.J. Watson once told me that you

can build a race car up to a point — like the frame, body, and some parts — and you can make money on it. But, if you finish it, chrome it, assemble all of it, and make it run, then it's a flat loser. Well, this is still the way I believe a race car should be built. People don't appreciate all the work that goes into a race car. Many builders today just slap a frame together (to keep their prices low to compete with other builders who are doing the same thing). They think they're doing OK, but they're not doing as well as they think. They're cutting prices so much that they will eventually reach a point where it won't be profitable any more. Costs are up and prices are down.

The Sprint car business is nasty.

"In the World of Outlaws, there is a car-of-the-week club," Grant continues. "Whatever car won last week . . . that's that they want. Steve Kinser won a lot of races in a certain kind of car. The guy who built it, Denny Mitchell, used to work for me. He's built a lot of cars because everyone wants a 'Steve Kinser car.' They don't realize it's a combination of things that makes it a winning car . . . the design, the driver, and money. Steve Kinser is still a winner, but all the other cars are not."

A single comment succinctly describes why Grant King reduced his racing activities: "You spend $500 a week for tires to win $1,000. You give half of the $1,000 to your driver. It just doesn't make sense."

Grant is first-generation Chinese. He was born in Victoria, British Columbia, Canada, of parents who left China to seek a better life in North America. The youngest of nine surviving children (a brother died in childhood), Grant learned to speak Chinese and English as a child, used chopsticks, and participated in other Chinese customs in the home.

"We practiced Chinese respect for the family, even though we were living in Canada," Grant states. "If a lot more families did this now, we'd probably be better off. This is sort of a dying thing now, but I wouldn't trade it for anything.

"Moving from China was very hard on my mother," he continues. "She enjoyed her life there and her family had some of

Ace Lane, Jr.

On the East Coast and in Western Pennsylvania they call these cars "Heavies". The King built Heavies gained a feared reputation on these tough circuits, helped in part by Ken Brenn' Jr's performance.

Grant's first trip to the Speedway was with a unique vehicle: The first rear-engine Offy, owned by Rolla Vollstedt, left. Len Sutton handled the car during some 1963 tire tests.

The late Doug Caruthers left, helped put King Midgets on the map as he utilized Gary Bettenhausen's chassis tuning knowledge to help the project along. They're celebrating an indoor victory, the first outing for the new car.

the good things. She told me about the beauty of the fruit trees in China and lived in her memories. She was panic-stricken when she got to Canada, still being almost a child, even though she was married. My father worked as a cook on a steamship. He was a professor and could have taught at a university, but didn't realize this.''

One of Grant's older brothers, Len, operated a garage in Victoria and Grant eventually went to work for him. "He taught me the trade,'' Grant says. "I had heard there was racing in town, but I never had the opportunity to see any of it. Then one day a customer of Len's brought a Sprint car to store in the garage over the winter. The minute the next season opened I went with them to help them run the car. I was still in school at the time and in machine shop class, instead of making screw drivers and chisels like everyone else, I was making race car parts. I've been chasing race cars ever since.''

Grant suspects that his family, especially his mother, did not approve of his racing activities because the sport had the reputation of attracting rough "leather jacket'' types. However, Grant continued with racing and after that first season built a new Sprint car for the Chinese car owner who stored his race car in Len's garage. The car had an aluminum body and a Model B Ford engine with a Miller-Schofield head. "It looked good and ran good,'' Grant recalls. "I didn't draw any plans, but built it as I went. All race cars are built that way and they're built like that right now.''

The personal contacts and experience he would gain over the next 14 years racing in the Northwest would be valuable in preparing him for Indianapolis. It was from those acquaintances that he brought several excellent rookie drivers to Indianapolis. They were Billy Foster, Art Pollard, Jim Malloy, and Tom Sneva.

Working with each of these rookies was especially rewarding for Grant, but he seems to have the greatest respect for Foster and Sneva. "They were super personalities,'' Grant exclaims. "They were fast and they made no phoney excuses. A lot of drivers can go fast but they cannot pass another car in a race. Both of these guys were passers. They were easy to work with and they had no hang-ups. They got in a race car and could squeeze every mile-per-hour out of it.''

The tools of his trade have changed drastically over the last 30 years. Above, Grant puts together a Speedway car tub in aircraft fashion.

It has been said that virtually anyone who's ever been involved in building USAC race cars has worked for King at one time or another. Indy 500 Yearbook publisher Carl Hungness built himself a Midget in Grant's shop and nearly made King crazy in the process. King wanted him to stick to the typewriter.

Grant King Racing was born out of Grant's need to earn money to support himself during his first Midwest racing seasons. Many crew members were not paid at all or were paid very little by the racing teams. This hardship was usually viewed as a dues-paying and learning experience. Grant started out building race car parts in 1964 "because no one back there (Midwest) was building them." He later expanded his activities to car-building for the same reasons.

After his early years at Indianapolis with Rolla Vollstedt, the Jim Robbins team, and Granatelli/STP, Grant formed his own Speedway team for the first time in 1970. He has operated independently ever since. In addition to the drivers from the Northwest, other

drivers associated with King teams at Indianapolis include Lee Roy Yarbrough, Greg Weld, Larry Dickson, George Follmer, Steve Krisiloff, Bentley Warren, Sheldon Kinser, John Martin, Bob Harkey, and Gary Bettenhausen.

Spotting good driving talent — often an unheralded and upcoming individual — has been a hallmark of Grant King. He evaluates the type of experience a driver has had, including the type of car and racing surface. "The worst kind are drivers that develop bad habits," Grant says. "Sprint drivers who drive a lot of dirt develop bad habits. The best drivers are pavement Sprint drivers, preferably those who have driven rear-engine Sprint cars. Tom and Jerry Sneva ran rear-engine Sprint cars. Sports car drivers can

be decent rookies at Indianapolis, but they often underestimate the talent it takes to run ovals.

"Being smooth is necessary for Indianapolis, and driving the pavement gives this to you," Grant continues. "A rear-engine car feels entirely different than a front-engine car. You have to drive it with finesse and can't horse it around like a Sprint car on dirt. A good driver must be chassis-wise.

"If a driver sits in the car and it feels good to him . . . fits him . . . that's the start. This will make him feel confident. Of course, the car has to run good and handle good and all drivers know they have to sort the car out and tell you how it's doing. Success is not always dependent on the car feeling good but, more often than not, when the car feels good the driver will go fast."

Grant has been associated with Sprint cars since he built his first Sprinter more than 30 years ago. This allegiance, however, came to an abrupt end in 1978 when he attended his final Sprint car race. He no longer owns a Sprint car. "I don't want to be typed with Sprint car racing," he says. "That tag still goes with me everywhere. At Daytona this year Donny Allison asked me how the Sprinters were doing. I told him that I didn't know. The point is that he looked at me and thought of Sprint car racing. Today I wouldn't even go across the street to see a Sprint race."

USAC's decision to ban the rear-engine spring car is called "narrow

Grant King-built Championship Dirt cars became the hot set-up during the Seventies. Here Al Unser in his Viceroy Spl. leads great dirt-tracker Greg Weld in the Hoosier 100.

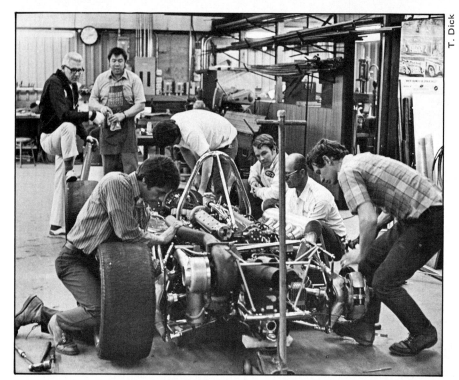

Left: King has managed to assemble a lot of talent over the years in his shop, and this photo depicts just a few of them. Car builder Jackie Howerton, left rear; mechanic Ted Hall, right rear; veteran builder (deceased) Wally Meskowski, kneeling next to driver Jimmy Caruthers (deceased). King and his next door neighbor A.J. Watson are at front.

minded" by Grant because it detracted from the prestige of the division that was traditionally the stepping stone to Indianapolis for drivers coming through the ranks. Rear-engine Sprint car experience is vital to a new driver coming to the Speedway Grant believes. "They've exploited Sprint cars today," Grant comments. "These cars were the start of our racing." Their importance as a stepping stone to Indianapolis is all but gone and their outward appearance — due frequently to shortcuts in order to keep prices down to compete with other car builders — have made Sprint cars figuratively and literally unattractive in Grant's eyes.

As things change in racing, one element appears to remain constant. Money and racing do not seem to come in equal measures. Racing demands more than its "fair share." Grant has experienced this phenomenon in dealing with some rather "indifferent" customers. One incident involved a customer calling his bank to stop payment on a $9,000 check he had just given to Grant for a new Sprint car. He later sent a $5,000 check because he believed this was the right price for the car. Another customer still owes Grant $100,000 for work done over several years. He plans to sue this customer. Yet another customer gave Grant a passenger car in lieu of cash payment for a race car. No title came with the car, so it could not be sold to help pay for the expenses of building the race car.

In 1970 when Grant fielded his first Indianapolis team, he really did not know how "alone" he would actually be. Two individuals, previously unknown to Grant, wanted to sponsor his team of Art Pollard and Greg Weld. "They wanted a racing operation," Grant relates. "They told some stories and did some manipulating and came up with a little bit of money that made them sound genuine. But, they sure wrote a lot of bum checks. We didn't know they were con men. Every time they gave me a check, it bounced. I've still got $40,000-$50,000 of their checks that are rubber. We ran with the purse money that year. We lost that. We lost everything." These sponsors left debts of $100,000 in their wake when they left town.

In addition to his activities as a car builder and car owner Grant found time to: promote the Pole Day Sprints at Indianapolis Raceway Park for nine years . . . become a Kentucky Colonel . . . have his Sprint car become the pattern for a scale model car kit . . . and sell individual sponsorships in small blocks all over the body of his Indian-

apolis car, the Spirit of Indiana, to involve race fans in a small way in the sponsorship of an Indianapolis car.

Despite some bitter disappointments in racing, there are moments that were highly satisfying for Grant King. "It is enjoyable to be able to create something from a piece of raw material, form it into the shape of a race car, and watch it go around the track. It's a real thrill when you do this yourself."

Grant has enjoyed the camaraderie among racing people which existed even though they competed keenly against one another on the track. This element was more apparent in racing ten years ago than it is today. Then, people enjoyed being with one another . . . whether it was during tire-testing at Phoenix with several other teams . . . going from garage to garage borrowing tools or parts at Indianapolis . . . or simply getting together for the pleasure of each other's company.

Thirty years ago in Len King's garage in Victoria, British Columbia, a young Grant King was being paid for a full week's work, a portion of which was not dedicated to the garage business, but to racing. "Len was really mad at my racing because it took so much time away from work in his garage. I was getting paid for a full week, but I'd spend a lot of time working on the race car. He was probably right in trying to persuade me from

Below: Grant has turned out everything from a quarter Midget (for his nephew) to his string of Championship Dirt cars. Above, Kerry Norris poses with one of the few King Three-Quarter Midgets.

fooling around with race cars. I should have gotten serious, but instead, I made a career out of racing. I probably could have done some other things and could have gotten rich, working as hard as I've had to in racing.

"This is a demanding business," Grant says. "It's hard on everybody and everything. The month of May at Indianapolis is the end result of a hell of a lot of hard work and heartaches."

Above right: Grant confers with Sheldon Kinser when he used to drive one of the King Speedway machines. Kinser was an Indiana Sprint hot-shoe and King gave him a Sprint car to run, later brought him to the 500 in a popular car called the Spirit of Indiana.

King had Roger Mears as a driver this year, but a late start put the team behind. Roger's speeds were too slow.

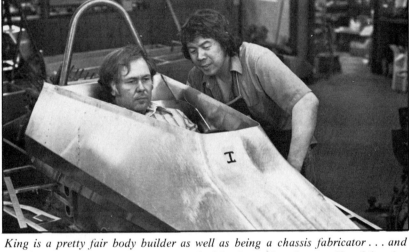

King is a pretty fair body builder as well as being a chassis fabricator . . . and there's a definite difference. Many can build a frame, but the art of hand forming aluminum into a race car body shape is almost a lost one with only few practioners in the entire country. Above, he checks fit with a stern faced John Martin.

Left and Below: Over the years Grant has occasionally duplicated some very successful Speedway cars as he hasn't been blessed with the funds necessary to purchase some of the entirely new, expensive designs. When A.J. Foyt saw two of Grant's entries he smiled and said, "Well, you built it at least as good as we did . . . maybe even better." Later A.J. & King swapped notes on the handling of the vehicles shown.

Duane Sweeny, Indy's New Flagman

by Al Stilley

Lucky to be alive. That's the best way to describe first-time Indianapolis 500 starter Duane Sweeney.

Slightly more than a year before the 1980 Indianapolis 500, it wasn't known if Sweeney would survive critical injuries suffered in an interstate accident en route to Texas World Speedway.

Sweeney suffered multiple injuries, including broken ribs, a punctured lung, a fractured skull, a broken hip and a partially shattered waist.

Sweeney, who was 57 at the time of the accident, recovered and actually started the 1979 Rex Mays 150 in Milwaukee in June.

Sweeney walks with a limp, mostly as a result of replacing his hip. He admitted that he "hobbled around" a lot in 1979, a year that he overcame serious injuries for the third time in his life.

The second time occurred in 1976 on a small plane flight to Milwaukee following a 100-mile USAC stock car race at the DuQuoin (Ill.) State Fairgrounds. Sweeney, two USAC officials, and a pilot miraculously survived a flaming plane crash which occurred while pilot Dick Schetter attempted to make a landing at the Hales Corners airport.

On his second approach near the airport, the plane suddenly lost power and a wing of the aircraft struck an auto dealership signpost, ripping off the wing and forcing the plane toward the showroom.

The light plane bounced and came to a halt against the auto dealership showroom with the cockpit tilted nearly upside down. The passengers were literally hanging by their seatbelts.

Sweeney's companions, Ralph Klevenow and Carl Lamers and Schetter managed to free themselves from the wrecked plane. They reacted quickly and assisted a dazed Sweeney from the plane moments before it became engulfed in flames. Sweeney and Klevenow were treated for cuts and bruises. Schetter and Lamers remained hospitalized for days.

That night, Sweeney went to the Hales

Corners Speedway, where he has served as chief starter for nearly three decades, and received a standing ovation when he was introduced to the crowd.

"I just know our experience around the race tracks helped save our lives," Sweeney recalled a few months after the accident. "I really believe that seeing things happen at race tracks and sensing what to do when the unexpected hits, really helped save our lives. I never thought of it that way before."

Sweeney's first ordeal in an accident occurred in 1941 when he was involved in a head-on collision. He went through the windshield and landed on the hood. Sweeney was hospitalized for two days for treatment of multiple cuts. Some of the scars from that crash are still visible on Sweeney's weathered face.

Sweeney, his wife Mary, and their family reside in the Milwaukee area where he is employed as a supervisor at Waukegan Engine-Dresser Industries.

He's been around race tracks most of his life. The route that brought him to the 1980 Indianapolis 500 took three decades.

He looks upon the Indianapolis 500 as many drivers look at it.

"Indy is the ultimate," Sweeney beams. "The drivers feel that way about

Indy and I've got the same outlook."

Sweeney admitted, too, that he had "big butterflies" before the start of the 64th Indianapolis 500.

The "big butterflies" were there because of the famed stature of the Brickyard itself, not because he felt incapable of handling the flagman's chores.

Standing atop the officials' tower on the west side of the front-stretch is far away from the Milwaukee area ballpark where Sweeney was club referee for the Waukegan Motor Club in the late 1940's.

The club later raced motorcycles in 1948. In 1951, Sweeney began flagging races one night at Hales Corners when the flagman failed to show up.

Over the next 10 years, Sweeney flagged races at Cedarburg and Franksville in his home state, O'Hare Stadium in Chicago and at Waukegan.

In 1962, Sweeney recalled that he flagged his first race at State Fair Park in West Allis, Wis. He later began flagging additional races sanctioned by the U.S. Auto Club, even though Hales Corners and the famed Milwaukee Mile remained as his "home" tracks.

In 1978, he became the chief starter for USAC championship events and USAC's stock car division. He is the chief starter for all 1980 Championship Racing League events.

His experience at flagging short track and major track races is invaluable.

"The flagman is 99 percent boss on the short track," Sweeney reflected during May at the Indianapolis Motor Speedway. "That's because you can see the entire track and quickly determine if anyone is in trouble."

He compared the start of a short track event to the start of the 1980 Indianapolis 500 in terms of a flagman.

"The cars have to be bunched up on the short track and they have to be going at about the same speed," Sweeney said. "If they're too fast at the start, some of them would go off the first turn. It has to be fast, but safe. On the short track, if they look good in the third turn then they'll be okay coming off the fourth turn."

At Indianapolis, Sweeney related an entirely different perspective.

"First of all, the starter can't see the whole track so it's a different situation," Sweeney explained. "If the front row looks good and if the intervals between the rows look good, then I give them the green. There is a point on the front-stretch that if the drivers have not seen the green flag, they know they aren't going to get it. You don't want to wave the green flag over their heads at the last minute."

Sweeney then revealed that, in his opinion, Bobby Unser (who started on the outside of the front row) might have jumped "a little bit" and that he was bothered by the slower cars in the rear of the field.

"The interval between the eighth and ninth rows was much too long, but the front of the pack looked good," Sweeney said. "There wasn't any sense in holding the field up because of the slower cars in back."

On race day, Sweeney had plenty of assistance from chief steward Tom Binford and referee Art Meyers who were stationed inside the starter's tower on the outside of the front-stretch.

"There are three important spots as the field comes down the front-stretch," Sweeney said. "Within a length of 150 yards, there is one spot where Binford says 'okay' and releases the field to me. At that point, I have about three to four seconds to make the most important decision in auto racing."

Sweeney was at the Indianapolis Motor Speedway to flag the two weekends of time trials and remained there throughout the week before the race itself. It was the period between time trials and the race that left quite an impression upon Sweeney about the professionalism of championship racing. He sat in on key meetings — the drivers' meeting with the full field, a rookies' meeting and a front row drivers' meeting.

"I learned more from the answers that the veteran drivers gave the rookies than anything else that took place that month," Sweeney said, while discussing the additional pressure on the entire starting field which included 10 rookies.

"They (the rookies) wanted it to be a safe start and a safe race," Sweeney continued. "That was very evident from the questions they asked. They were very enthusiastic to pick the minds of the veterans and to make the race safe. It showed me that the rookies wanted to do the right thing and they wanted to know

as much as they could learn about actual race day conditions."

"I was particularly impressed with Johnny Rutherford during those meetings," Sweeney stated. "He told the rookies they had been driving for most of the month in front of empty grandstands. He told them, 'With people filling the grandstands, this will be the smallest race track you've ever raced on.' His comment didn't really strike me until about 20 laps after the race started. It was then that I realized the front-stretch seemed to get bigger and longer. It seemed awfully small when the race started."

Sweeney also revealed that the front row drivers explained to the rookies that they should get off the throttle slowly in anticipating the "bunch-up" under the yellow light. They informed the rookies that 150 mph would seem like 50 mph after turning laps in excess of 180 mph.

Surprisingly, the veteran flagman expressed his dislike of working from a

flagstand atop the field. He explained that his philosophy is based on years of short track experience.

"I'm a firm believer of working a race from the ground. You don't see policemen directing traffic at an intersection from a helicopter. It's the same way at a race track. If you're on the ground, you can control the field when you have to," Sweeney said.

Realistically he added, "At Indianapolis, the cars are going so fast and they are so small that it's too difficult to see them from the ground and really know what you're looking at. This is a race that you have to work above the field."

Being named the chief starter of the 1980 Indianapolis 500 created another problem for the personable Sweeney. He needed two checkered flags in addition to

his regular set of starters' flags which are sewed new each year by his wife.

"This year she had to sew two checkered flags because one of the flags is signed by all the drivers in the starting field and presented to the winner at the victory Banquet," Sweeney explained.

The checkered flag that Rutherford received on the night after the race was hand sewed by Mrs. Sweeney, who rarely goes to the race track.

There is a Sweeney who is already following in dad's footsteps at Hales Corners. Duane's 21-year-old son Mark started flagging races at Hales Corners in 1980. He has been a scorer at Hales Corners for the past several years.

It's just possible there could be a Sweeney around the Brickyard for many years to come, although Duane Sweeney's career as a flagman is one of the most respected in motorsports today.

Sweeney has earned much of that respect from fellow officials and drivers, although he admits that he does not fraternalize with the drivers.

"It just seems like you're asking for trouble if you fraternalize with them too much," Sweeney revealed. "My job is up there on the starting line. If a driver has a gripe, it's best to go off to a corner somewhere and discuss it in a professional manner."

Down through the years, Sweeney has witnessed happiness and sorrow at short tracks and major tracks throughout the U.S.

He still admits that he sees "spots" at the famed Milwaukee Mile where the accident occurred that took the life of Ronnie Duman and where Jim Hurtubise got burned so badly.

"I can see those spots every time I go up on the flag stand at Milwaukee," Sweeney sadly recalled.

Sweeney has waved the checkered flag hundreds of times throughout his career as a flagman, leaving scores of drivers happy from the short track to the big track. One year at Milwaukee, he even waved the checkered flag one lap too soon during a USAC stock car race.

Undoubtedly, Sweeney received great satisfaction by waving the checkered flag for the first time at the winner of the 1980 Indianapolis 500, Johnny Rutherford. It took around three and one-half hours from the time he waved the green flag to start the 64th annual Indianapolis 500 until he waved the checkered flag.

On the day after the race, Sweeney recalled that final act by stating, "At that moment, I had a feeling of total self-satisfaction."

[171]

Tough Job, Tough Man

JOHN COOPER:
New Speedway President

by Carl Hungness

If you've never met new Speedway President John Cooper, walk up to him and shake his hand. You'll soon discover that he's first a race fan and secondly an executive. In fact, it would be fair to say that John Cooper is a race addict. If you happen to be a casual race fan, the addiction to racing is something that you probably don't understand.

There's a special feeling, call it a high if you will, when you hear the drone of an engine straining on its way toward a turn. If you're an addict you know all about the feeling you get when you see two, three, maybe even four drivers go into a turn side by side. You can know about each driver's desire to win. You can understand the mechanic's desire for his car to do well. And you're familiar with the car owner's desire to watch his machine outperform all others.

When you're a race addict like John Cooper, it's very difficult to join the everyday business world and muster up the type of desire you find around most any race track in the world. If central casting were calling for a Colgate-Palmolive executive type, they could send in Cooper and he'd look right in place heading a board meeting and talking about toothpaste distribution.

John R. Cooper has spent his time in executive board meetings and has been a respected decision maker. But he's also spent some time sweeping out garages at the Speedway and knows that he has a bit of gasoline in his veins. He knows well the inner excitement you can feel when you see an underdog, or a rookie, or a race-scarred veteran do well.

Back when he was a teenager, he managed to land a job as crewmember for Rodger Ward (sweeping the garage) and shortly thereafter began a life-long friendship with many participants of the Fifties era.

After college (Northwestern) and a stint in the Navy, John worked for the then newly formed United States Auto Club (USAC). He had previously done some public relations/promotion work with a few race promoters during his college days. Like so many others before and after him, Cooper just wanted to be involved in the sport. Salary wasn't important. Later he gained some advertising agency experience and was involved in Chrysler's racing program for four years. He was becoming well rounded in the world of wheels.

He struck out on his own ("I've always had a little bit of entrepreneur spirit inside me," he grins) and landed a contract to help promote Sprite's involvement in Championship racing. His friendship with car owner Lindsey Hopkins helped him along the way and the Sprite promotion was later judged to be one of the most successful ever run by a beverage company. Long time fans will recall that the Sprite cars were painted green, long a dreaded racing color in the U.S., and were piloted by Roger McCluskey, Wally Dallenbach and Mel Kenyon. Overall, the Coca-Cola company was happy with John's work and his initial involvement with the world-wide corporation would eventually lead to another opportunity with the corporation.

The troubled Ontario Motor Speedway offered Cooper the reigns to run the beautiful California facility and John responded with what has to be termed the most successful race run there to date: The 1972 California 500. For once the grandstands were full. Nevertheless, John is quick to give credit to the sport itself for helping to draw fans.

"We were lucky in one way," he says. "We had the first 200 mile per hour lap in qualifying and that seemed to get Los Angeles excited. And in a place like LA where there's so much going on all the time it's hard to get the city's attention focused on any one thing."

Later, Cooper learned about the world of stock car racing through an executive position with NASCAR. He was also chosen as a lobbyist to represent the auto racers of the U.S. in Washington when there was talk during the 1973-74 gasoline shortages that auto racing might have to come to a halt. He hasn't received an overwhelming amount of publicity for his behind the scenes work, but the movers and shakers within the sport have had his respect for many years.

For a while it looked like John Cooper would have to be content to be a race fan and sometimes board member of a sanctioning body. He had accepted what looked like a career position from Coca-Cola to create a sports department.

"I was handling everything, from taking care of Coke's involvement with high schools all the way to their Olympic activities."

Then a couple of years ago, Tony Hulman died and the person known as Tony's right-hand man, Joe Cloutier, was named president of the Speedway. Cloutier didn't really need the additional responsibility, for he had just recovered from a heart attack and had his hands full trying to maintain his duties at Hulman and Company, the Terre Haute based Wholesale Grocery firm that built Tony's fortune. Cloutier always had a hand in Speedway business, but he was in the autumn of his career and the Speedway now needed a full time president. Cooper had first met Tony and Mrs. Hulman during his early USAC days and also became friends with Tony's daughter, Mari George at the same time. John was both surprised and flattered when he was offered the president's post and like all good race addicts, decided to chuck his secure post with Coca-Cola to once again be involved with his first love.

Although the grandstands are always full on race day and the Indianapolis 500 is generally known as the world's largest single day sporting event, giving Cooper the post of president in 1980 was like dropping the proverbial hot potatoe in his lap. Knowledgeable race fans are familiar with the split that occurred in Championship racing some 18 months ago that caused formation of the Championship Auto Racing Teams (CART) as a separate sanctioning body from USAC. The split caused a thick air atmosphere during the 1979 "500" and countless lawsuits and protests were heard throughout the month. Enter John Cooper.

First, the automobile racing press lauded his appointment and gave him a vote of confidence that is rare indeed. It has been said many times over that it is almost impossible to get a group of racers to agree on almost anything. But both CART and USAC members gave John their best wishes. Maybe it was a nice way of saying, "Ok, now we've got someone to really take pot-shots at . . . let's see how you'll hold up when it gets down to decision making."

Cooper not only held up, he built a foundation that looks like it'll make him a skyscraper in the industry. He began to act as mediator between the two warring factions and made a base proposal to end the split. The outcome of Cooper's plan was the formation of the Championship Racing League whereby the two groups went back together under one roof. For now, in the summer of 1980 the roof is more like a tent, but it appears as though everyone is at least trying to work together. You can walk into Cooper's office and he exudes an air of respectability about the sport that is necessary for a man in his position. You know he speaks some words of wisdom simply because he's been down the road.

You can also bump into him at a dirt track Midget race and say, "Hey Coop, what's happenin'? What do you think of this new kid out there . . . " and John will probably tell you that he reminds him of a particular star in his early days. Plus, he'll enjoy the performance as much as you will. He can kick tires and lean on roll bars with the best of them.

Cooper is a refreshing personality in the racing business, as he doesn't practice what is commonly known as the executive shuffle. Ask the man a direct question, and you'll get a direct answer. If he isn't knowledgeable in some facet of the business (such as a highly technical, mechanical question) he won't attempt to skirt the issue and looks at problems as minor challenges in everyday work clothes.

It is possible to put two men side by side, ask them both the same question, and have them give the same precise answer. One man you may doubt, while the other will come across as someone you want to have faith in, believe, and let your problems rest with. Cooper fits in the latter category.

In his prior career, John has never been considered as a visible decision maker and we asked him if it bothered him to now be in a position where his actions will be judged by the racing fans and press.

"No," he replied, "it doesn't bother me. You know, I've never been involved in making car specifications, and that's always a major hassle in this sport. But I do know it's possible to write specifications for race cars that will fit more than one brand of engine or one type of chassis."

Nevertheless, he realizes that what is good for the sport is good for the Speedway and he's continually involved in behind-the-scenes conferences that affect all of Championship style racing. In 1980, for example, the Indianapolis Motor Speedway is deeply involved in the promotion of the 500 mile race held at Pocono and some of John's energy is being directed toward making that event a healthier one. Throughout the day he can expect to receive phone calls from a wide array of race interested sources

---

"I think we'll have to do a little better job in tooting our own horn"

---

ranging from an irate Championship driver to a company desiring involvement with the world's largest single day sporting event. Like many members of pro auto racing, Cooper is extremely accessible, a situation that solves as many problems as it creates.

"Sometimes you feel like you're living with a telephone in your hand," he grins.

Since he's taken over at the Speedway following the USAC-CART split, he hasn't yet been able to devote all his attention to Speedway improvements.

"As we all know," he says, "some of the participants have been unhappy with Championship racing in general, not particularly the 500."

John recognizes the fact the Speedway has become an American institution, and institutions in general have built traditions. That the gates are still open to the place year 'round is evidence enough the policies and practices are successful. However, we're glad to hear Cooper expound on the premise that some "progressive changes, within the boundaries of tradition," are in order. We pointed out the facts that Speedway cars have been largely responsible for American passenger cars utilizing wider tires, turbochargers, and to some degree, alcohol mixed with gasoline. However, neither the Speedway nor Championship racing in general has received their due credit for these mechanical innovations that have largely affected America's largest industry.

"You're right," he notes. "I think we have to do a little better job in tooting our own horn, and I'm sure we will in the future."

One shouldn't expect to see any drastic changes in the policies of the Indianapolis Motor Speedway, but we do imagine that the old adage of "Well, we've always done it that way in the past . . . no reason to change is there?" will not particularly hold true under Cooper's reign. There has always been a program of continual improvement at the 500 plus acre facility since Tony Hulman acquired it in 1946. John Cooper doesn't foresee any slowdown of activity in the improvement department, and from all indications it appears as though the Eighties will be the best decade yet for the Speedway.

Although the 1980 "500" was held in the worst recessionary times since the Great Depression, the purse was higher than ever before. New programs are being instituted for the Museum that should draw more visitors throughout the entire year. The track is becoming increasingly popular as a meeting place for old car clubs to hold annual events. Radio and television interests are as good as ever. And for the past several months the rumor has persisted that the Indianapolis Motor Speedway just might become the site of an annual NASCAR stock car race. While the purists of open-cockpit racing might yell foul, it would be a break in tradition to run a second event at IMS, it seems only reasonable that the world's most famous racing facility would host more than one event per year.

Hopefully, John Cooper has moved his wife Jane and two kids, Charlie 10, Cathy 13 to their most permanent home yet. Some executives might envy Cooper for having a 27 hole golf-course right outside his window, but John isn't a participant. He's more into family oriented spectator sports and can be found at an occasional hockey or basketball game. Somewhere along the line he says he'd like to buy a boat and spend some time away from the roar of the crowd. For now though, it looks like one of racing's happiest marriages between John Cooper and the Indianapolis Motor Speedway are setting up for some smooth sailing into the 1980's. They may not call him Cap'n Cooper yet, but give him a little time.

No News is Bad News

by Ann Miller

Each May, the world of sport focuses keen attention on the Indianapolis Motor Speedway. Thousands of writers, photographers, and broadcasters descend on the famed Brickyard to cover the greatest and richest speed classic of them all. Soon after their arrival, most seek out a non-descript cement block building just a few steps south of Gasoline Alley. There, at the IMS News Bureau, these sports journalists "set up shop" ready to relay all the on- and off-track happenings to race fans everywhere. And there to assist them in the never-ending game of "beat the deadline" is the competent staff of the Bureau: Bob Laycock Sr., Wilson D. "Bill" York, Don Foltz, Bob Clidinst, and Tom Bush.

At first thought, their job seems pretty "cush". They get to sit around all month in air-conditioned comfort, sipping cold ones and visiting with friends they haven't seen for a year. They simply pass out a list of qualifiers after "time trials"

and post the unofficial results after the race. Easy, right?

Wrong. For these five gentlemen, there's little sitting or visiting and no "cold ones." They're too busy:

● They issue concise, complete, accurate, up-to-the-minute reports on virtually everything that occurs at the track, starting on opening day with entry lists and data on how many cars have passed United States Auto Club technical inspection; through lap speeds during practice periods; on through qualifications, carburetion day, race day, and beyond.

● Act as liaisons between Speedway officials and the media, releasing official rulings and notifying the press of news conferences.

● Answer as Clidinst put it, "every question a newsman ever thought of dreaming up" about 500's past and present, garage area rumors, and facts, figures, and statistics, ad infinitum.

● Investigate accidents.

● See that all the essential, ultra-modern electronic equipment provided in the press room (typewriters, broadcast hook-ups, wire service transmitting machines and the like) are in good working condition.

● Distribute other information, such as the promotional "press kits from accessory companies and racing teams; the USAC "Daily Report"; announcements on awards presentations; and the indispensible *500 Fact Book*, filled with biographical sketches on the drivers and car designers, Speedway records, etc.

For years, Bob Laycock compiled this book himself; the 1980 edition he co-authored with Bill Donaldson. Associated with the IMS Publicity office for thirty years, Laycock has been in charge of the News Bureau since 1953. The noted racing historian terms the staff's job a "joint effort." Overall responsibility for the press room is his, while York "pretty

Bob Laycock, left, and Bill York are two dedicated Speedway staffers whose work is invaluable.

much operates the room on a day-to-day basis" according to Laycock. He calls Bush the "doorman" who "sees that the people who come in are entitled to come in." Foltz mans the phones in the office, while Clidinst is stationed at the starting line to report all the on-track developments. "We have a direct line there, a "ring down", explains Laycock," everytime he picks up the receiver it rings in our office. Every time there's a lap speed or a new car that enters the course he immediately gets on the phone and gives us the information. We post it on the black board inside the press office . . . and we also keep a board on the outside window of the press room for the public."

The most notable news each day is condensed into the USAC "Daily Report" put together by USAC personnel at the news bureau. "Jep Cadou is responsible for the preparation of the reports and Sue Jordon does the typing," informs USAC's chief timer and scorer on the Sprint circuit since 1963. These reports are available to newsmen each day soon after the track closes at 6 p.m. On qualification days, the "Report" contains a complete rundown of all attempts plus driver quotes. During the race, a "Report" sheet is released after every 40 laps, listing the race leaders at the end of every 10 laps, cars out of the race, reasons for yellow flags, and other vital statistics.

Glancing around the orderly, newly-remodeled press workroom, Laycock recalled the News Bureau's early days. "We started out under the Tower Terrace seats with a dirt floor and an ice-filled water cooler," he says. "Then we got new facilities under the Tower Terrace (now occupied by Goodyear Public Relations) when it was built. The present News Bureau building was constructed in 1970, with plenty of room to expand to the back if the need arises.

Inside, the click-clack-ding of the typewriters chimes with the almost constant ring-ring of the phones. The pit-side public address system is piped in, and it is not unusual to see reporters standing underneath the speakers, microphones uplifted, catching the comments of drivers and officials. Although the Speedway issues between 3-4,000 media credentials every May, the facility is most utilized by local and regional newswriters. The Indianapolis newspapers, the *Star* and the *News*, have offices and a darkroom in the building. A lounge, once the site of the post-race interview and innumerable card games, was removed during the recent

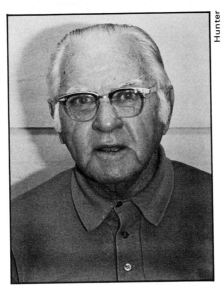
Tom Bush always has a ready smile.

Don Foltz handles the phone in May.

Bob Clidnst works the pits all month.

refurbishing for more workspace and a more business-like atmosphere. "Yes, we did take out the room that was used strictly for socializing", remarks Laycock. "At certain times . . . we've really been crowded. The people that needed to work didn't have room and there was too much noise for them to concentrate." He pauses and sighs, "Sometimes it's hard to keep the people out of here that are just in here for a good time and aren't necessarily working."

Bill York, calm and capable like Laycock, took his rookie stripes off in this business a long time ago. A 22-year veteran of the Speedway News Bureau, he has also handled press room and statistics chores for the Indiana Pacers since 1967. He states that 50-100 newsmen use the room during practice periods, but for qualifications and the race that number "jumps into the thousands." However, he claims that the busiest days for him are the Friday before the first day of qualifications and the three or four days prior to the race, when "the media people are preparing leads building up to the big day itself." After the winner's interview, now held in a room at the very south end of the Tower Terrace, and the post-race pandemonium, the job isn't over yet. Says York, "The next morning we come in and get the official finish and start compiling all the statistics for the Victory Dinner — the "Rookie-of-the-Year" award and things of that nature."

With all the many people the staff deals with each year, there's bound to be a few "run-ins." "Thankfully," observes York," all but one or two of these incidents have been amicably settled." There have been humorous moments as well. Of these, the president of Hoosier Handling, Inc. particularly mentions the excuses given by latecoming media — legitimate or otherwise — on why they need credentials. "I've heard quite a few stories," he chuckles.

In 1971, one of these latecomers delayed York from leaving for the one minute of trackside watching he "will not miss" — the start of the race. "It was a Godsend," he now relates. "I was late getting down there so I didn't get to my usual spot on the photo stand. I was standing on the steps of the (photo) wagon when I saw that the pace car wasn't going to get stopped. I scurried out of the way of the car — I injured a wrist or an elbow, I don't know how I did that, I guess it was on the hood of the car. The late Elmer George and I were the first two guys there to help Chris Schenkel, the astronaut, Pete Conrad and, of course, Mr. Hulman. The force of the impact had taken them all down into the well of the seats. We pulled them out and made sure they were alright."

In 1964, life started out to be "the pits" for Bob Clidinst. It's still that way, as he keeps his colleagues back in the press office abreast of all the happenings on the racecourse: e.g. the number of cars on the oval and their significant lap speeds. He also advises the Bureau on the time of, and reasons for, all yellow light situations. If the yellow signals an accident, the press room goes "on location." From his starting line post, Clidinst hitches a pace car ride down to the south end of the Tower Terrace where he joins Laycock and York, who have hustled over from the media center. Then they, and any sportswriters who want to go along, take one of two press vans (the other is for photographers) to the site of the wreck. Clidinst and York check the marks on the track surface, and on the wall if there was contact. They measure the distance of car's slide and determine the number of spins. Laycock checks the condition of the driver(s) involved and the extent of damage to the cars. Afterwards, all three confer, decide what actually transpired in the incident, and release the information to the press. Only occasionally do they consult with the USAC observers in the area of the accident. "Actually, asserts Clidinst, a custom designer of model race cars and airplanes," it entails very little 'interpretation'. Once you learn what those marks mean, there is very little possibility of error."

Meanwhile, Don Foltz is minding the store in the inner office of the News Bureau. During the month, he probably puts in more time on the phone than all the teenagers in Indianapolis combined. An employee of Hulman and Co. in Terre Haute, he is also the president and director of the Clinton State Bank in Clinton, Ind. This ex-Indiana state legislator and former director of the state's Department of Natural Resources has been an integral part of the press room staff for 15 years. Foltz says he gets calls from the general public in addition to those from in- and out-of-town writers. A lot of the questions concern rules and technicalities, "like how can you start 33rd when you've qualified another car," he laughs. This answering service has even been used by elbow-benders at local pubs, who usually phone in Donald Davidson-type stumpers. Says Foltz, "we try to accomodate everybody, even if it is some kind of bet." Although a number of queries involve a little researching, he

An always smiling Jep Cadou is one of the world's most knowledgeable race writers.

maintains that the staff gets "most of them answered."

Dubbed "the centurian" by York, Tom Bush fills other roles besides his main task of bouncer. In a way, he's kind of a handyman, secretary, public relations worker, and policeman all rolled into one. A lively septuagenarian, Bush clearly enjoys his duties in the press room. The retired postal worker first began working at the Speedway in 1921, at the age of 18 as a ticket seller. After a long stint in the Safety Patrol, guarding the garages and the pit gate, he came to the News Bureau in 1975. He contends that the reporters are "just like the people in the stands. You get some new ones, but mostly it's the same ones that come back year after year."

Although they are all dedicated and enthusiastic fans of auto racing, none of

the staff members really get a chance to just sit and enjoy watching the cars on the track. Instead, they are all caught up working in the always exacting, often exhausting, and sometimes exasperating occupation of accommodating the media. In spite of it all, York insists that, when the month of May is over, he and his press room associates "start looking forward to next year." Indianapolis Motor Speedway Vice-President and Director of Publicity, Al Bloemker, whose department oversees the News Bureau, has words of praise for the staff. "They do an almost perfect job," he says. "They know what the media wants and they give it to them, quickly and accurately." Without a doubt, the staff of the IMS News Bureau adds to the Speedway's well-deserved reputation of putting on the best show in motorsports.

The press room on a slow day. When it's busy there are wall to wall writers.

Names & Numbers

Mahoney

by Dave Scoggan

"Names and numbers of all the cars and drivers" has long been a popular shout of entry list hawkers at the Speedway. But this year, you would have needed a computer to keep track of some of the identity changes in chassis. No less than two cars appeared on the track with three different numbers, while others went from backup (T) status to front-line duty (and sometimes numerical surgery).

Sharing the "sleight-of-brush" award for 1980 were the Patrick Racing Wildcat of Tom Bagley, and the Armstrong Mould Lola of Tom Bigelow. The Armstrong Lola started the month as #45, debuted by Howdy Holmes on May 5. When Bigelow gave up on his new Orbitor I #3, he assumed the Lola and changed to the single digit. Tom qualified Lola #3, while Holmes made an unsuccessful fourth day attempt with the now — #45 Orbitor I. For the race, the Lola bore the traditional Armstrong "43", since Howdy's original #43 also failed to qualify.

Tom Bagley's Wildcat began May life as #70, colored red, white and blue. When Gordon Johncock crashed his newer Wildcat in practice, the #70 car was transformed into #20 by Pole Day morning. Gordie decided not to qualify the car however, so Bagley earned a starting spot in car #20. By next track appearance, the racer sported #40 and was painted in the blue and yellow scheme of Kent Oil.

Adding to the confusion from the Patrick camp was Johncock's eventual PC6, qualified as the Kent Oil #40T, but repainted and raced as the North American Van Lines #20. Also, the Phoenix shoed by Gordon Smiley as a red, white and blue #70 was debuted by Tom Bagley on May 8 as the Kent Oil #40.

Hurley Haywood experienced trouble with his #99 Drake V8 about the time teammate Johnny Parsons began working with the #15T V6 Chevy. Suddenly, 15T sprouted a #99 nose cone and Mr. H.H. behind the wheel. Hurley made the show in V6 #99, while the original Drake V8 quietly sat at the end of the last day qualifying line bearing #55 and pink striping.

Even old "Super Tex" played the numbers this year. A.J.'s primary car was the Foyt/DOHC-powered #14 Parnelli, with his "backup" Cosworth designated 14T. When time ran out on the Foyt engine experiment, the "T" quickly vanished from the Cosworth. Safely but slowly qualified, A.J. then renumbered the DOHC to 16 for George Snider to steer; Cosworth power also came to Ziggy's aid.

Tom Sneva's practice crash in the #9 O'Connell Phoenix was to have placed him in the #81 Woodward McLaren, but when Vern Schuppan got rained out of a qualifying attempt in the #89 O'Connell backup car, Sneva returned to his now-available first choice. Tom's yellow McLaren first showed on Carb Day without a number, but later became #9.

One number switch caught some people completely off guard — and the change occurred before the month began. Phil Caliva's Alsup McLaren-Offy originated as #49, but was voluntarily changed to #47. When Caliva smote the third turn wall on May 15, both the Indianapolis *Star* and *News* reported that Phil was driving a "Chaparral-Cosworth," which just happened to be #47 on the original entry list. (Just shows you can't believe everything you read in the papers, although we're sure Phil Caliva wishes he could!)

Mahoney

GROUND EFFECTS

A Half Hour History of the Latest Chassis Innovation to Invade the Speedway.

Andretti's 1978 Formula I car led the revolution.

by Philip LeVrier

The old saying, "History repeats itself" has been a proven fact at the Indianapolis 500 many times over. Railbirds at Indy patiently sit back and watch as every few years a new technical innovation or formula for a winning car will pop up and set the pattern for car builders to follow. This is one of the many things that make the classic race so interesting. In the last twenty years alone, we've seen the "laydown" Offy show its stuff in 1957 and '58, the domination of the A.J. Watson-built roadsters, the development of the Cosworth engine, but nothing like the rear-engine revolution of the 1960's when Colin Chapman, Jimmy Clark and Dan Gurney made the Offy roadster an endangered species.

Most car owners and drivers had seen the handwriting on the brick wall ever since Jim Clark's Lotus-Ford finished second in 1963 and they were forced to purchase the new Ford-dual overhead cam V-8 engine bolted into a small 1,300-pound Lotus chassis. Of the 33 qualifying cars at Indy in 1965, only four were front-engine Offy roadsters, and nobody was surprised to see Clark lead 190 of 200 laps to win in Colin Chapman's creation.

Once again, Colin Chapman has changed the thinking at Indy — although less dramatically than in 1965. For the last few years Chapman has been concentrating on the Grand Prix circuit with Mario Andretti driving, and both achieved their goal of a world championship title in 1978 with a combination of Andretti's driving skills and a revolutionary new chassis designed by Chapman on a "ground effect" concept.

Chapman's new car was based on the theory that a race car could be designed to take advantage of the airstream *under* the car as well as the airstream over the top and he came out of secret testing with a new, sleek, clean-shaped Lotus 78, powered by a Ford Cosworth engine. The car sported sidepods and was referred to as a "wing car" and its secret was underbody aerodynamics.

The secret of the Lotus 78 was that the car was designed so that air flowed in

Jim Hall revolutionized Champ car racing.

through the pods mounted on the sides of the chassis and is subjected to a venturi pressure differential action which results in the chassis being sucked down on the ground for better traction.

Chapman's next car, the perfected Lotus 79 was a true ground effect car, with wide sidepods and a more aerodynamically designed full body which created the low pressure area needed for better suction and increased traction. It ran away with the 1978 Grand Prix season as rival GP car builders scurried to design their own "wings cars".

By the 1979 Grand Prix season Colin Chapman had succeeded in completely changing the look of the Grand Prix car. It now featured small front wings, a pointed nose with the driver sitting way up front, side skirts and fully covered engines. The idea is to take advantage of surface cooling down the monocoque body, smoother air flow, and aerodynamic side pods creating negative lift and especially the theory of taking up as little air flow room as possible under the car.

One way Chapman discovered to control the amount of air flow under the car was with the use of side skirts. The "skirts" are extensions at the bottom of

The new cars from the Patrick stable were impressive. Note the low "sidepods" and skinny nose.

Wendt

the chassis which prevent air from getting under the car and destroying the venturi effect. The skirts are designed to run as close as possible to the track to add to the down-force vacuum under the tub of the car.

By the end of the '79 Grand Prix season the ground effect technical innovations were changing with every race as car builders experimented with different shaped pods and movable side skirts. Even Colin Chapman got passed up as his Lotus was overshadowed by new ground effect machines, especially the weird-looking 1979 Ferrari 312T4 designed by Mourno Forghieri, which went on to capture the world title with Jody Scheckter at the wheel. However, one of the factors responsible for Ferrari's superiority in 1979 was its ground effects features.

Back in the United States, Al Unser and Jim Hall of Midland, Texas showed up with the first ground effect car in champ racing. Ironically, ground effects were first successfully used by Jim Hall in 1970 in his Chaparral 2-J Can-Am car. But that car used a snowmobile engine to create a suction in the enclosed rear section of the car.

Jim Hall's Indy car was designed by John Barnard, who designed the 1978 world championship-winning Lotus 79 of Mario Andretti. Outwardly, the new Chaparral and the Lotus bear a striking resemblance. The beautiful yellow Pennzoil Chaparral utilized full ground effects and at Indy in 1979, Al Unser ran away at the beginning of the race and built up a comfortable lead. The car really stuck to the track and it looked as though Unser would chalk up the victory until a cracked transmission seal caused him to drop out at the halfway point. Roger Penske's semi-ground effect cars dominated the CART season, won Indy and the CART title for Rick Mears. Mechanical problems plagued the Chaparral all season and not until the final race at Phoenix, was Unser finally able to get all the problems worked out and record the first victory for the car.

Bobby Unser, driving for Roger Penske, almost won the 500 when brother Al dropped out, and one of the many drivers who admitted Al Unser's car was the one to beat in 1980. It certainly looked that way as the car reached its potential and Jim Hall came out of the season with a full year of testing the car.

With Jim Hall showing that ground effects was the only way to go at Indy in 1980, it looked like the '80 champ car season was going to be the most innovative since Colin Chapman presented the rear engine Lotus as the design for success. Over the winter, the Indy car builders were busy preparing new ground effects cars in time for Indy; either copied after the Chaparral, the Lotus 79, or the Penske PC-7 semi ground effects chassis.

To prepare for the 1980 '500' there was a lot of testing being conducted in California with Rutherford getting in over 500 miles of testing in the Chaparral. Roger Penske was also testing his new full ground effect Penske PC-9. With Penske's experience in the semi-ground effects PC-7, he was surely the favorite to pick at Indy should the Chaparral fail again. Penske's team of Bobby Unser and Rick Mears were running 1-2 late in the '79 race and were headed for the first two-car team victory at Indy since 1962 when Unser suddenly dropped out. Mears went on to win the race in his PC-7. For 1980, Penske had formed a "super team" with Bobby Unser, Rick Mears and Mario Andretti all to be supplied with new ground effect PC-9s.

But Penske had to test his new car and iron out the bugs while Jim Hall already had a full season of testing. The 1980

It's refreshing to see the body work fully enclose the engine once again.

Al Unser's new Longhorn mount looked great but had some definite problems.

Chaparral was basically the same car as in 1979 with the only change being the driver. A lot of detail development had been made but "There's nothing completely new," owner Hall said. "It's been a matter of updating what we learned from last year."

Ex-Chaparral pilot Al Unser showed up as the driver for another Texas car owner, Bobby Hillin, who sunk a lot of money into a new ground effects car designed by Ed Zink. The new car was based on the Frank Williams/Patrick Head chassis that Alan Jones drove to five Formula One firsts in 1979 and the 1980 Grand Prix opener.

With all of the testing going on, there was a lot of excitement about the new wave of race cars that were coming to Indy. The year was going to be a comeback for American designers and the fans were to be rewarded with cars that actually looked like race cars again. Instead of looking like stripped-down super modifieds or go-carts, the cars featured full bodies and bold, aesthetic paint jobs.

Rumors began to surface that Dan Gurney was testing a new ground effects Eagle. The new car was far more different than anything that had ever emerged from his California shops. The new Eagle was based on a design by John Ward. It was his initial attempt at a championship ground effects car, and it was an attempt at a different approach to Jim Hall's ground effects ideas.

The Eagle was fabricated by Ward and chief mechanic Wayne Leary, and had a distinctive appearance with its narrow tub designed to use a minimum of frontal area to achieve better aerodynamics. From the cockpit back, the car flared out into a square tail and wing that covered the engine. The fuel tank was located

directly behind the driver rather than along his side. This not only permitted a narrower configuration but centered the weight of the fuel in the middle of the chassis.

The design is a proven Formula One racing idea with the fuel tank location helping to preserve handling characteristics by not having the balance of the chassis disturbed as much, as the weight of the fuel gets lighter as it is used.

But the unique thing about the car's design was John Ward's ground effects solution. He sealed off the air beneath the car rather than have it flow under the machine in a venturi effect as in the Chapman-Hall concept with the wide side pods.

In doing this, he created a low pressure area at the *rear* of the car which creates the down force which exemplifies ground effects. In addition, the rear end was swept upward like the Chaparral so the ground effects is experienced along the length of the car.

Gurney was also experimenting with a rocker arm 355-cubic inch V-8 Chevy engine similiar to NASCAR stock car racing engines.

Mike Mosley shook the car down in California tests at only 180 mph with the Chevy engine. It moved much quicker with a Cosworth powerplant but in USAC competition, Gurney planned to use an "All-American Effort."

At the Championship Racing League opener at Ontario, Johnny Rutherford and Chaparral were in a class by themselves. In his initial appearance for Jim Hall, gentleman Johnny left little doubt he was the man to beat after making a mockery of the pole position competition by out-qualifying the field by 3 miles an hour.

Rutherford secured the No. 1 starting

spot with a lap of 196.803. Bobby Unser gave Roger Penske's new ground effects PC-9 its baptism and qualified second fastest at 193.473.

The third new development in ground effects chassis was Bobby Hillin's brand new Longhorn LR-1 driven by Al Unser for third best speed.

It was an exciting showroom as teammates Gordon Johncock and Tom Bagley were also wheeling debut ground effects Wildcats for owner Pat Patrick and Dan Gurney's new Eagle was unveiled.

Mike Mosley had done quite a bit of testing in the needle-nosed, ultra clean Eagle and had it up to speed after some early chassis problems. In a familiar ground effects puzzler, the Eagle was not getting consistent down force because of the chassis lifting in the turns and too much air was disturbing the suction. This problem was overcome by adding thin body structures to the lower outside forward sections of the tub supported by dihedral supports in an attempt to give a greater sealing effect to the chassis and in effect, desensitizing the car.

There were some "out-dated" McLarens and Parnellis in the Ontario field but most of the top positions were filled by the proven semi-ground effect Penske PC-7s and PC-6s.

When the race got under way, Lone Star J.R. was virtually uncontested in the only American sophomore ground-effects machine. However, Bobby Unser in the debut of Roger Penske's initial full ground-effects chassis was pretty impressive. Unser was able to stay close to Rutherford and as the two began to lap slower cars on the eighth lap. Unser even managed to take the lead away from the Chaparral but lasted only six laps before a punctured radiator ended his afternoon.

Spike Gehlhausen's semi-ground effects car surprised many and he was picked as a dark horse.

Although nicely constructed, Sherman Armstrong's new Orbiter didn't get the bugs worked out in time.

Al Unser in the Formula One-flavored racer, was never a factor for the lead and was sidelined with transmission trouble while running fifth.

In the two other ground effects cars, Gordon Johncock finished best with a third in Pat Patrick's new Wildcat. Mike Mosley dropped out when his Cosworth engine went sour.

After their victory at Ontario, Hall & Co. quickly brought their Chaparral 2-K to Indy for more tire tests. They had spent three winter months extensively testing the car and it was perfect. In more than 600 miles of practicing, the car had not suffered a failure of any type. As Rutherford said, their number one priority was to make the car reliable. Obviously, the truly professional racing team from Texas was well ahead of the competition.

While testing at Indy in April the Chaparral team was joined by master mechanic George Bignotti who showed up to test his new Phoenix. The beautiful car was more streamlined than a normal ground effects car. Its parts were built in England and the machine was assembled in George Bignotti's shop in Indianapolis.

Jerry O'Connel, owner of Tom Sneva's reliable old McLaren ordered a new Phoenix to be built by English craftsman John Thompson who was also rumored to be building a ground effects car for Salt Walther.

Indy railbirds were grinning like possums with all these new cars being readied for the 64th running of the 500. The last couple of Indianapolis races have been especially interesting from the technical standpoint because of the wide variety of cars and engines in the field. A few years ago all the cars looked alike and many used the same engine. In 1980, there was an unusually broad variety of

engines and chassis designs. Twenty-five different types of chassis were entered — 20 Penskes, 11 McLarens, 10 Eagles, 10 Lightnings, 7 Wildcats and one or more of 20 other varieties — plus a variety of American stock-block engines along with the Cosworth and Offy power-plants. There was even talk that Porsche was going to be involved in the race to give it that international flavor.

As predicted, Jim Hall's Chaparral had the clear advantage when the track opened for practice in early May. The now-dubbed "Yellow Submarine" captained by Rutherford was running as wild as a Texas jackrabbit as the other 89 cars entered tried to play catch up.

Opening day crowds got a glimpse at space-age racing when Sherman Armstrong wheeled out the Jiffy Mix Orbitor/Cosworth driven by Howdy Holmes. Armstrong had decided to follow Hall and Hillin and picked out a Formula-One proven design. He contracted March Engineering of England to create a pair of cars for veterans Tom Bigelow and Howdy Holmes. The John Barnard (Chaparral) designed creation was a true ground effects car with the short, stubby nose and the square side pods and the driver's position located far forward. Holmes was second on the track and he soon got the full-bodied car up to fast speeds before experiencing engine problems.

Unfortunately, Tom Bigelow's twin Orbitor II wasn't ready in time to qualify and he soon vacated the cockpit in favor of the Lola he drove in 1979.

Another car that looked similiar to the Orbitor was Janet Guthrie's slick Texaco Lightning/Cosworth. The car was clearly the classiest-looking set of wheels beside Jim Hall's Chaparral and both Janet and Johnny Parsons orbited the track in true

Star Wars fashion as only their Darth Vader helmets protruded above the car's non-windshield.

Lindsey Hopkins also put his bunny decal on a new Lightning built by Dave Klym. The aerodynamic car was assigned to Johnny Parsons with a choice of three engines — a V-6 turbocharged Chevy, a V-8 Drake and a Cosworth.

On the second day of practice, Al Unser gave yet another look at futuristic racing when he arrived in the white No. 5 LR-01 Cosworth and Gordy Johncock presented Bignotti's new full-bodied ground effects Phoenix. Tom Bagley and Tom Sneva also had new Phoenix racers and these five cars featured the smallest rear wings seen at Indy in ten years.

Dan Gurney entered his new ground-effects Eagle for driver Mike Mosley, powered by a Chevrolet stock-block normally aspirated 5.6-liter Chevy engine similiar to a NASCAR powerplant. There had been hints that dapper Dan Gurney was going to show up with a wingless wing machine. There was a lot of applause when the crew pushed the new Eagle out to the track for practice runs. Although very popular because of the All-American effort, the car turned out to be as cantankerous as some of the CART/USAC graffit on the Gasoline Alley bathroom walls.

The heavy artillery was rolled out when Bobby Unser, Rick Mears and Mario Andretti all took to the track in their new Roger Penske PC-9s designed by Geoff Ferris. This was truly one of the most formidable racing teams ever seen at the Speedway and was certainly going to give Rutherford some trouble with the three to one odds. The cars were all powered by eight cylinder turbo-charged Cosworth DFX engines and had been tested at Ontario at better than 200 mph.

The new Penske machines were the prettiest ground effects cars to arrive.

Penske also had two backup PC-7s in his stable after selling the rest to the competition. The PC-7 semi-ground effects cars were still quite competitive. Hoosier hope Spike Gelhausen was fastest in the Penske/Cosworth with which Bobby Unser almost won the 1979 "500". The car was updated by chief mechanic Derek Mower and extensively tested in California over the winter.

Tim Richmond, Pancho Carter, Dennis Firestone and Bill Alsup all had PC-7s while Dick Ferguson, Salt Walther, Jim McElreath and John Mahler were seen in PC-6s. Sporty car driver Bill Whittington had a PC-7 that was converted into a full-bodied ground effects car with the addition of a PC-9 rear-end by Bob Sparshot, who helped build Jim Hall's Chaparrall.

Even with all the new space-age cars and proven Penske chasis, there were many favorites to chose from in the lower income bracket. The perennial favorite being Roger Rager in his stock-block Chevrolet Wildcat. Roger and road racer Bill Tempero's cars featured full-bodies with fabricated "K-Mart ground effects" and were true crowd pleasers with their rumbling "Chivie" mills rattling the grandstands and giving old timers a chance to remind the younger race fans of the good old days of the thundering Novis.

The two veteran Parnelli chassis chauffeurs, A.J. Foyt and Danny Ongais also appeared on the track in their same cars. It would have been great for the fans if A.J.'s crew had pushed out an exotic new Coyote-orange Formula One ground effects car, but unfortunately this didn't happen.

Ongais was supposed to drive a new experimental Porsche-powered Interscope ground effects car designed by ex-Eagle designer Roman Slobodyjnski. But the German firm yanked its engine from the field in a dispute over turbo boost regulations.

Foyt was also upset over the pressure relief valve on his turbo-charger and after withdrawing from the Ontario race in a five-year-old Parnelli/Cosworth, the rumors were rampant about the four-time Indy King's plans. Surely ole A.J. had something up his sleeve.

It appeared that A.J.'s answer to the ground effects craze was his Foyt V-8 engine run under USAC's 48-inch boost rules. After a few practice laps in the updated Parnelli/Foyt, A.J. and crew made a hasty retreat to Gasoline Alley and traded the Foyt engine for a Cosworth (which the grand old Texan soon got up to 192-plus, much to the crowd's delight).

Within a few days of practice, Johnny Rutherford was consistently fastest and was openly confident. He admitted the car was dialed in and he was "ready to go racin'." To put a cap on the statement, he took the back-up Chaparral out and ran even faster! With his one-sided victory at Ontario and two dialed-in ground effects cars, Lone Star J.R. was certainly the firstest with the mostest.

The "Yellow Submarine" continued to lead the speed parade, but members of the Penske stable soon zoomed within fairly close range of the Chaparral on their first day on the track. Defending champion Rick Mears and 1978 World Grand Prix Champion Mario Andretti both came within challenging range of

Rutherford on the same day they made their 1980 track debuts and, like last year, it was shaping up to be another Chaparral/Penske duel.

Before race day a new fact was discovered about the new ground effect concept — leg injuries sustained during crashes. Gordon Johncock and Tom Sneva both crashed their new cars in practice and sustained leg injuries.

Johncock destroyed his new Phoenix when the car broke loose without warning. He blamed the crash on the USAC rule which took away the articulating or sliding skirts on the ground effects cars. He said the car leaned in the turns when the unmovable skirts trapped the air and when the car flattened out the air escaped, disrupting the car's handling. The 1973 Indy champ said sliding skirts as used in Grand Prix racing, would alleviate these problems. Another problem caused by the solid rubber skirts was the amount of rubber they left on the track. After a week of practice the turns were soon coated with a dangerous slick coating of skirt rubber.

Al Unser's Formula-One copy LR-01 was also experiencing chassis handling problems and Englishman Frank Durney, who served as the aerodynamics chief for the Williams team and designed the car, had to be flown in to help sort out the problems. He also complained about the skirt rules. In the opener at Ontario, CART rules allowed moving skirts and Unser was third fastest, but USAC rules called for solid skirts. Gurney said the car was the only true ground effects car in the field and relied on articulating skirts for success.

Johnny Rutherford continued to show the way in his Pennzoil Chaparral but the Penske "Super Team" was knocking on the door when Mario Andretti emerged as a definite pole contender with a 190-plus lap in his Essex Penske PC-9. Rutherford surprised no one on the first day of qualifications when he posted a 4-lap average of 192.256 mph to capture the pole position. J.R. had a margin of more than 1 mph over second quick Mario Andretti at 191.012.

Rutherford actually made the run in the backup Chaparral. The No. 1 machine burned a magneto wire during the morning practice session, melting down the cap.

When the side-skirt smoke (and rain) cleared after qualifications it was also no surprise to see all three of the new Penske cars driven by Andretti, Bobby Unser and Rick Mears occupying starting berths in the first two rows.

Other ground effects cars weren't as

quick and didn't appear to be contenders. In many cases, the cars weren't finished in time for the extensive testing that was needed. Johnny Rutherford pointed out that; "Everybody that has ground effects now is going through the same things that Hall did a year ago."

Al Unser qualified on the fourth row in the Longhorn LR-01 and Pat Patrick's two remaining ground-effects cars were survivors of a rough month. After wheel problems on the Phoenix, Tom Bagley was in Johncock's Wildcat, which had done well in its debut at Ontario. The winged Wildcat IV was drawn up by Bob Riley (of A.J. Foyt Coyote fame) and George Bignotti. The car was unique in that it featured wings on the *side* of the side-mounted pods, which act as wings and control the flow of air underneath the car, rather than having air flow through the pods. Bagley crashed the already qualified car on Carb Day and although repaired in time for the race, it wasn't fully dialed in. Teammate Johncock made the field in an old Penske PC-6 semi-ground effects car and rookie Gordon Smiley put the new Phoenix in the middle of the field.

Dan Gurney's No. 48 struggled to qualify and Janet Guthrie in the ultra-modern Lindsey Hopkins Lightning failed to make the show as did Howdy Holmes when a side pod panel came off and cut his rear tire, sending him into the wall. It was ironic that the concept that should have put him into the race caused him to miss the show.

It was predictable to find that half of the first 18 qualifiers were Penskes and it was also predicted that the 1980 race would be a repeat of the '79 show with the battle between the Chaparral and the Roger Penske stable.

When the field finally took the green flag, the yellow Pennsoil screamer of Johnny Rutherford quickly shot to the front followed by Bobby Unser and Mario Andretti. Despite having a fairly stout advantage over the entire field, Rutherford had his hands full in the early stages with Unser, Andretti, Rick Mears and Pancho Carter — all in Penske cars.

With a three to one advantage over Rutherford, Roger Penske figured his three new machines had a good shot at winning the race should anything happen to J.R. But a monopoly is not always a good thing, and it was Rutherford's day as mechanical problems and a tire problem ruined Penske's hopes for a third Indy triumph.

Al Unser in the new Dairy Queen

Dan Gurney's new Eagle looked small, skinny compared to the rest of the field.

Even though it wasn't in the race, Dave Klym's work on the 55 was first class.

LR-01 found out that he didn't have more burger than bun and dropped out with engine woes as did Tom Bagley in the Wildcat and Gordon Smiley in the Phoenix.

The persnickety Eagle dropped out of the race early after making several "mosquito spraying" laps. The aluminum rocker arm engine in the Eagle was not turning the RPMs it should have been and it was sad that Gurney announced he was going to drop out of champ car racing until he could find a sponsor and much needed bucks.

Johnny Rutherford, the hands-down favorite after winning the pole position and dominating the race at Ontario, lived up to expectations by leading 124 of 200 laps. Rutherford, who began his Indy career before the demise of the Offy-roadster, helped to establish a new

era at the Brickyard — the era of ground effects, when he joined the three-time Indy winners club.

Rutherford's dominance in qualifying and the race both at Ontario and Indy appeared to be a very clear forecast for the Indy-car set and for the next couple of years we're going to be seeing an exciting new revolution — the American development of ground effects at Indy — all inspired by Colin Chapman's Lotus 79 ground effect car.

History has repeated itself once again at Indianapolis and the stage is set until the next technical revolution which will perhaps put a Penske PC-9 or a Chaparral on the last row of the qualifying field, just as Bobby Grim's front-engined Watson-built roadster sat behind all those rear-engine Fords in 1968.

The Oldtimers

Jack Fox photos

Chief Steward Tom Binford
was given the Bill Klein award.

Ira Hall, center, a chipper 89 years old, talks with builders
Harry Templeton and Frank Kurtis.

Mary Owen received a plauque
for her continuing help in May.

An impressive array of yesterday's talent lines up to pose and
reminisce about the 1950 winning car.

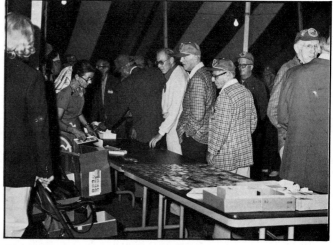

The Oldtimers tent should be "bugged" as there are dozens of
memorable stories to be heard every year.

by Jack C. Fox

Every year they come back to the scene of former triumphs and disappointments to relive their racing dreams with those who shared them. The annual "500" Oldtimers Club gathering, topped by the big Bar-Be-Que, is a big event in the lives of yesteryear's drivers, riding mechanics, car owners, crew men, officials and Speedway employees who have been (or were) associated with the "500" at least 20 years ago.

Headquarters for the club during the month of May is a big mobil home parked to the rear of the press building (courtesy of Dick Huddleston and Lew Worcel) where members can sit around and bench race as well as enjoy luncheon and snacks as dispensed by Marge Hauss

and Mary Owen who help out as "den mothers."

The Monday evening before the race the Bar-Be-Que is held for approximately 350 members (some of whom fly into town just for this event). Hook Drugs springs for the meal and it is a good one. Each year the Speedway Museum sends over one of the historic race cars from their collection and this year it was Johnny Parsons' winner from 1950. Parsons posed for photos behind the wheel while some of the older drivers lined up behind him. Perhaps the oldest driver — chronologically — on hand was Ira Hall, a very strong and healthy 89. Oldest driver — competitively — was Tony Gulotta who drove a Miller in 1927 followed by Babe Stapp, a member of the Duesenberg Team in 1927. Babe suffered

a serious coronary several days after the Bar-Be-Que but, at last report, was progressing nicely. Several regulars were in the pits with various problems this year which prevented their attendance. Freddy Mangold, Russ Catlin, Pete DePaolo, Walt Ader and Clay Ballinger were among those missing.

As usual the club presents awards and this year three new members were inducted into the Hall of Fame — David Bruce-Brown, Walter Christie and George Robertson — all of whom were active before World War I. The L.W. "Bill" Klein Award went to Lindsey Hopkins, Jack Beckley received the AP Parts Award and Oldtimers plaques were given to Tom Binford, Keith Andres, Bill Dredge, Johnny Williams, Marge Hauss and Mary Owen.

Crocky Wright, one time motorcycle and Midget racer now works in the Museum.

Mahoney Photos

Talented broadcasters all, these fellas make up a part of the Syndicated Sports Network. From left: Paul Scheuring, Mike Venable, Ron Biddle, Gary Lee and Gary Byers.

SPEEDWAY PEOPLE

Don Hein, Indianapolis based TV sports commentator is a knowledgeable regular. Below: Bob Hurt, Indy driver who was injured years ago, was a May visitor again and showed a bit more improvement.

Attractive Gloria Novoteny works on the Speedway Radio Network all year 'round.

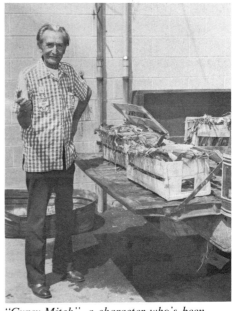

"Gypsy Mitch", a character who's been around the Foyt garage for many years usually brings a load of corn for the Gasoline Alley crews.

USAC's public relations man Paul Reinhart, left, and John Cooper, Speedway president shown chatting in the pits.

Goodyear racing tire boss Leo Mehl chats with a now retired Roger McCluskey. McCluskey looked downright spiffy in his role as USAC's Competition Director.

Two graying oval track veterans, retired Wally Dallenbach, left, and a still very active Mel Kenyon.

Kevin O'Neil with Indy's WIBC radio station is a familiar face.

Ace photographer Jim Schweiker recorded for Penske and Gould again.

Left, Cathy Rude is next femme Indy hopeful. Melanie Simon on the right.

SPEEDWAY PEOPLE

"Holy Cow!" Milt Harper is an annual Indy sight.

Halibrand Athletic Club members pose with 1980 "Kitty" winner. From left: Ted Halibrand, winner Linda Calhoun who is an IMS Motel waitress, Don Watkins, Bob Falcon, and Butch Jackson.

This is not your everyday farm girl, it's foxy looking Alice Mosley.

Speedway Prexy John Cooper in a confab with ABC's Jim McKay, left, Dennis Lewin and NBC's Sean McManus. Racing TV coverage looks like it will be healthy in the 80's.

Jerry Sneva talks with one of motorsport's most knowledgeable and interesting writers, Jerry Miller.

Grounds Super Charlie Thompson, left and Indy 500 Museum director Jack Martin are both dedicated to the track.

Racing filmmaker Dick Wallen was back.

"We won!" Pennzoil PR man Bill Dredge.

IMS photogs Ron McQueeney, left, and Jack Duffy. Both do memorable work.

[187]

IMS-Link

SPEEDWAY PEOPLE

Sam Posey & Herm Johnson

Unsung heroes of the Speedway, the Technical Staff, headed by Jack Beckley (5th from left).

Mahoney Photos

'60 winner Jim Rathmann is now a Chevrolet-Cad dealer.

IMS-Bergquist

Hard-working Tom Hays aids many Midwestern ovals.

USAC Midget Champ Steve Lotshaw chats with Jerry Sneva.

IMS-Hunter

STP's Ralph Salvino is always a welcome part of the Indy 500 scene.

IMS-Bergquist

Track announcer Tom Carnegie's voice is unmistakable over the P.A. system.

IMS-Willoughby

Indy's track safety man Jerry Decius never gets the credit he and crew should.

Officials Don Garner, left, and Bob Cassady were pleased at having a quiet month.

California car builder Dave Klym built a beautiful car for the Hopkins team.

Car owners Rose and Pete Wysard brought a clean Speedway car this year but lady luck kept them out of the starting field.

Foyt mechanic Howard Gilbert, left, with three time winner Mauri Rose.

ABC's Bill Fleming takes a break.

Yearbook publisher Carl Hungness and his crew from left, Terri Gunn, Justyn Blackwell, John Mahoney, Wilma Steffy, Marie Willis and Ray Toms.

Mahoney

Indy's Joe Cloutier, a man with a dry sense of humor must enjoy mechanic Smokey Yunick's straightforward attitude.

Mahoney

Pit gate guard Joe Ray checks for proper (and genuine) credentials.

Mahoney

Speedway, Ind. attorney Tom Deal "stooges" with the Watson team.

Carla Carter and Dana Capels score Pancho's practice laps in relative comfort.

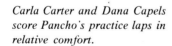

Mahoney

deBrier

Speedway owner Mary Hulman is very active at Indy throughout the month of May.

deBrier

Sheldon Kinser raps with a now retired Freddie Agabashian. Freddie says he is still thoroughly enjoying himself, rebuilds cars, plays golf, etc.

SPEEDWAY PEOPLE

Lindsey Hopkins, left, has been an owner at Indy for 30 years. He's chatting with Ted Hollingsworth.

Two dedicated racers, Johnny Vance, left and Reynold MacDonald depicted this year's mood.

The photo shop's Donna Wolf.

Right: Clint Brawner and brother Larry are working on a genuine roadster!

Rube came back and played some poker.

Sherman Armstrong and Paul Leffler at ease during the golf tournament.

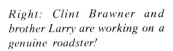

Steve Szentivanyi pulls his weight at IMS.

Kay Totten-Spivey is a stringer for the Indianapolis Star newspaper.

Mahoney

Herb Porter, better known to Gasoline Alley residents as Horsepower Herb, sharing office time with Danny "O".

Meadows

One of Indianapolis' best known D.J.'s "Adam Smasher found time to attend the 64th annual 500 Mile Race.

SPEEDWAY

Mahoney

Chet Coppuck, TV sportscaster in Indy is one of racing's true supporters.

Mahoney

The Pace car room's Pat Cronin needed help from her niece Pat this year: tennis problem.

Mahoney

West Coast attorney Don Bringgold is always an interested observer.

An always good natured Aldo Andretti and former 500 winner Parnelli Jones renew acquaintances again in Gasoline Alley.

Meadows

Mahoney

Carl Gehlhausen helped his son Spike achieve his dream of running at Indy and now Spike is making him very proud.

Bubby Jones was a visitor. Ol' Bub is racing CRA Sprinters in California.

PEOPLE

The man on the left has thrilled thousands of Sprint car fans and had Indy regulars rooting too: Ralph Ligouri. Rookie Phil Caliva is getting some advice.

C.M. Dibble has been spending his month of May at the Speedway for over 25 years.

Indy's Bill Donaldson, relaxes: Rare.

Our old friend, "Mr. First In Line," Larry Bisceglia, was back for 1980.

Kim Hood and Tom Cochran of PM Magazine produced some nice work on the May doings.

Pals Billy Vukovich (left) and Tim Coffeen.

Award Time

Dave Rippey, President of Sun Oil Co. (center) presents Mark Donohue's 1972 winning Sunoco Spl. to the IMS Museum. From left are Karl Kainhoffer (Penske engine builder); Jack Martin, Museum Director; Roger Penske and IMS President John Cooper. In the photo at right, the car rests on a '500' Festival Float before going to the museum.

1980 members of the ''11th Row Society'' Tom Sneva, Tom Bigelow and Gary Bettenhausen are joined by Gary LaFollette and Art Harris (right).

AARWBA honorees include (from left) Bill Marvel, Dale Burgess, Bob Russo, Bill Eggert, Jep Cadou, Charlie Brockman, George Moore and Bob Laycock.

Tim Richmond receives the Indiana dairymen's 6th annual ''Fastest Rookie'' award from Myrna Hazel, state manager of the American Dairy Association of Indiana and Paul Page, ''Voice of the 500''.

American Red Ball Scholarship award winner Rick Mears is joined by Paul Page (left), Board Chairman Robert L. Hiner and President Elmer H. Ostermeyer, far right.

Tom Bagley accepts the Cecil C. Peck Award for race car fabrication presented by Orval Strohl, Chairman of the Board of the Peck Company. The winning car was Bagley's Kent Oil Wildcat No. 40.

Rookie driver Ronnie Shuman accepts the Hoosier Coal & Oil "Almost Made It" check for $2,000. Ron was next in line to qualify when rain ended time trials.

Speedway President John Cooper (right) and Museum Director Jack Martin pose beside the new National Automobile Dealers Association "Milestone Award".

Tom Bigelow and his Armstrong Mould team accept their Miller Pit Stop first place award while sampling the sponsor's product.

Phil Harmes (left) receives the Locktite Award for the "Oldest and Best Preserved Photo Collection" from 1979 winner Bruce Craig. The presentation took place at the Auto Racing Collector's Convention. Organizer Jack Middleton is at right.

[195]

speedway network

The faces behind the voices on the world's largest radio network.

Luke Walton

Russ Arnold

Paul Page

Lou Palmer

Chuck Marlowe

John DeCamp

Howdy Bell

Donald Davidson

Bob Forbes

Jerry Baker

Bob Jenkins

Darl Wible

Ron Carrell

Doug Zink

PRIZE MONEY

COMPLETE PRIZE FUND FOR THE 1980 INDIANAPOLIS 500-MILE RACE

Indianapolis Motor Speedway $1,186,700.00*
Citizens Speedway Committee (Parade) 10,000.00
Citizens Speedway Committee (Lap Prizes). 40,000.00
Accessory Prizes 266,525.00*

$1,503,225.00*

*New records. Former records, $1,009,154.54 and $1,271,954.54 respectively.

(1980 Total is $231,270.46 more than previous record last year)

ACCESSORY PRIZES

Aeroquip	$ 1,500.00	Miscellaneous	$ 1,325.00
AFNB	5,000.00	Miller Brewing	28,300.00
American Dairy Association	3,000.00	Monroe	4,100.00
AMS/OIL	2,000.00	Motorola	1,500.00
Anheuser-Busch, Inc.	10,000.00	NADA	10,000.00
Bell Helmets	400.00	Cecil C. Peck	1,000.00
Borg-Warner	5,000.00	Pennzoil	10,000.00
Canon, USA	1,000.00	Premier	3,400.00
Standard Oil Dealers	2,500.00	Premier D/A	1,000.00
Champion	57,500.00	Raybestos	3,050.00
Citicorp	2,000.00	Renner's Express	1,000.00
Ditzler-PPG	3,000.00	Rockwell	10,000.00
Earl's Supply Co.	1,700.00	A.C. Rupp	250.00
Extra Mile Award	1,000.00	S-K Tools	1,500.00
Gabriel	24,000.00	STP Corp.	7,000.00
Gould	3,000.00	STP Mueller	500.00
Heli-Coil	1,200.00	Sears	9,000.00
Hillman Jewelers	800.00	Sid Collins Award	500.00
Hinchman Uniforms	500.00	Simpson Sports	2,000.00
Hoosier Coal & Oil	2,000.00	Stant Manufacturing	1,200.00
Hurst Performance	1,000.00	Stewart-Warner Award	500.00
Ideal	1,000.00	Stewart-Warner	800.00
Indiana Oxygen	500.00	Sunnen	1,500.00
Indiana SAE	1,000.00	Thermo King	500.00
Ingersoll-Rand	3,000.00	Valvoline	3,000.00
Kingsford	10,000.00	Vanderwell Products	4,000.00
Loctite	6,500.00	Worth	1,000.00
Machinists Union	6,000.00	WRTV	500.00
Mallory	2,000.00		

TOTAL ACCESSORY PRIZES: $266,525.00

Merchandise won by race participants included:

The Pontiac Pace Car
The Thornton Bardach Checkered Flag Ring
Eight Seiko Digital Chronographs from Hillman Jewelers
Tool Sets from the Ingersoll-Rand and S-K Companies

Trophies were presented to race participants by the following companies:

American Dairy Association	Miller Beer
AFNB	National Automobile Dealers Assn.
Borg-Warner	Cecil C. Peck
Budweiser	Premier/DA Lubricant Co.
Sid Collins Memorial Fund	Raybestos-Manhattan
Hoosier Coal & Oil	Renner's Express
Indiana Oxygen	Stewart-Warner
Indiana SAE	STP
Kingsford Division	Thermo King
Loctite	WRTV
Machinists Union	

by Jerry Miller

Early in the month, some lovers of fun poured red paint off an Indianapolis interstate overpass onto cars speeding along underneath.

When police arrived at the overpass, they found an empty paint bucket and a hastily painted sign that read: "Indy 500 — The Sickest Spectacle in Sports." They did not find the slap-dash artists who had tried to turn the interstate into a modernistic landscape painting, a highway-sized version of those splotchy mosaics that always stare at you in the lobbies of corporate headquarters.

The surrealists of the interstate had a point. Not the one on their sign. The Indianapolis 500 isn't sick. The New Mexico prison riots, John Wayne Gacy, snuff movies — now, they're sick.

The 500 is merely surrealistic, like the handiwork of those Picassos of the cloverleafs, a switchback in the flow of reality, a mirror reflection in a fun house, a Fellini movie. It is outside the real world and its real sickness.

Spike Jones, of all people, was right about the 500. He saw it precisely for what it was — a dance of the hours. The bleat of horns, the tinkle of fragile glass breaking, a police whistle in an insane asylum, red paint splashed over the hood of a Cordoba.

It is insanity on holiday. Grown men zip themselves into fire-resistant masquerade costumes, shoe-horn themselves into fire-conducive beetle shells, and tie time's tail in a knot. They aren't sick. They aren't even crazy. They are — you got it — surreal.

They are the deformed heroes of a *vita* that isn't *dolce*, pregnant women in a Miss America contest. They are shaped by the crippled hands of infamy, minor gods made out of Pla-Doh.

They go 200 miles an hour and spit in the eye of Death, whose eyes are always closed, anyway. They are not lunatics, though, only fools with rubber faces and the earwig of freedom crawling in their ears.

Grown men and women who pay money to watch this burlesque of immortality — now maybe they're a little crazy. But, of course, normality is a meaningless term within the confines of a funny farm.

The 500 isn't a sickness. It isn't even a spectacle or a sport. It is a dance with a two-headed bear. It is arm wrestling with the American dream. It is the production-line daydream of Western civilization.

Cars slash past at speeds only a madman could concoct, like thirty-three Dr. Jekylls with horsepower foaming in their test tubes. Death supposedly waits behind the retaining walls like a circus animal on the loose. But death, too, is a meaningless term within the bubble of a moment.

It is a wish you can touch. It is a vision you can hold in your arms for one dance. It is childhood in a bottle, the black hole in death, Ingrid Bergman on a foggy runway. Here's looking at you, kid — but look fast and never directly into the sun that dangles like a cheap ring, turning the finger of a cloud green.

It is a death-sicle on a stick, cotton candy that goes up your nose like burning fuel. It is enough empty beer cans to recarpet the earth, enough fried chicken and hot dogs to feed the starving children of Oz.

It is the Waltons with a screw loose, Apple Pan Dowdy laced with hash.

It is a one-hit hallucination. It is better than being sick. It is health food that doesn't taste like a bale of hay, a roaring drunk who never has to go to the bathroom. It is craziness armed with a water pistol.

Its meaning is up for grabs, Bo Derek at a white slavery auction.

Splash red paint on it — it will wear it. It doesn't care. Call it sick — it won't even notice. It is already mad and babbles like an idiot, but it understands itself better than reality.

Leave it be, like a brainless child on a jungle gym. It is the surreal Indianapolis 500. It is not hurting anyone but itself.

PIT STOP REPORT *(Continued from Page 91)*

(Continued from Page 91)

CAR NO.	STOP NO.	LAP NO.	REASON	TIME IN SECONDS
28th Place — TOM BAGLEY				**Kent Oil**
40	1	15	Fuel only	10
	2	29	Fuel pump drive broke Out of Race	
				TOTAL TIME: 10
29th Place — SPIKE GEHLHAUSEN				**Winton Sales**
35	1	15	Fuel only	9
	2	20	Hit Wall Out of Race	
				TOTAL TIME: 9
30th Place — BILL WHITTINGTON				**Sun Systems**
94	1	10	Spun, Hit Wall — Out of Race	

CAR NO.	STOP NO.	LAP NO.	REASON	TIME IN SECONDS
31st Place — DICK FERGUSON				**AMS/Oil Special**
26	1	10	Accident — Out of Race	
32nd Place — MIKE MOSLEY				**Theodore Racing Eagle**
48	1	3	Fuel, Head gasket replaced, Board man crossed pit lane, man over wall, no fireproof clothes	3638
	2	5	Valve cover gasket bad, men over wall without fireproof clothes, Oil leak Out of Race	
				TOTAL TIME: 3638
33rd Place — LARRY CANNON				**Kraco Car Stereo**
95	1	2	Broken connecting rod — Out of Race	

Official Entry List

Car	Driver	Entrant and Car Name	Chief	Chassis/Engine
1	Rick Mears	Penske Racing Inc./The Gould Charge	D. Soppe	PC-9/Cosworth
2	Bill Vukovich	Leader Cards, Inc./	A. J. Watson	Watson/Offy
3	Tom Bigelow	AMI Racing Division/Armstrong Mould Inc.	P. Leffler	Orbitor-1/Cosworth
4	Johnny Rutherford	Chaparral Racing Ltd./Pennzoil Chaparral	S. Roby	Chaparral/Cosworth
5	Al Unser	Longhorn Cars Inc./	G. Huening	LR-01/Cosworth
6	Jimmy McElreath	Shirley McElreath/McElreath Special		Penske/Cosworth
7	Jerry Sneva	AMI Racing Division/Hugger's Beverage Coolers	P. Leffler	Lola/Cosworth
8	Dick Simon	Vollstedt Enterprises Inc./	C. Rogers	Vollstedt/Offy
9	Tom Sneva	Jerry O'Connell/	J. Phillips	Phoenix/Cosworth
9T	Tom Sneva	Jerry O'Connell/	J. Phillips	McLaren/Cosworth
9X	Tom Sneva	Jerry O'Connell/	J. Phillips	McLaren/Cosworth
10	Pancho Carter	Alex Morales Co./Alex XLNT Foods Special	J. Capels	Pc-7/Cosworth
10T	Pancho Carter	Alex Morales Co./Alex XLNT Foods Special	J. Capels	Lightning/Cosworth
11	Bobby Unser	Penske Racing Inc./Norton Spirit	L. Gerrish	PC-9/Cosworth
12	Mario Andretti	Penske Racing Inc./Essex	B. Sprow	PC-9/Cosworth
14	A. J. Foyt Jr.	A. J. Foyt Enterprise/Gilmore Racing Team	J. Starne	Parnelli/Cosworth
15	Johnny Parsons	Lindsey Hopkins/Hopkins Special	M. Devin	Lightning/Cosworth
15T	Johnny Parsons	Lindsey Hopkins/Hopkins Special	M. Devin	Lightning/Offy
16		A. J. Foyt Enterprise/Gilmore Racing Team	J. Starne	Parnelli/Foyt
17		Vollstedt Enterprises Inc./	R. Vollstedt	Vollstedt/Offy
18	Dennis Firestone	Jack L. Rhoades/Scientific Drilling Controls		Penske/Cosworth
19	Dana Carter	Jack L. Rhoades/Scientific Drilling Controls	M. Luther	McLaren/Offy
20	Gordon Johncock	Patrick Racing Team/North American Van Lines Pacesetter	G. Bignotti	PR-001/Cosworth
21	Tim Richmond	Mach I Racing Enterprises/Hawaiian Tropic	J. Barnes	PC-7/Cosworth
21T	Tim Richmond	Mach I Racing Enterprises/Mach I Racing	J. Barnes	PC-7/Cosworth
22		Leader Cards Inc./	A. J. Watson	Watson/Chevy 355
23		Shirley McElreath/McElreath Special		Eagle/Offy
24	Sheldon Kinser	Leader Cards Inc./Genesee Beer Wagon	A. J. Watson	Watson/Cosworth
25	Danny Ongais	Interscope Racing/Interscope Panasonic Porsche	P. Casey	Interscope P-01/
25T	Danny Ongais	Interscope Racing/Interscope Panasonic Porsche	P. Casey	P6B/Cosworth
25X	Danny Ongais	Interscope Racing/Interscope Panasonic Porsche	P. Casey	P6B/Cosworth
26	Dick Ferguson	Steve & Richard Sanett/Aero Electronics Special	J. Eisert	PC-6/Cosworth
28	Herm Johnson	Cliff Menard Racing/	J. McCormack	Lightning/Offy
29	Billy Engelhart	Beaudoin Racing Enterprises/		Wildcat/DGS
30	Phil Threshie	Arizona Racing Associates/I.A.M. Special	C. Looper	ARA-IAM 1/Chevy 355
31	Phil Threshie	Arizona Racing Associates/I.A.M. Special	C. Looper	ARA-IAM 1/Chevy 355
32		Walter Medlin/	T. Smith	Eagle/Offy
34		Wysard Motor Co./Wysard Motor Co. Special	J. Sullivan	Wildcat/DGS
35	Spike Gehlhausen	Fletcher Racing Team/Winton Sales	D. Mower	PC-7/Cosworth
36	Mike Mosley	Dan Gurney-Teddy Yip/Theodore Racing Eagle	W. Leary	Eagle/Cosworth
37	Ross Davis	Davis-Abramson-Land/The Enterprise	H. Dierks	Wildcat/DGS
38	Jerry Karl	Willie Compton/Tonco Trailer Co.	L. Parks	McLaren-Karl/Chevy 355
39	Jerry Karl	Willie Compton/Tonco Trailer Co.	L. Parks	McLaren-Karl/Chevy 355
40	Tom Bagley	Patrick Racing Team/Kent Oil	G. Bignotti	PR-002/Cosworth
41	Bill Alsup	Alsup Racing Team/	C. Peroutka	PC-7/Cosworth
41T		Alsup Racing Team/	C. Peroutka	McLaren/Offy
42	John Wood	Mergard's 20th Century Enterprises/	E. Meinking	Eagle/Offy
43	Howdy Holmes	AMI Racing Division/Armstrong Mould	P. Leffler	Orbitor II/Cosworth
44		AMI Racing Division/	P. Leffler	Lola/Cosworth
45	Greg Leffler	AMI Racing Division/Starcraft R.V.	P. Leffler	Lola/Chevy V-6
46		AMI Racing Division/	P. Leffler	Wildcat/DGS
47		Chaparral Racing Ltd./Pennzoil Chaparral-Lola	S. Roby	Lola/Cosworth
48	Mike Mosley	Dan Gurney-Teddy Yip/Theodore Racing Eagle	W. Leary	Eagle/Chevy 355
49		Chaparral Racing Ltd./Pennzoil Chaparral	S. Roby	Chaparral/Cosworth
50		Kenneth Mahoney/BFM Enterprises	K. Mahoney	Manta/Offy
52	Bobby Fisher	James Kallner/Eagle Magnetic	D. Cecil	Eagle/Chevy 355
53	Al Unser	Longhorn Cars Inc./	G. Huening	LR-01/Cosworth
54		Stephen Barber/Cryogenic Associates	H. Higuchi	Eagle/Offy
55	Janet Guthrie	Lindsey Hopkins/Texaco Special	D. Klym	Lightning/Cosworth
55T	Janet Guthrie	Lindsey Hopkins/Texaco Special	D. Klym	Lightning/Drake-8
56	Jim Hurtubise	Kenny Moran/Moran Electric	A. Krueger	Mallard/Offy
57	Tom Frantz	Tom Frantz/Frantz Auto Body	J. Tennant	McLaren/Cosworth
58	Spike Gehlhausen	Fletcher Racing Team/Winton Sales	D. Mower	Lightning/Cosworth
59		Hoffman Auto Racing/Hoffman Auto Racing	G. Hall	Lightning/Offy
61		Penske Racing Inc./	J. McGee	PC-7/Cosworth
62	Ed Finley	Bob Olmsted/Bob Olmsted's V-12	B. Olmsted	Eagle/Volker
63		Penske Racing Inc.	J. McGee	PC-7/Cosworth
65	Bill Tempero	Bill Tempero/Wood Power Systems-Spirit of Colo.	D. Adair	Eagle/Chevy 355
66	Roger Rager	Gail and Roger Rager/Advance Clean Sweep	B. Henderson	Wildcat/Chevy 355
			W. Houser	
67	Frank Weiss	Buddie Boys Racing Ent./The Canadian I	D. Kasella	McLaren/Offy
68	Buddie Boys	Buddie Boys Racing Ent./The Canadian II	D. Kasella	Rascar/Chevy 355
69	Joe Saldana	Hoffman Auto Racing/Hoffman Auto Racing	G. Hall	PC-7/Cosworth
70		Patrick Racing Team/	G. Bignotti	Wildcat IV/Cosworth
72		National Engineering Co./Warner Hodgdon Racing	D. McCormack	McLaren/Cosworth
73	Roger Mears	National Engineering Co./Warner Hodgdon Racing	D. McCormack	Spirit/AMC
75	Bob Harkey	O'Hanlon's Racing Team/O'Hanlon's L'il Cheaper	W. Woodward	March/Chevy 355

76	Vern Schuppan	Walmotor Inc./	J. Walther	PC-6/Cosworth
77	Salt Walther	Walmotor Inc./	G. Walther Jr.	PC-r/Cosworth
78	Ron Shuman	Gary Stanton/Stanton Racing Products	G. Stanton	PC-6/Cosworth
79		Hoffman Auto Racing/Hoffman Auto Racing	G. Hall	Spyder/Offy
80	Larry Dickson	RP Racing Enterprises/	C. Looper	Penske/Cosworth
80T	Larry Dickson	RP Racing Enterprises/Polak Construction	C. Looper	ARA-IAM 1/Chevy 355
82	Rick Muther	Pacific Coast Racing Team Inc./	R. Hunter	PC-6/Cosworth
83		A. J. Foyt Enterprise/Gilmore Racing Team	J. Starne	Coyote/Foyt
84		A. J. Foyt Enterprise/Greer Special	J. Starne	Coyote/Foyt
85		Wayne Woodward/O'Hanlon's L'il Cheaper	W. Woodward	Curtis/Offy
86	Rick Muther	Pacific Coast Racing Team Inc./	R. Hunter	Lightning/Offy
90		Patrick Racing Team/	G. Bignotti	PR-003/Cosworth
91	John Mahler	Intercomp Racing/	B. Finley	Eagle/Offy
92	John Mahler	Intercomp Racing/	B. Finley	PC-6/Offy
93	Don Whittington	Road Atlanta Racing/Sun System Special	G. Bartils	Parnelli/Cosworth
94	Bill Whittington	Road Atlanta Racing/Sun System Special	G. Bartils	Parnelli/Cosworth
95	Larry Cannon	Cannon Racing Team/	P. Thrasher	Wildcat/DGS
96	Bill Whittington	Road Atlanta Racing/Sun System Special	G. Bartils	McLaren/Cosworth
97		Agajanian-Purcell Racers/Agajanian-Purcell	G. King-E. Baue	King/Chevy 355
98		Giuffre Bros. Crane-Agajanian/Giuffre Bros.	G. King-E. Baue	King/Chevy 355
99	Hurley Haywood	Lindsey Hopkins/	M. Devin	Lightning/Chevy V-6
	Tony Bettenhausen	Tony Bettenhausen Enterprises/		McLaren/Cosworth

Something's wrong here. Gary Bettenhausen walks around the Speedway looking for a ride and you walk around with a scowl on your face because you missed the show. Now what we oughta' do is make a trade: You take over Bettenhausen's Sherman Armstrong ride and I'll arrange it so Gary gives you his Sprint car rides. And I'll make him promise to never again drive them. Then Gary will take over your car and pretty soon he'll have a tough decision to make because Penske or a Pat Patrick will probably call him up. But first you have to promise an apology to Lindsey Hopkins. I feel confident that the old gent will accept it graciously. He'll probably even offer to buy you a Midget and gently tell you to go get yourself some experience racing, not driving. It's been a good number of years since we've seen Lindsey's name on a Midget and that division could use a shot in the arm. You go bump around a few real race tracks, not some airports with pylons marking the turns and then you come back to Indy. The first thing you sit in will feel first class.

* * *

After Tom Sneva hit the wall with his new mount for the 1980 event, he half-jokingly, half-seriously said, "I hope the car's a total loss . . . and can't find another like it." About the new ground effects vehicles Sneva said, "I'm not a big advocate of ground effects. It is more expensive, less safe and doesn't make you any more competitive." . . . Car owner Jack Rhoades appears as though he might become a regular at Indianapolis. The Columbus, Indiana aircraft sales merchant arrived at the Speedway this year with two rookies, Dennis Firestone and Dana Carter. Although both drivers wiped out their cars, Firestone eventually made the race, Rhoades said he was going to talk to Speedway officials about obtaining the same garages next year so he could decorate them and really do the job right next year. Any guy who gives a pair of rookies is OK in our book . . . While handsome rookie Tim Richmond was making the veterans (and scads of screaming teeny-boppers) turn their heads, Roger Rager was winning one of the most important personal battles of his life. Rager has been a racer since he was 14 years old, driving go-karts. He's raced on more quarter and half-mile dirt ovals than you can expect him to remember, in conditions ranging from beautiful to deadly. Like hundreds of other American circle track racers, Rager's life-long dream was to make the show at Indianapolis. He said after qualifying,

"I hope this proves that you can make this race and you don't need a million dollars to do it. Maybe this will show a lot of other guys like me who don't know the right people or don't know how to play the politics game that they can make it without all that. There are a lot of good drivers out there who aren't here, just because they don't know the right people."

We'd like to be able to give him more than a free copy of the Indianapolis 500 Yearbook for his efforts. Nice job Rager.

* * *

While Tim Richmond was taking the lion's share of publicity throughout the month of May as a rookie, likable newcomer Gordon Smiley was on pins and needles wondering whether or not he'd be granted a ride in one of the Patrick team cars as previously promised. Gordon's cause was aided through his use of public relations man Bob Starck, a Lincoln, Nebraska chap who realizes the value of the printed word. Their combined efforts paid off as Smiley rapidly got up to speed and qualified well. Car owner Pat Patrick has to be lauded for his attitude as well: "We've got to bring up some young talent on the Championship Trail," the Michigan oilman said, "and the only people you can look toward to do it is the car owners."

We wish Patrick's statement were shared by the bulk of the car owners, but the inherent economic situation of campaigning an Indy car makes the giving away of rides a financial improbability. It should be noted that no matter how many people attend the Indianapolis 500, we can't forget that pro auto racing as a whole must be a subsidized sport. Put simply, we don't attract enough fans in the grandstands to support the sport. Sponsors and patrons have become a necessary entity and those owners who treat racing as a business have proven to be the most successful among their lot in the past decade.

* * *

It has been said that anyone with a roll of paper, a typewriter and a barrell of ink can become a judge of a particular participant's performance. We shall thus take this opportunity to voice our considered opinion that it is becoming a little too easy for a rookie to be accorded a chance to drive at Indianapolis (once he has obtained a car). The case of the Whittington brothers comes to mind. Although we don't doubt they may both have enough coordination to become adequate race car drivers, we don't think they were quite ripe for big time auto racin' yet. They had previously demonstrated this fact at Daytona, and while they weren't to be considered a hazard at Indy, a few more miles in Championship cars would have them, and their competitors, feel more comfortable.

Something definitely seems to be amiss when conversation among students of the sport produces comments such as, "Who's he . . . never heard of him before . . . where'd he get his experience?" While it is true that a driver must first be approved by the sanctioning body and then must pass a rookie test, we believe that there is no substitute for experience in a Championship car. Another rookie for example, had trouble simply keeping the engine running on pit stops this year. His crew chief motioned for him to "jazz" the throttle slightly, keep the RPM's up enough so the engine wouldn't die. According to the chief, our driver simply floored the throttle pedal during pit stops . . . a circumstance which can lead to all sorts of explosions. Suffice it to say the driver was displaying action something other than professional. One need only to think of the consequences of putting a car in the grandstands at the 500, something that isn't out of the realm of possibility, and maybe the standards for an open-wheel, open-cockpit driver might be raised to an acceptable level.

* * *

Several seasons back, mechanic Danny Jones found himself working with then Midget driver Billy Engelhart. You could hang around their pit and see that there was one of those rare communications going on: Driver respected the mechanic and vice-versa. The mechanic would make a suggestion and there was no argument from the driver. They talked about making the car work better. And it did. They talked, like most Midget and Sprint drivers do, about someday getting a chance to run at Indianapolis. This year they were among the most happy qualifiers to be found. Mechanic Jones wouldn't take much credit for work on the car, "After all," he said, "you get a car and engine from Jud Phillips (Tom Sneva's Chief) and if you can't make it work, you ain't worth much." Nevertheless, Jones is as thorough a wrench turner as you'll find in Gasoline Alley and he can take credit for not making the car go any slower than it had in the past. Engelhart has travelled thousands of miles, through some dismal times as well as some smiles en route to Indy and it's nice to see a man fulfill one of his dreams. They're a good team, we hope there's enough bucks around to bring them back next year.

* * *

We thought the dust was beginning to settle between the warring factions of USAC and CART (the Championship car owners who split from USAC to form their own sanctioning body) and pit lane talk this year centered around the fact that it was indeed nice to talk racing rather than lawsuits. For a time in the early summer of 1980, the Championship Racing League (CRL) functioned as the outgrowth of the two groups and we had hoped that attention just might become centered around putting spectators in the grandstands at the rest of the races along the Championship Trail. As this column is being written in July, there is once again a split. It appears as though CART will run the Champ Trail, we don't know who will sanction the 500 in 1981 and the general good feeling of everyone working toward the same goal is long forgotten.

It appears to this quarter that the doctrine of laissez-faire just flat won't work in Championship auto racing. Although we do live in a democracy, we can't obtain enough stabilization to allow the people to rule themselves in Indy 500 style racing. A quick survey of other forms of big-time racing in this country seems to bear out our point. Wally Parks, founder of the NHRA (drag-racing group) has always been known as head man. Bill France, Sr. NASCAR founder is the person who ultimately stops the buck in his organization. Now his son is following in his place. John Bishop wields a friendly hatchet in the successful IMSA (road racers) organization. But the Sports Car Club of America (SCCA) is plodding along as usual running both amateur and professional events, and they're not attracting many really well-known names. SCCA is goverened by a board and the executive director doesn't have much switch pulling power. Neither does USAC's main exec, Dick King.

Up until the mid-Fifties the American Automobile Association (AAA) sanctioned Indy and the Championship Trail. The board was made up mostly of businessmen who weren't continually taxed to their decision making qualities.

Then it was a simpler time. The Indianapolis 500 was made up of Offenhausers and roadsters that didn't garner half million dollar sponsorships. Each year was a virtual repeat of the last, at least since the end of the Second World War. Then over 50 spectators were killed at LeMans (could happen at Indy, right?) and the AAA said "No thank you," to sanctioning any more auto races. USAC was formed and after Henry Banks had been carrying on for some ten years, he too noticed that his title of Director of Competition left something to be desired in terms of having some power, devoid of intervention by the USAC board.

Quiet and complacent, Henry had seen change come about in his sport. The rear engine revolution had taken place, Ford Motor Company had invested heavily in 500 style racing, television was a little more interested . . . the sport was becoming a business. Henry suggested to the board that an executive director be hired and given some meaningful power. Of course Henry thought he'd be the first man they would ask, but the suggestion fairly well backfired. USAC said thanks for your years Hen', and they brought in one Bill Smyth. Henry was shuffled upstairs and told to run the USAC Properties division, a blessing in disguise to him. He couldn't make a hard-nosed dictator or even a stern executive director. He's too nice a guy . . . has too many friends in the sport that he'd feel badly saying no to. Thus, Smyth was put in the hot seat. He instituted a couple of good programs, drummed up some sponsors and was drummed out of office within a few years.

Dick King has weathered the storms as well as any man can be expected and the USAC Board has seemingly given him as fair a reign as they know how. Nevertheless, there's always been a board to report to, and compared to the old AAA Contest Board, the USAC Board of Directors has been mellow.

Rather than dissect the USAC Board, which one must

remember is made up of very dedicated, well-meaning individuals, we believe that the power to run Championship auto racing should ultimately lie in the hands of one individual. It is becoming increasingly clear that there are some inherent problems with boards governing Championship racing. They can become their own worst enemy through the normal, every season changes that occur in this technological business. The problem is basic: We have continual engineering advances that must be monitored in order to present a reasonably competitive program to the paying public. Rules have to be written and re-written covering everything from the amount of turbo-charger boost allowed, width and height of wings, whether or not we're going to allow wings, amount of fuel, etc., etc. . . . enough to fill a rule book. Other sports don't have this continuing, and often times, nagging problem. Any individual change in baseball rules, for example, is a major point of contention. True, we've just witnessed a labor problem in baseball, but that game isn't beset by constantly changing engineering advances.

The ironic thing about our continuing mechanical changes is that they should be used to our advantage rather than the cause of bickering. American passenger cars now have wide tires, tubrochargers and alcohol is partially used for fuel. Every one of these engineering advances was first proven on a Championship car yet we've seen virtually no publicity whatsoever in the past decade that the race tracks of America are the birthplace of such innovations.

As we enter the 1980's it would be nice if we were concentrating on the promotion of putting spectators in the grandstands rather than worrying about what organization is going to be responsible for making rules governing the sport. For a while in the summer of 1980 it appeared as though the CRL board had come up with a very workable set of specifications (based on specs initiated by USAC) but once again, there was something amiss because as of this writing we don't know what the long-term outlook is for Championship racing. And for this writer at least, that's an unsettling feeling.

Our suggestion for the solution has been posed before: Hire Andy Granatelli and give him a three year contract. Tell him he can't: 1) Own a car; 2) a racetrack; 3) be involved with a product or service. To our way of thinking he's simply the best huckster available who has the best interest of the sport at heart. There are others who might be adequate in a friendly dictator position, such as a Roger Penske, but they're all involved with a vested interest in the sport. Granatelli is blessed (or cursed) with some far-out ideas such as turbine power, regulating engine sizes through a fuel formula, etc. but overall, his prior performance record shows that he has enough moxie about him to sell whatever it is he's trying to promote. He can identify with the problems of race car ownership as well as those that mechanics, drivers and promoters experience simply because he's served in every capacity himself.

With Granatelli at the helm I don't think that our great American institution, the Indy 500 (and the rest of the Championship races) would be dominated by engines and chassis made in England. It's a sad enough state of affairs to have to watch the parking lots fill with imported Japanese cars and motorcycles and then watch foreign cars win the races. Somewhere along the line we mis-placed our good old American ingenuity. I'd hate to have to be the guy to explain the current predicament to the original Henry Ford if he were granted a day back on this planet. Not only have we been surpassed in the technology of the wheeled-vehicle (we produce one motorcycle in this country) but we can't even keep our own house in order when it comes time to race 'em.

Performance Records

MARIO ANDRETTI, Nazareth, Pennsylvania

Indianapolis 500 Record (Passed Driver's Test 1965)

Year	Car	Qual.	S	F	Laps	Speed or Reason Out
1965	Dean Van Lines	158.849	4	3	200	149.121
1966	Dean Van Lines	165.899	1	18	27	Engine
1967	Dean Van Lines	168.982	1	30	58	Lost wheel
1968	Overseas Natl. Airways	167.691	4	33	2	Piston
1968*	Overseas Natl. Airways		28		10	Piston
	*(Rel. L. Diclson)					
1969	STP Oil Treatment	169.851	2	1	200	156.867
1970	STP Oil Treatment	168.209	8	6	199	Flagged
1971	STP Oil Treatment	172.612	9	30	11	Accident
1972	Viceroy	187.167	5	8	194	Out of fuel
1973	Viceroy	195.059	6	30	4	Piston
1974	Viceroy	186.027	5	31	2	Piston
1975	Viceroy	186.480	21	28	49	Accident
1976	CAM2 Motor Oil	189.404	19	8	101	Running
1977	CAM2 Motor Oil	193.351	6	26	47	Broken Header
1978	Gould Charge	194.647	33	12	185	Flagged
1980	Essex	191.012	2	20	71	Engine

TOM BAGLEY, Centre Hall, Pennsylvania

Indianapolis 500 Record (Passed Driver's Test 1978)

Year	Car	Qual.	S	F	Laps	Speed or Reason Out
1978	Kent Oil	190.941	14	27	25	Overheating
1979	Dairy Queen/Kent Oil	185.414	15	9	193	Running
1980	Kent Oil	185.405	13	28	29	Pump Drive

GARY BETTENHAUSEN, Monrovia, Indiana

Indianapolis 500 Record (Passed Driver's Test 1968)

Year	Car	Qual.	S	F	Laps	Speed or Reason Out
1968	Thermo-King	163.562	22	24	43	Oil cooler
1969	Thermo-King	167.777	9	26	35	Piston
1970	Thermo-King	166.451	20	26	55	Valve
1971	Thermo-King	171.233	13	10	178	Flagged
1972	Sunoco McLaren	188.877	4	14	182	Ignition
1973	Sunoco DX	195.599	5	5	130	Running
1974	Score	184.492	11	32	2	Valve
1975	Thermo-King	182.611	19	15	158	Accident
1976	Thermo-King	181.791	8	28	52	Turbocharger
1977	Agajanian-Evel Knievel	186.596	21	16	138	Clutch
1978	Oberdorfer	187.324	31	16	149	Blown Engine
1980	Armstrong Mould	182.463	32	3	200	Running

TOM BIGELOW, Whitewater, Wisconsin

Indianapolis 500 Record (Passed Driver's Test 1973)

Year	Car	Qual.	S	F	Laps	Speed or Reason Out
1974	Bryant Heat-Cool	180.144	23	12	166	Flagged
1975	Bryant Heating	181.864	33	18	151	Piston
1976	Leader Card	181.965	32	14	98	Running
1977	Thermo-King	186.471	22	6	192	Running
1978	Armstrong Mould	189.115	18	21	107	Stalled
1979	Armstrong Mould	185.147	30	14	190	Running
1980	Armstrong/Jiffy Mix	182.547	31	8	198	Running

LARRY CANNON, Danville, Illinois

Indianapolis 500 Record (Passed Driver's Test 1973)

Year	Car	Qual.	S	F	Laps	Speed or Reason Out
1974	American Financial	173.963	33	24	49	Stalled
1976	American Financial	181.388	10	17	97	Flagged
1977*	Mergard 20th Century					
	*(Relieved John Mahler for 8 laps)					
1980	Kraco Car Stereo	183.253	14	33	3	Broken Camshaft

DUANE (Pancho) CARTER JR., Brownsburg, Ind.

Indianapolis 500 Record (Passed Driver's Test 1974)

Year	Car	Qual.	S	F	Laps	Speed or Reason Out
1974	Cobre Firestone	180.605	21	7	191	Flagged
1975	Cobre Tire	183.449	18	4	169	Running
1976	Jorgensen Steel	184.824	6	5	101	Running
1977	Jorgensen Eagle	192.452	8	15	156	Blown Engine
1978	Budweiser Lightning	196.829	21	24	92	Header
1979	Alex XLNT Foods	185.806	17	20	129	Wheel Bearing
1980	Alex XLNT Foods	186.480	8	6	199	Running

BILLY ENGELHART, Madison, Wisconsin

Indianapolis 500 Record (Passed Driver's Test 1976)

Year	Car	Qual.	S	F	Laps	Speed or Reason Out
1980	Master Lock	184.237	22	11	193	Running

DICK FERGUSON, Los Angeles, California

Indianapolis 500 Record (Passed Driver's Test 1979)

Year	Car	Qual.	S	F	Laps	Speed or Reason Out
1980	AMS Oil	182.880	15	31	9	Accident

DENNIS FIRESTONE, Gardena, California

Indianapolis 500 Record (Passed Driver's Test 1980)

Year	Car	Qual.	S	F	Laps	Speed or Reason Out
1980	Scientific Drilling	183.702	24	16	137	Transmission

A. J. FOYT, Houston, Texas

Indianapolis 500 Record (Passed Driver's Test 1958)

Year	Car	Qual.	S	F	Laps	Speed or Reason Out
1958	Dean Van Lines	143.130	12	16	148	Spun Out
1959	Dean Van Lines	142.648	17	10	200	133.297
1960	Bowes Seal Fast	143.466	16	25	90	Clutch
1961	Bowes Seal Fast	145.907	7	1	200	139.130
1962	Bowes Seal Fast	149.074	5	23	69	Accident
1962*	Sarkes Tarzian		17		20	Starter
	*Rel. E. George, 127-146					
1963	Sheraton-Thompson	150.615	8	3	200	142.210
1964	Sheraton-Thompson	154.672	5	1	200	147.350
1965	Sheraton-Thompson	161.233	1	15	115	Gearbox
1966	Sheraton-Thompson	161.355	18	26	0	Accident
1967	Sheraton-Thompson	166.289	4	1	200	151.207
1968	Sheraton-Thompson	166.821	8	20	86	Engine
1969	Sheraton-Thompson	170.568	1	8	181	Flagged
1970	Sheraton-Thomp ITT	170.004	3	10	195	Transmission
1971	ITT-Thompson	174.317	6	3	200	156.069
1972	ITT-Thompson	188.996	17	25	60	Engine
1973	Gilmore Racing	188.927	23	25	37	Conn. rod
1974	Gilmore Racing	191.632	1	15	142	Gearbox
1975	Gilmore Racing	193.976	1	3	174	Running
1976	Gilmore Racing	185.261	5	2	102	Running
1977	Gilmore Racing	194.563	4	1	200	161.331
1978	Gilmore Racing	200.122	20	7	191	Flagged
1979	Gilmore Racing	189.613	6	2	200	Running
1980	Gilmore Racing	185.500	12	14	173	Valve

SPIKE GEHLHAUSEN, Speedway, Indiana

Indianapolis 500 Record (Passed Driver's Test 1976)

Year	Car	Qual.	S	F	Laps	Speed or Reason Out
1976	Spirit of Indiana	181.717	25	33	0	Oil Pressure
1978	Hubler Chev./WIRE	190.325	16	29	23	Accident
1979	Sta-On/Guarantee/ WIRE	185.061	31	10	192	Running
1980	Winton Sales	188.344	4	29	20	Accident

HURLEY HAYWOOD, Ft. Lauderdale, Florida

Indianapolis 500 Record (Passed Driver's Test 1979)

Year	Car	Qual.	S	F	Laps	Speed or Reason Out
1980	Guarantee/Sta-On/ KISS 99	183.561	25	18	127	Turbocharger

GORDON JOHNCOCK, Hastings, Michigan

Indianapolis 500 Record (Passed Driver's Test 1965)

Year	Car	Qual.	S	F	Laps	Speed or Reason Out
1965	Weinberger Homes	155.012	14	5	200	146.417
1966	Weinberger Homes	161.059	6	4	200	143.084
1967	Gilmore Broadcasting	166.559	3	12	188	Spun Out
1968	Gilmore Broadcasting	166.775	9	27	37	Gearbox
1969	Gilmore Broadcasting	168.626	5	19	137	Piston
1970	Gilmore Broadcasting	167.015	17	28	45	Engine
1971	Norris Industries	171.388	12	29	11	Accident
1972	Gulf McLaren	188.511	26	20	113	Valve
1973	STP Double Oil Filter	192.555	11	1	133	159.036
1974	STP Double Oil Filter	186.750	4	4	198	Flagged
1975	Sinmast	191.652	2	31	11	Ignition
1976	Sinmast/Goodyear	188.531	2	3	102	Running
1977	STP Double Oil Filter	193.517	5	11	184	Valve Spring
1978	N. American Van Lines	195.833	6	3	199	Penalized 1 lap
1979	N. American Van Lines	189.753	5	6	197	Running
1980	N. American Van Lines	186.075	17	4	200	Running

JERRY KARL, Manchester, Pennsylvania

Indianapolis 500 Record (Passed Driver's Test 1972)

Year	Car	Qual.	S	F	Laps	Speed or Reason Out
1973	Oriente Express	190.799	28	26	122	Flagged

Performance Records

Year	Car	Qual.	S	F	Laps	Speed or Reason Out
1974	Ayr-Way/Lloyd's	181.452	19	19	115	Accident
1975	Jose Johnson	182.537	20	13	161	Running
1978	Machinist Union	187.549	28	14	196	Flagged
1980	Tonco Trailer	183.011	28	21	64	Clutch

GREG LEFFLER, Winchester, Indiana

Indianapolis 500 Record (Passed Driver's Test 1980)

Year	Car	Qual.	S	F	Laps	Speed or Reason Out
1980	Starcraft R.V.	183.748	23	10	197	Running

JIM McELREATH, Arlington, Texas

Indianapolis 500 Record (Passed Driver's Test 1962)

Year	Car	Qual.	S	F	Laps	Speed or Reason Out
1962	Schulz Fueling	149.025	7	6	200	138.653
1963	Bill Forbes Racing	149.744	6	6	200	140.862
1964	Studebaker STP	152.281	26	21	77	Magneto
1965	John Zink Urschel	155.878	13	20	66	Rear End
1966	Zink-Urschel-Slick	160.908	7	3	200	143.742
1967	John Zink	164.241	11	5	197	Flagged
1968	Jim Greer	165.327	13	14	179	Stalled
1969	Jack Adams	168.224	7	28	24	Engine Fire
1970	Greer-Foyt	166.821	33	5	200	152.182
1973	Norris	188.640	33	23	54	Conn. rod bolt
1974	Thermo-King	177.279	30	6	194	Flagged
1977	Carrillo Rod	187.715	20	23	71	Waste Gate
1978	Circle City Coal	188.058	26	20	132	Engine
1979	AMAX Coal Co.	185.883	19	35	0	Valve
1980	McElreath	186.249	11	24	54	Accident

RICK MEARS, Bakersfield, California

Indianapolis 500 Record (Passed Driver's Test 1977)

Year	Car	Qual.	S	F	Laps	Speed or Reason Out
1978	CAM2 Motor Oil	200.078	3	23	103	Engine
1979	Gould Charge	193.736	1	1	200	Running
1980	Gould Charge	187.490	6	5	199	Running

MIKE MOSLEY, Fallbrook, California

Indianapolis 500 Record (Passed Driver's Test 1967)

Year	Car	Qual.	S	F	Laps	Speed or Reason Out
1968	Zecol-Lubaid	162.499	27	8	197	Flagged
1969	Zecol-Lubaid	166.113	22	13	162	Piston
1970	G. C. Murphy	166.651	12	21	96	Cracked Block
1971	G. C. Murphy	169.579	19	13	159	Accident
1972	Vivitar	189.145	16	26	56	Accident
1973	Lodestar	198.753	21	10	120	Conn. rod bolt
1974	Lodestar	185.319	6	29	6	Engine
1975	Sugaripe Prune	187.833	5	26	94	Piston
1976	Sugaripe Prune	187.588	11	15	98	Running
1977	Sugaripe Prune	190.064	9	19	91	Timing Gear
1978	Alex-XLNT Foods	188.719	25	17	147	Gearbox
1979	Theodore Racing	186.278	12	3	200	Running
1980	Theodore Racing	183.449	26	32	5	Gasket

DANNY ONGAIS, Costa Mesa, California

Indianapolis 500 Record (Passed Refresher Test 1977)

Year	Car	Qual.	S	F	Laps	Speed or Reason Out
1977	Interscope Racing	193.040	7	20	90	Lost Power
1978	Interscope Racing	200.122	2	18	145	Engine
1979	Interscope/Panasonic	188.009	27	4	199	Running
1980	Interscope/Panasonic	186.606	16	7	199	Running

JOHNNY PARSONS, Indianapolis, Indiana

Indianapolis 500 Record (Passed Driver's Test 1973)

Year	Car	Qual.	S	F	Laps	Speed or Reason Out
1974	Vatis	180.252	29	26	18	Turbocharger
1975	Ayr-Way/WNAP	184.521	19	19	140	Trans. Shaft
1976	Ayr-Way/WIRE	182.843	14	12	98	Running
1977	STP Wildcat	189.255	11	5	193	Flagged
1978	First Natl. City T.C.	194.280	8	10	187	Flagged
1979	Hopkins	187.813	9	32	16	Piston
1980	Wynn's	187.412	7	26	44	Piston

ROGER RAGER, Mound, Minnesota

Indianapolis 500 Record (Passed Driver's Test 1978)

Year	Car	Qual.	S	F	Laps	Speed or Reason Out
1980	Advance/Carpenter	186.374	10	23	55	Accident

TIM RICHMOND, Ashland, Ohio

Indianapolis 500 Record (Passed Driver's Test 1980)

Year	Car	Qual.	S	F	Laps	Speed or Reason Out
1980	Uno/Q95 Starcruiser	188.334	19	9	197	Out of fuel

JOHNNY RUTHERFORD, Ft. Worth, Texas

Indianapolis 500 Record (Passed Driver's Test 1963)

Year	Car	Qual.	S	F	Laps	Speed or Reason Out
1963	U.S. Equipment Co.	148.063	26	29	43	Transmission
1964	Bardahl	151.400	15	27	2	Accident
1965	Racing Associates	156.291	11	31	15	Rear End
1967	Weinberger Homes	162.859	19	25	103	Accident
1968	City of Seattle	163.830	21	18	125	Fuel Tank
1969	Patrick Petroleum	166.628	17	29	24	Oil Leak
1970	Patrick Petroleum	170.213	2	18	135	Brkn. Header
1971	Patrick Petroleum	171.151	24	18	128	Flagged
1972	Patrick Petroleum	183.234	8	27	55	Conn. rod
1973	Gulf McLaren	198.413	1	9	124	Flagged
1974	McLaren	190.446	25	1	200	158.589
1975	Gatorade	185.998	7	2	174	Running
1976	Hy-Gain	188.957	1	1	102	148.725
1977	First Natl. City T.C.	197.325	17	23	12	Bent Valves
1978	First Natl. City T.C.	197.098	4	13	180	Flagged
1979	Budweiser	188.137	8	18	168	Running
1980	Penzoil Chaparral	192.256	1	1	200	Running

DICK SIMON, Salt Lake City, Utah

Indianapolis 500 Record (Passed Driver's Test 1970)

Year	Car	Qual.	S	F	Laps	Speed or Reason Out
1970	Bryant Heating-Cooling	165.548	31	14	168	Flagged
1971	TraveLodge		33*	14	151	Flagged
	*Qualified by J. Mahler					
1972	TraveLodge	180.424	23	13	186	Flagged
1973	TraveLodge	191.276	27	14	100	Piston
1974	TraveLodge	184.502	10	33	1	Valve
1975	Bruce Cogle Ford	181.892	30	21	133	Running
1976	Bryant Heating	182.343	16	32	1	Rod
1977	Bryant Heating	185.615	30	31	24	Overheating
1978	La Machine	192.967	10	19	139	Wheel Bearing
1979	SANYO	185.071	20	26	57	Clutch
1980	Vt. Amer./Silhouette/ Regal 8	182.788	29	22	58	Lost Wheel

GORDON SMILEY, Garland, Texas

Indianapolis 500 Record (Passed Driver's Test 1980)

Year	Car	Qual.	S	F	Laps	Speed or Reason Out
1980	Valvoline/D'Head Ranch	186.848	20	25	47	Turbocharger

JERRY SNEVA, Spokane, Washington

Indianapolis 500 Record (Passed Driver's Test 1977)

Year	Car	Qual.	S	F	Laps	Speed or Reason Out
1977	21st Amendment	186.616	16	10	187	Running
1978	Smock Material	187.266	32	31	18	Ring & Pinion
1979	Natl. Engineering AMC	184.379	21	31	16	Turbocharger
1980	Hugger's Beverage Holders	187.852	5	17	130	Accident

TOM SNEVA, Spokane, Washington

Indianapolis 500 Record (Passed Driver's Test 1973)

Year	Car	Qual.	S	F	Laps	Speed or Reason Out
1974	Raymond Companies	185.147	8	20	94	Ring, Pinion
1975	Norton Spirit	190.094	4	22	125	Accident
1976	Norton Spirit	186.355	3	6	101	Running
1977	Norton Spirit	198.884	1	2	200	160.918
1978	Norton Spirit	202.156	1	2	200	161.244
1979	Sugaripe Prune	192.998	2	15	188	Accident
1980	Bon Jour Jeans	185.290	33	2	200	Running

GEORGE SNIDER, Bakersfield, California

Indianapolis 500 Record (Passed Driver's Test 1965)

Year	Car	Qual.	S	F	Laps	Speed or Reason Out
1965	Gerhardt	154.825	16	21	64	Rear End
1966	Sheraton-Thompson	162.521	3	19	22	Accident
1967	Wagner-Lockhead	164.256	10	26	99	Spun Out
1968	Vel's Parnelli Jones	162.264	29	31	9	Valve
1969	Sheraton-Thompson	166.914	15	16	152	Flagged
1970	Sheraton-Thomp ITT	167.660	10	20	105	Suspension
1971	G. C. Murphy	171.600	21	33	6	Stalled

Performance Records

Year	Car	Qual.	S	F	Laps	Speed or Reason Out
1972	ITT-Thompson	181.855	21	11	190	Flagged
1973	Gilmore-Racing	190.355	30	12	101	Gearbox
1974	Gilmore Racing	183.993	13	28	7	Valve
1975	Lodestar	182.918	24	8	165	Running
1976	Hubler Chevrolet	181.141	27	13	98	Running
1977	Simon Assoc./ Greenwood Center	188.976	13	24	65	Valve
1978	Gilmore Racing/ Citicorp	192.627	23	8	191	Flagged
1979	Spirit of Neb./ KBHL-FM	185.319	35	33	7	Valve
1980	Gilmore Racing	185.385	21	15	169	Engine

AL UNSER, Albuquerque, New Mexico

Indianapolis 500 Record (Passed Driver's Test 1965)

Year	Car	Qual.	S	F	Laps	Speed or Reason Out
1965	Sheraton-Thompson	154.440	32	9	196	Flagged
1966	STP Oil Treatment	162.272	23	12	161	Accident
1967	Retzloff Chemical	164.594	9	2	198	Flagged
1968	Retzloff Chemical	167.069	6	26	40	Accident
1970	Johnny Lightning 500	170.221	1	1	200	155.749
1971	Johnny Lightning 500	174.622	5	1	200	157.735
1972	Viceroy	183.617	19	2	200	160.192
1973	Viceroy	194.879	8	20	75	Piston
1974	Viceroy	183.889	26	18	131	Valve
1975	Viceroy	185.452	11	16	157	Conn. rod
1976	American Racing	186.258	4	7	101	Running
1977	American Racing	195.950	3	3	199	Flagged
1978	First Natl. City T.C.	196.474	5	1	200	161.363
1979	Pennzoil	192.503	3	22	104	Transmission Seal
1980	Longhorn Racing	186.442	9	27	23	Cylinder

BOBBY UNSER, Albuquerque, New Mexico

Indianapolis 500 Record (Passed Driver's Test 1963)

Year	Car	Qual.	S	F	Laps	Speed or Reason Out
1963	Hotel Tropicana	149.421	16	33	2	Accident
1964	Studebaker STP	154.865	22	32	1	Accident
1965	STP Gas Treatment	157.467	8	19	69	Oil Line
1966	Vita Fresh Orange Juice	159.109	28	8	171	Flagged
1967	Rislone	164.752	8	9	193	Flagged

Year	Car	Qual.	S	F	Laps	Speed or Reason Out
1968	Rislone	169.507	3	1	200	152.882
1969	Bardahl	169.683	3	3	200	154.090
1970	Wagner Lockhead	168.508	7	11	192	Flagged
1971	Olsonite Eagle	175.816	3	12	164	Accident
1972	Olsonite Eagle	195.940	1	30	31	Distributor
1973	Olsonite Eagle	198.183	2	13	100	Conn. rod bolt
1974	Olsonite Eagle	185.176	7	2	200	Running
1975	Jorgensen Steel	191.073	3	1	174	149.213
1976	Cobre Tire	187.520	12	10	100	Running
1977	Cobre Tire/Clayton Dyno-Tune	197.618	2	18	94	Oil Line
1978	Arco Graphite Eagle	194.658	19	5	196	Flagged
1979	Norton Spirit	189.913	4	5	199	Running
1980	Norton Spirit	189.994	3	19	126	Ignition Coil

BILL VUKOVICH, Coarsegold, California

Indianapolis 500 Record (Passed Driver's Test 1968)

Year	Car	Qual.	S	F	Laps	Speed or Reason Out
1968	Wagner Lockhead	163.510	23	7	198	Flagged
1969	Wagner Lockhead	164.843	26	32	1	Broken Rod
1970	Sugaripe Prune	165.753	30	23	78	Clutch
1971	Sugaripe Prune	171.674	11	5	200	Running
1972	Sugaripe Prune	184.814	18	28	54	Rear End
1973	Sugaripe Prune	191.103	16	2	133	Running
1974	Sugaripe Prune	182.500	16	3	199	Flagged
1975	Cobre Tire	185.845	8	6	166	Flagged
1976	Alex Foods	181.433	9	31	2	Conn. rod
1977	Gilmore Racing	186.393	23	17	110	Broken Wing Strut
1979	Hubler/WNDE/ Th. King	187.042	34	8	194	Running
1980	Hubler Chev/WFMS	182.741	30	12	192	Running

BILL WHITTINGTON, Ft. Lauderdale, Florida

Indianapolis 500 Record (Passed Driver's Test 1980)

Year	Car	Qual.	S	F	Laps	Speed or Reason Out
1980	Sun System	183.262	27	30	9	Accident

DON WHITTINGTON, Ft. Lauderdale, Florida

Indianapolis 500 Record (Passed Driver's Test 1980)

Year	Car	Qual.	S	F	Laps	Speed or Reason Out
1980	Sun System	183.927	18	13	178	Running

Photographs

If you would like copies of photographs in this Yearbook, most can be purchased from the respective photographer whose name appears in small type alongside the photo. Please address your requests to the individual photographer and not to the Yearbook.

Steve Snoddy
2405 Larman Dr.
Indianapolis, IN 46227

Jack Gladback
RR 3 Box 51
New Palestine, IN 46163

David Knox
RD 1 Box 52
Parkesburg, PA 19365

Arnie deBrier
123 Barclay
Cherry Hill, NJ 08034

Any photo marked "IMS"
Indianapolis Motor Speedway
Photo Shop/Ron McQueeney
Speedway, IN 46224

John Mahoney
2710 Coldstream Ln. 1-B
Indianapolis, IN 46220

Tracy Talley
2012 Oxnard
Downers Grove, IL 60515

Phil Whitlow
1900 S. Walnut
Bloomington, IN 47401

Jim Cooling
4517 N. Mitchner
Indianapolis, IN 46226

Jim Alvis
10303 Broadway
Indianapolis, IN 46280

Bob Kluesner
2008 Lake St.
Vincennes, IN 47591

Jim Dawson
RR 2 Box 353
Muncie, IN 47302

Rick Lane
216 W. Parkwood
Springfield, OH 45506

Larry Shuman
4625 Lynnfield #1016
Indianapolis, IN 46254

Danny Laycock
RR 1 Box 93
Danville, IN 46122

Tom Dick
8033 Wysong
Indianapolis, IN 46219

Ralph Tippy
6200 W. Tidwell #2306
Houston, TX 77092

Don Larson
1013 Tuckahoe
Indianapolis, IN 46260

Steve Margison
RR 1 Box 325
Shelbyville, IN 46176

Ken Coles
32507 Rosslyn
Garden City, MI 48135

Driver Biographies

by Jep Cadou

Mario Andretti

Frustrated by two seasons of miserable performance of his Grand Prix equipment since he won the 1978 World Championship in Formula I, Mario Andretti made a sterling bid for victory in the 1980 Indianapolis 500.

The dry statistics show that he finished 20th, completing only 71 laps before engine failure eliminated him. But they don't begin to tell the story.

After missing the 1979 500 because it conflicted with his commitment for the Grand Prix of Monaco, Mario came to Indianapolis with what he termed "the best car I've ever had here." The beautiful silver, blue and red #12 Essex Penske/Cosworth was indeed as fast as it was pretty. Mario put it in the middle of the front row at 191.012 mph. On carburetion-test day, he had the fastest unofficial speed with a full tank of fuel.

He was running well in the race, having taken the lead in a three-way battle with Johnny Rutherford and Bobby Unser, when the beauty turned beast just quit running.

One of those unfortunate souls like Parnelli Jones who could well have won three or four 500's instead of just one, Mario scored his sole triumph in his backup Hawk in 1969 after crashing his primary Lotus in spectacular fashion coming out of Turn-4 in practice.

Born in Trieste, Italy, Mario started racing in Formula Junior cars with his twin brother, Aldo, when they were 13. After his family moved to the United States, Mario started driving modified stocks in 1958 at 18. He won over 20 races during the ensuing three years. Joining USAC in 1964, he drove in 20 Sprint races, finished third in the standings and attracted the eye of a wise chief mechanic named Clint Brawner. Clint brought him to the Speedway in 1965 and Mario proceeded to finish third, win Rookie-of-the-Year and then go on to take the 1965 USAC National Championship. Mario won other USAC titles in 1966 and 1969, but ill luck dogged his Speedway attempts. He did manage sixth place in 1970 and eighth in both 1972 and 1976.

Mario, wife, Dee Ann and children Michael, Jeffrey and Barbara Dee live in Nazareth, Pa.

Tom Bagley

One of the very few race drivers possessing a master's degree (Penn State), Tom Bagley earned a bachelor's degree in physics at Drexel University after attending grade and high school in his native Pittsburgh, PA.

Tom started racing in 1971, driving a Formula Ford. He moved into Super Vees in 1972, winning three races. In 1975, Tom finished in the runner-up position in Super Vee point standings and won a special award from Robert Bosch Corporation. He won five Bosch VW Gold Cup races and the series championship in 1976. In 1977, Bagley ran the USAC Mini-Indy series, won two races and finished the season as co-champion with Herm Johnson. He also was active in Formula Atlantic and Trans-Am, Can-Am and Camel GT series that year.

Bagley made his first 500 field in his initial attempt in 1978, placing 25th when he was eliminated by overheating after 25 laps. He moved up to a ninth-place finish in 1979.

Bagley had the misfortune to crash on carburetion-test day this year and his car had to be repaired for the race. It lasted only 29 laps before a pump drive broke and put him out, in 28th place.

Tom and wife Sally live in Centre Hall, PA.

Gary Bettenhausen

This was the 500 that restored the confidence of the gutty Dutchman that they call "der Schmucker" in Gasoline Alley.

At 38, no longer one of the young lions of USAC, Gary roared all the way from 32nd starting position to finish third in the world's premier auto race in a

[207]

Wildcat with an "obsolete" four-cylinder engine. He quickly followed that up with a hair-breath win over his old racing buddy, Pancho Carter, in a Dirt Championship race at DuQuoin, Ill. six days later, as if to prove it were no fluke.

We could see that Gary's fine competitive edge had returned when he pressed Pancho to the limit before finishing second to Carter in a Sprint feature at Indianapolis Raceway Park two weeks before the 500.

The Indianapolis performance was Gary's finest since 1972. That was the year he should have won the 500, but his teammate, Mark Donohue, did win it. Gary had a comfortable lead at 175 laps when ignition trouble slowed him and he finally stopped on the course on his 183rd lap. He thoroughly dominated that race, leading 138 laps and turning in the fastest leading lap of the race.

His only previous top-five finish before this year came in 1973 and was something of a statistical curiosity. Gary drove car #5, started in fifth place and finished fifth. That year, he won the event which still ranks as the fastest race in USAC Championship history, winning at Texas World Speedway at 181.918.

Gary's career received a setback on July 4, 1974, when he flipped in practice for a Dirt Championship event at Syracuse, N.Y., causing nerve damage which left him with restricted use of his left arm, and put him out of action for nearly five months.

But he was back strong in 1975, running in four USAC divisions and winning two Sprint and two Midget features. Mechanical problems dogged him at the 500, putting him out of the 1976, 1977 and 1978 events after a crash sidelined him in 1975.

Oldest son of the late Tony Bettenhausen, who was killed in a 1961 Speedway practice crash while testing a car for buddy Paul Russo, Gary started racing go-karts in 1961 and moved into USAC Stocks at the Yankee 300 in May of 1963. In 1965, Gary moved into Midgets. By 1967, he was driving Sprint cars.

The year 1968 was a big one for Gary. He qualified for his first 500 and was running ninth at 43 laps when he ran over some debris from an accident and was eliminated by a punctured oil cooler. He had three second-place finishes in Championship events and was runner-up in the USAC Sprint division, winning seven features. He also won two Midget events. Gary won Sprint Championship in 1969 and 1971 as he and Larry Dickson combined in the unforgettable "Larry and Gary Show."

Bettenhausen and wife Wavelyn have three sons, Gary Jr., and twins Cary and Todd. They live at Monrovia, IN.

Tom Bigelow

Anyone who knows Tom Bigelow personally can well understand why the eighth-place finisher in the 1980 Indianapolis 500 has one of the largest fan clubs in all of auto racing.

Bigelow is just an absolutely superior person. He always has time to talk to his fans and sign autographs. He is never to busy to say hello or offer a kind word to someone who needs it.

This stocky resident of Whitewater, WI. also is one of the all-time greats of USAC Sprint racing. He is the record holder in career feature victories and captured the USAC Sprint championship in 1978 after three runner-up finishes.

While his record in the Championship cars has been less spectacular, the 40-year-old driver has seven straight appearances in the 500, with a best finish of sixth in the 1977 running.

A Wisconsin native, Tom got his start running Midgets with the Badger Midget Racing Association in 1957. He joined IMCA in 1965 and finished fourth in their Sprint standings and third in Midget points.

He moved up to USAC in 1967, and in 1968 managed to win three USAC Midget features. The first of his long string of USAC Sprint triumphs came in 1969, a year he also won the Houston (TX.) Astro-Dome Midget championship.

Tom passed three phases of his Indianapolis driver's test in 1970 but mechanical trouble prevented him from completing it. He finally passed the test

in 1973 and qualified but was bumped from the field. He first made the 500 in 1974 and drove to a 12th place finish, being flagged at 166 laps.

In 1979, Tom had two runner-up finishes on the USAC Championship Trail, in 200-milers at Texas World Speedway and Milwaukee.

He and wife Randy, who live in Whitewater, WI., have three children, Donald, Alan and Becky Bee. Tom drives a truck in the off-season.

Larry Cannon

Larry (Boom Boom) Cannon came up short on ammunition this year.

His Kraco Car Stereo Special was able to complete only two laps before camshaft problems put him out, placing 33rd and last.

An early exit was nothing new for the Boomer. In his rookie year of 1974, Larry last 49 laps before his car stalled, placing him 24th. He was 17th in 1976 when he completed 97 laps. He drove 8 laps of relief for John Mahler in 1977.

A native of Danville, Ill., which he still calls home, Larry started racing stock cars in 1959, moved into Super Modifieds and won many races in that type of competition before joining USAC in 1969.

He competed in Sprint and Midget divisions, winning one Sprint race and one Midget event.

In 1979, Larry completed the first two phases of his driver's test before crashing into the wall on the northeast turn. He finally passed his driver's test at the Speedway in 1973 but made no qualification attempt.

He made the 500 field for the first time in 1974.

Cannon and his wife, Linda, have two children, Jodie and Jill.

Pancho Carter

Pancho Carter was the center of the only real controversy arising out of the 1980 running of the Indianapolis 500. Did he finish sixth, the position which he was awarded and paid for, or second, as he alleges?

The hassle arose over an incident on the 58th lap of the race with Pancho in the lead at the time due to a pit-stop shuffle. The question is whether Pancho was waved around the Pontiac Turbo Trans-AM Pace Car as he contends or whether USAC Steward Bob Cassaday gestured to hold Pancho back, as Cassaday contends.

At any rate, Carter was penalized one lap and that relegated him to sixth spot — a difference of some $89,000 from the runner-up position.

Another of the brilliant group of second-generation drivers at the Speedway, Pancho is the son of Duane Carter Sr. and Arza. He is the half-brother of Johnny Parsons, to whose father, 1950 winner Johnnie Parsons Sr., Arza was married before she was wed to Carter Sr.

One of the most exciting open-cockpit drivers you could find, the 30-year-old Pancho enjoys the unique distinction of having captured USAC Midget, Sprint and Dirt Championship driving titles. He was the 1972 Midget titleist, won Sprint crowns in both 1974 and 1976 and captured the 1978 dirt championship. Pancho won Indy 500 Rookie-of-the-Year honors in 1974 with a seventh-place finish. He was fourth in 1975 and fifth in 1976.

He narrowly escaped death in a tire-testing crash at Phoenix, AZ. in 1977 which has left him with a permanent limp. He made a courageous comeback to the sport, posting back to back Sprint victories at Indianapolis Raceway Park and Winchester in early spring of 1978 after being told by doctors he would probably have to sit out that whole season. He won Dirt Championship events at Syracuse, N.Y. and DuQuoin, IL. on the way to the title. Mechanical failures sidelined him in the 1977, 1978 and 1979 500's.

Pancho and wife Carla live in nearby Brownsburg, Indiana and have one son, Duane Carl.

Billy Engelhart

Billy Engelhart is a most persistent fellow and it looks like it may finally be beginning to pay off for the likable guy from Madison, WI.

At 38 Engelhart is a veteran of 15 years of racing. He first tried to crack the 500 field in 1976, but didn't make it until 1980.

His 11th place finish was not spectacular but was far better than his 1979 finish when he wound up in the hospital with a fractured left leg suffered when he hit the wall in the Southwest turn during practice.

Engelhart got his start in Super Modifieds in the Milwaukee area in 1966. He won "Rookie-of-the-Year" honors with the Badger Midget Racing Association in 1967 and a similar honor in his first year in the USAC Midget Division in 1969.

Billy captured the famed Turkey Night Grand Prix Midget event in 1971 and finished second in USAC Midget points

in 1972. In 1973, he added a second Turkey Night victory and also won the prestigious Hunt Hundred at Terre Haute, IN.

Engelhart passed an Indianapolis driver's test in 1976, but was called in from his only qualification attempt after only one lap, running too slow to make the field.

In 1977, Engelhart won a USAC Sprint feature at Winchester, IN. and finished seventh in Sprint points. His biggest victory came in the 1978 Hoosier Hundred and he finished fifth in Dirt Championship points.

Divorced, Billy is the father of one son, Herbie.

Dick Ferguson

Another of the graduates of the road racing circuits who are making their mark at Indianapolis, Ferguson made three stabs at qualifying for the 500 in 1979 and apparently was in the field at one time.

But he was disqualified because his car owner had cheated on USAC turbo-charger boost rules, without Fergie's knowledge.

This year, the 30-year-old Los Angeles resident qualified on opening day, taking a day's low speed of 182.880 which many observers along pit row considered somewhat shaky. But it stood up admirably.

Ferguson lasted only nine laps before he was eliminated when Bill Whittington bounced off the first turn wall and left him with "nowhere to go but off the track." Ferguson slid into the inside guard rail, washing out his AMSOIL Special.

Born in New York City, Dick went to

high school in Los Angeles and then studied at the Ferrari Factory School in Maranello, Italy. He was a Formula Ford champion in 1970 and 1971. He moved into Super Vees in 1974 and won the Super Vee Gold Cup that year. In 1975, he continued Super Vee competition and also had two Formula Atlantic victories.

Ferguson won the Formula Atlantic Long Beach Grand Prix in 1978. He moved into USAC Championship competition in 1979, running at Texas and Ontario before making his first Indianapolis attempt.

Dick is married to Zenia Ferguson.

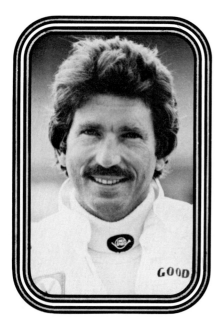

Dennis Firestone

One of a growing number of top drivers coming to the 500 from the Mini-Indy ranks, Dennis Firestone won that series in 1979, capturing five victories and three seconds in eight races.

Recovering from a practice crash when he strayed into the grass while running about 90 miles an hour on the second turn, spun and hit the wall, Firestone qualified the second weekend for 24th starting spot.

He finished 16th, being eliminated after 137 laps by transmission problems.

Born in Townsville, Australia, Firestone grew up in America and attended San Jose State College in Calif. He also enjoys skiing and boating. The 35-year-old six-footer is president of a trucking company.

He started racing in Formula Fords at Riverside, CA. in 1971. He won the 1974 and 1976 South Pacific Formula Ford Championships and the 1976 Formula Ford National Championship. In 1976 and 1977, Firestone captured 23 straight

races in the Formula Ford and Formula Atlantic series. He won the Kimberly Cup as the SCCA's outstanding driver.

Firestone place second in the 1978 Mini-Indy series and was named "Rookie-of-the-Year." He drove his first championship event at the CART 500-miler at Ontario in 1979, failing to finish.

Separated, Dennis is the father of three daughters.

A.J. Foyt

The 1980 Indianapolis 500 was not one of A.J. Foyt's happiest days. He showed something of his frustration over the public address system when he commented that USAC's boost rules made the race seem like "a hurd of turtles."

But Foyt continued to set records on May 25 just as he does every time he sets his tires on the sacred asphalt and sybolical "Yard of Bricks" at Indianapolis.

Foyt extended his string of consecutive Indianapolis 500 appearances to 23 races, dating all the way back to 1958. He thus became the first man ever to drive in the 500 in four different decades — the 50's, 60's, 70's and 80's.

The modest sum of $29,512.24 which he received for his 14th place finish, eliminated by valve problems after 173 laps, boosted his all-time Speedway winnings record to $1,347,694.97.

Only man ever to win the Indianapolis 500 four times, Foyt captured his races in 1961-1964-1967-1977. He was second in 1976 and 1979, third in 1963, 1971 and 1975. He was seventh in 1978 and eight in 1969.

Tabbed by most followers of auto racing as the greatest driver ever to sit in

a racing car, Foyt also holds victories in the 24 Hours of LeMans and the Daytona 500. He is the only person who ever has won all three of these keystone events of motor racing. He also holds a number of sports car victories.

A seven-time USAC National Driving champion, Foyt also is a four-time Indianapolis pole-winner. He became the first man ever to win two USAC National titles in a single season when he added the 1979 USAC Stock title to his Indy-car diadem. He has a record total of 66 National Championship victories at this writing.

He and wife Lucy live in Houston, TX. and have three children, A.J. III, Terry Lynn and Jerry Zan. When A.J. isn't racing automobiles, you'll usually find him racing his string of horses. His son is his trainer.

Spike Gehlhausen

Daniel William (Spike) Gehlhausen was one of the early sensations of the 1980 Indianapolis 500-mile race period.

He showed surprising speed in practice right from the start and posted the fourth fastest qualifying time, earning the inside starting spot in the second row.

But his victory bid was short-lived as he crashed in the first turn after only 29 laps, placing 29th. That was the same spot in which he finished in 1978 when he crashed on the second turn after only 23 laps.

Spike's best finish so far is a 10th place, achieved in 1979.

Gehlhausen started driving Midgets in the St. Louis Auto Racing Association in 1971. He ran in the Car Owners Racing

Association in 1973 and moved up to USAC Midgets in 1974.

Spike was 10th in the 1975 Milwaukee 150 in his first Championship start and was later named the 1975 USAC Championship Rookie-of-the-Year. He qualified for the 1976 Indianapolis 500 handily but pulled into the pits before completing a lap, with his gauge showing no oil pressure and was through for the day, placing 33rd.

Spike and wife Carolyn live in Speedway.

Hurley Haywood

Only man in history to score a sweep of the 24 Hours of LeMans, the Daytona 24 Hours and the Sebring 12 Hour races, Hurley Haywood made an outstanding record in road racing before coming to Indianapolis.

The 32-year-old Jacksonville, FL. resident endured a difficult rookie 500 which saw his car twice catch fire in the pits and eventually succumb to turbo-charger problems after 127 laps, to finish 18th.

The blond-haired Haywood was born in Chicago and now makes his home in Jacksonville, FL. He is a business administration graduate of the University of Jacksonville.

He was the IMSA champion in 1971 and 1972. He has won the 24 Hours of Daytona four times, in 1973, 1975, 1977 and 1979. He won at Sebring in 1973 and scored his LeMans victory in 1977. Most of his road racing success has been achieved in Porsches.

Haywood came to Indianapolis first in 1979 and passed his rookie test. He had an initial qualifying lap of 190-plus, but

his speeds steadily decreased after that and he missed the starting field.

Gordon Johncock

One of the guttiest little guys you could find anywhere, 43-year-old Gordon Johncock ran the 1980 "500" with a cast on a fractured left ankle and still managed to finish fourth, less than a car length behind third-place Gary Betten-hausen.

Overcoming the injury, suffered in a practice crash before qualifying, enabled Johncock to keep unbroken a string which reached 16 consecutive years of 500 participation this year.

He was the winner of the tragedy-marked 1973 running, which was plagued by bad weather and three fatalities and finally was cut to 332.5 miles by merciful rains.

Johncock made a supreme bid for a second Indianapolis victory in 1977 in a classic duel with his close racing friend, A.J. Foyt. Gordy was leading with only 16 laps to go and apparently had the victory sewed up when a crankshaft broke. In sportsmanlike manner, Gordy pulled off into the infield in the first turn so as not to oil down the racing surface. Then, he took a frustrated dive into the creek there.

Johncock was a terror on the high-banked pavement in Sprint cars after making an outstanding record in Michigan-based Modified competition. He set a world half-mile record at Winchester, IN. in 1964 and also broke into Championship racing that year.

Johncock finished fifth in his initial

Indianapolis 500 in 1965 in a Weinberger Homes roadster. It was a vintage year for rookies, with third-place finisher Mario Andretti gaining Rookie-of-the-Year honors. Johncock moved up to fourth in 1966. He spent less time on the race track than anyone. But that was the year of a big first-lap accident. There was then a rule that crews could not work on cars during the red-flag period. So, Gordy remained in the pits for about three minutes after the restart, while his crew worked on body damage. He finished only 1 minute and 48 seconds behind winner Graham Hill.

Johncock didn't finish an Indianapolis race from then until his 1973 victory. He was fourth in 1974, third in both 1976 and 1978 and sixth in 1979. He is married to Lynda and now has moved back to Coldwater, MI. from Phoenix, AZ. He is the father of five children.

Jerry Karl

Smiling Jerry Karl, who never has the best of equipment but often makes the race, updated a McLaren chassis and dropped a stock-block Chevy in it to make his 1980 Indianapolis effort.

His bid lasted only 64 laps before he was ousted by clutch problems, placing 21st.

Karl started driving Midgets at Freeport, Long Island, N.Y. in 1960 and ran with the American Racing Drivers Club until 1966, when he also started competing in the URC Sprint circuit. He won three Sprint races in his initial year with that group, finished third in the point standings and was named co-Rookie-of-the-Year with Al Loquasto and Denny Zimmerman.

[211]

Karl drove his first USAC Championship race at Dover, Del., in 1969, finishing 10th. He passed three phases of his Indianapolis driver's test in 1970, but mechanic problems kept him from completing it. In 1971, he drove some Indy practice laps but didn't get started on his test. Finally passing the test in 1972, Karl was unable to qualify. He finally made the race in 1973 in Smokey Yunick's Chevy-powered Oriente Express and finished 26th after a pit stop of one hour and 36 minutes to change a turbocharger. His best finish was a 13th in 1975. He hit the wall on the Northeast turn in 1974. In 1979, Jerry qualified but was bumped from the starting lineup.

He and wife Linda and their three children live in Manchester, PA.

Greg Leffler

This 29-year-old resident of Winchester, IN., surprised many close followers of auto racing when he won the USAC Sprint championship in 1979.

But his 10th place finish in the 1980 500 was really no surprise because he did a thoroughly strong and consistent job in the practice and qualifying period leading up to the race.

A bachelor, Greg is the son of Paul Leffler, long one of the top USAC Sprint mechanics and recently also a top Indy-car wrench. Greg began racing on the USAC Sprint circuit in 1972 and finished ninth in the point standings that year. He won his first Sprint feature in 1975 and also had single victories in 1976 and 1977.

In 1978, Greg captured three Sprint features and finished sixth in the point standings. In 1979, he took six features en route to the title.

He made his debut in the Championship cars at Milwaukee that year but a practice crash kept him from making a qualifying attempt.

Jim McElreath

Believed to be the oldest man ever to start the Indianapolis 500 at 52, Jimmy McElreath lasted only 54 laps this year before crashing on the southwest turn and placing 24th.

McElreath began his racing career right after the end of World War II in 1945, driving stock cars in the Dallas region near his Arlington, TX. home. He had been running well in the IMCA ranks in 1961, when he was offered the ride in Lindsey Hopkins' "Gray Ghost" dirt championship car for the 1961 Hoosier Hundred. McElreath turned in a fine performance to finish third and finished out the season driving for Hopkins.

In 1962, McElreath qualified for his first 500 with the seventh fastest overall speed in the field and finished the race in sixth position to win Rookie-of-the-Year honors in a unanimous ballot. His best Indianapolis finish was a third in 1966. He was fifth in both 1967 and 1970 and sixth in 1974.

McElreath became known as the "Ray Harroun of Ontario" when he won the inaugural running of the California 500 in 1970. McElreath has a total of five National Championship victories. Three came in 1965 when he finished third in the point standings. He was runner-up to Mario Andretti in 1966 points, winning one race.

McElreath and his wife Shirley lost their only son, James, in a Sprint accident at Winchester, IN. several years

ago. Now they have a racing son-in-law in the person of Tony Bettenhausen Jr., who married one of their two daughters, Shirley. Their other daughter is Vicky.

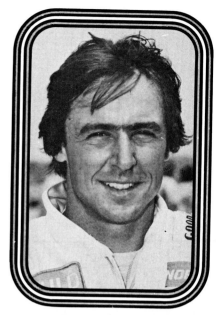

Rick Mears

One of the fastest-rising stars of the Championship firmament, Rick Mears reached the pinnacle in only his sophomore year at Indianapolis with his 1979 domination when he won both the pole and the race.

He was well on his way to a second-place finish this year when a flat tire caused him an extra pit stop and ropped him one lap behind to a fifth place finish. That has to be a comedown for this 28-year-old Bakersfield, CA. resident but he is obviously going to be around winning races for a long time to come.

Mears came to the Speedway from an unusual background, that of Off-Road racing. After starting out in Sprint Buggies at Ascot Park in Gardena, CA., Rick moved into Off-Road competition in 1972, attracting much attention when he beat Parnelli Jones in a Japanese event. Rick won seven Class I Off-Road races in 1973. He moved into Formula Vee and Supervee competition in 1975.

Rick drove his first Championship race for Bill Simpson in 1976 at the California 500, finishing eighth. He got a ride for the 1977 Indianapolis 500 and passed his driver's test, but mechanical problems ended his qualifying bid. A chance meeting with Roger Penske on a motorcycle safari resulted in a business association with Mears driving for Penske starting with the 1978 season. He earned the outside starting spot on the front row with a 200.078 qualifying average and earned Co-Rookie-of-the-Year honor with Larry Rice, running fifth before mechanical problems sidelined him.

His 1979 victory was followed up by Mears becoming the first — and probably only CART driving champion.

Mears and wife Dina Lynn have two children, Clint and Cole.

Mike Mosley

Soft-spoken Mike Mosley got in only about as many laps this year as he does words in his average interview — five.

Mosley was in the pits with the race barely underway and stayed there for many painful laps while the crew tried to diagnose what was wrong with the engine of his Aluminum stock-block Eagle. It turned out to be a gasket failure.

That put him out with only 32nd place to show for the effort of himself, car owner Dan Gurney and chief mechanic Wayne Leary. Such luck is nothing new for Mosley at Indianapolis.

He was running at the end only in his rookie year of 1968 when he finished eighth and in 1979, when he was second in his finest Indianapolis performance.

Mike crashed spectacularly in the fourth turn in both 1971 and 1972 and retired from racing later for a brief time.

Starting in Three Quarter Midgets, in 1961 Mike moved into CRA Sprints in 1964. In 1966, he won six CRA features and finished second in the point standings.

Mosley passed his driver's test at the Speedway in 1967 but crashed in practice and made no qualifying attempt. He made his Championship debut with a seventh place finish at Trenton, N.J. and won one USAC Sprint feature.

He qualified an A.J. Watson creation in 1968 and brought it home in eighth place.

Mike, wife Alice and a son, Michael II, live in Fallbrook, CA.

Danny Ongais

You might figure that Danny Ongais, one of the most quiet and retiring of Speedway drivers, would be the principal in an almost-unknown Indianapolis 500 accident.

Few of the many thousands who were still around at the end of the race realized that Ongais brushed the wall at the north end of the track on the very last lap of the 500.

That was probably the most spectacular thing that Danny did all month. It was a year that was somewhat out of character for Ongais, usually one of the hardest chargers and most spectacular of performers in his "Black Beauty" Interscope/Panasonic Specials. Perhaps, his Panellis are getting a little long in the tooth. But, for whatever reason, Ongais blended into the pack this time.

He was a 16th place starter, never a real factor in the race, and finished seventh, one lap behind the leaders.

A native Hawaiian and former motorcycle champion in that country, Ongais was a legendary drag-racing driver long before he made his Indianapolis debut in 1977. He won national championships in AA Gas Dragsters in 1963 and 1964 and captured the AAA Fuel title in 1965. He also was the first driver to exceed 200 mph on European drag strips. Danny ran in SCCA Amateur road racing in 1974 and won 12 races in 15 starts. He ran the Formula 500 series in 1975 and 1976,

finishing fifth in points the latter year. In his first USAC Championship start, he was 28th in the 1976 California 500. He started seventh in the 1978 Indianapolis race and second in 1978, but was eliminated both years by engine problems. In 1979, he finished fourth after starting way back in 27th. He had to qualify on the final day after crashing on the scheduled opening day of time trials and spending several days in the hospital.

Ongais is single and lives in Costa Mesa, CA. He also is active in endurance and sports-car racing.

Johnny Parsons

Johnny Parsons got to enjoy a thrill on May 25 never before possible for a 500-mile race driver — starting behind his own father.

With 1950 winner Johnnie Parsons driving the Pontiac Trans-AM Pace Car, the 35-year-old son took off from the inside spot of the third row in the fastest-qualifying four-cylinder car, a laydown Offy.

But Parsons had mechanical woes and lasted only 44 laps before piston trouble put him out, in 26th spot.

Young Parsons started racing Quarter Midgets in the Indianapolis area at the age of 12. He won 45 races in them and then switched to go-karts when he was 16. At 18, he started running Three-Quarter and full Midgets.

Parsons, after competing with BCRA, URA and NMRA, started running USAC in 1968, driving in both Sprint and Midget events. He finished seventh in his first Championship start at Sacramento, CA. in 1970. In 1970, he ran four Championship races and took the pole for the Hoosier Hundred.

He passed his driver's test at the Speedway in 1973 but made no qualification attempt. He made the starting field for the first time in 1974, but was eliminated by turbo-charger trouble after 18 laps. His best finish was fifth place in 1977 in a Bignotti Wildcat.

Divorced, Parsons is the father of two children. He lives in Indianapolis.

Roger Rager

Roger Rager caused something of a minor sensation when he qualified his Advance Clean Sweep Wildcat, powered by a Chevy stock-block which came out of a schoolbus engine with 70,000 miles on it, at more than 186 mph for the 10th starting spot.

He had the thrill of leading the race when he stayed out for a couple of extra laps on the first pit-stop shuffle. Then, disaster struck when veteran Jim McElreath lost control and hit the wall in the southwest turn, taking Rager out with him.

Roger, who had completed 55 laps, placed 23rd, in his rookie year at the 500.

Born in Lincoln, Neb., Rager was captain of his highschool football team at Gering, Neb., and won all-state honors. He started racing go-karts at 6 and was the Nebraska State Champion in 1962 and 1963. After racing hobby stocks, dragsters and Super Modifieds, he joined the IMCA Sprint circuit in 1968 and race Sprinters all over the U.S. In 1973, Roger went to South Africa to race Sprint cars and was introduced to a vacationing airline stewardess. A whirlwind romance ensued and Roger and Gail Rager were married a week later. They have three children, and live in Mound, Minn.

Rager joined the USAC Sprint circuit in 1976 and was selected as its Rookie-of-the-Year, finishing 23rd in the point standings. He drove his first Championship race at Trenton, N.J. in 1976 and finished 20th.

Rager passed a Speedway driver's test in 1978, but was unable to qualify for the race. In 1979, he practiced in a stock-block Eagle at Indianapolis, but failed to make the field.

Tim Richmond

We first tabbed this youngster as a comer when he won the very first race he ever started in the ferocious competition of the USAC Mini-Indy series. That triumph, achieved in the 1978 series opener at Phoenix, AZ., also was the very first time that Tim Richmond ever raced in a rear-engined car and his first USAC competition.

He also was impressive in his first USAC Sprint program at Indianapolis Raceway Park in 1978, winning his heat race and moving up from a 19th place start to finish ninth in the 40-lap feature. He finished fourth in a 50-lap feature at Salem in his next start and later was named USAC Sprint Rookie-of-the-Year. In the Mini-Indy series, he placed ninth with four top-ten finishes in the six races he ran.

His first Championship start came at Michigan International Speedway in July of 1979. Richmond lasted only four laps before engine problems put him out. But he finished eighth at Watkins Glen, N.Y. He ran his first 500-miler at Ontario Motor Speedway in September of 1979 and had the fastest qualifying time of the four-cylinder cars, but a broken ring-and-pinion gear forced him out after 39 laps.

He was a month-long sensation at Indianapolis, right from when he posted the fastest speed of opening-day practice through his ninth place finish in the race which won him Rookie-of-the-Year honors. He had the fastest overall, unofficial practice speed of the month at 193.5, was the fastest rookie qualifier and crashed spectacularly on "Pole Day," necessitating a second-weekend qualification and 19th place start.

Single, Tim is a resident of Ashland, OH. He started racing in Go-Karts at a tender age and learned to fly airplanes at 14.

Johnny Rutherford

We first got to know Johnny in the early 1960's at a Speedway watering hole then known as Mates White Front. He and another Johnny, his buddy whose last name was White, were running the dusty byways of the IMCA and used to stop by occasionally for a beer and some conversation. He was a pleasant and intense young man with a severe crew-cut and an unconcealed aspiration to someday be running — and winning — at the big track just across the street and a little west of the White Front.

Now, after his third Indianapolis 500 victory, the man we now know as "Lone Star J.R." belongs to the ages.

Rutherford was really something of a late-bloomer in Indianapolis car racing. True, he did win a National Championship race at Atlanta, GA. way back in 1965. But he didn't score again in the victory column until 1973. His big break came when he hooked up with Team McLaren, the British racing outfit that he drove for in his Indianapolis 500 triumphs of 1974 and 1976. The former year, Rutherford performed a feat which many had thought was virtually impossible. He came from a 25th place start all the way to Victory Lane.

In his 1976 victory, J.R. did it "the easy way." He started on the pole. And, that was the same starting niche which he occupied for his third victory this year. That was his second conquest of the season in his new "ride," the gleaming yellow Pennzoil Chaparral. He had thoroughly outclassed the field in a season-opening Championship Racing League 200-miler at Ontario, CA., earlier.

Rutherford would probably have an unbroken string of 18 Indianapolis 500 appearances going for him were it not for a Sprint car accident at Eldora Speedway, Rossburg, OH. in 1966, which threatened to nip his career in the bud. Both of his arms were broken when his Sprinter flipped down the back stretch and out of the ball park. Crashing was not an entirely new experience for the driver who was known as "Wreck-a-ford" in his salad days. But, breaking both arms was. It kept him out of the 1966 "500".

J.R. also had been involved in the 1964 Indianapolis fourth turn accident which took the lives of Eddie Sachs and Dave MacDonald. In that one, he was "an innocent bystander who suddenly had no place to go."

His first victory in 1974 also was his first Indianapolis finish. He had, however, made his presence known dramatically in 1970 when he missed the pole by 1/100ths of a second in a car that was several years old and not figured as even a front row contender.

Johnny found a bride, as well as fame and fortune, at the Speedway. Blonde Betty was a nurse on the Speedway medical staff when she caught Johnny's eye and they started dating. She now serves as his scorer and they are the parents of two children, John IV and Angela Ann.

Rutherford, now 42, got his start in racing at the Devil's Bowl Speedway in Mesquite, TX., not far from his present Fort Worth home, in 1959. He started out in modifieds and then switched to IMCA Sprint cars. His first Championship ride was in the Hoosier Hundred of 1962. In February of 1963, John drove a Chevy stock car for Smokey Yunick at Daytona Beach, FL., set a new track record in qualifying and won a 100-mile qualifying race.

Dick Simon

Dick Simon has one of the most interesting backgrounds of all the 500-mile race drivers.

He had been a ski jumping champion, parachute champion, multi-engine pilot, president of his own insurance company and road racing champion before arriving on the Indianapolis scene.

Starting his racing career in Super Modifieds, he won the 1965 Salt Lake Valley Racing Association championship. Dick drove a Lola in the 1969 SCCA Continental Championship, finishing eighth in the series.

Simon started his first Championship race at Phoenix, AZ. in March of 1970. In his first Indianapolis attempt, he started 31st and was flagged in 14th position after 168 laps.

Simon has yet to finish in the top 10 after 11 Indianapolis starts. He placed 22nd this year, losing a wheel and being sidelined after 58 laps by the resulting damage, though he was able to bring his car around to the pits.

A resident of San Juan Capistrano, CA., Dick is married to Melanie Simon. He has five children by a former marriage. He is now 46 years old.

Gordon Smiley

Certainly one of the most impressive of Indianapolis 500 debuts of 1980 was turned in by road-racing graduate Gordon Smiley. Gordon didn't even get onto the track until the second week of practice but quickly got up to speed and qualified at a 186.848 average, the ninth best overall speed.

His car caught fire due to turbo-

charger problems and was eliminated after 47 laps, placing 25th.

Smiley is a four-time SCCA champion and also won an Aurora Formula One title. Dedicated to his profession, Smiley follows a rugged physical fitness program prepared by the Royal Canadian Air Force and also plays racquetball often.

In 1979, Smiley joined the John Surtees works team for the Aurora Formula One series in Europe. Driving a new, ground-effects car, he was a consistent front-runner and won the Silverstone, England, event. That caught the attention of U.E. (Pat) Patrick who offered Smiley a ride in the Ontario 200 in April. Smiley started 14th and finished sixth in his first-ever oval race.

Smiley and wife Barbara live in Garland, TX.

Jerry Sneva

Blessed with the "best car I ever had here," Jerry Sneva struck a blow in his friendly sibling rivalry with brother Tom when he out-qualified Tom by 2½ miles an hour and won a starting spot in the middle of the second row for the 1980 "500".

But, alas, Jerry's luck was not to last. The #7 Lola/Cosworth, sponsored by Huggers Beverage Holders, got away from Jerry and spent itself on the first turn wall during his 131st lap — long after brother Tom had sailed past Jerry all the way to lead the race.

Like Tom, Jerry is a former champion of the Canadian American Modified Racing Association, having won that title in 1974. At 32, he is 13 months younger than Tom. He also is an all-around athlete, having played highschool football, basketball and hockey, and also being an outstanding golfer.

Jerry started out racing modified stock cars in the Spokane area, where he still lives, in 1968. He joined the CAMRA ranks in 1971 and won Rookie-of-the-Year honors. He finished fourth in CAMRA point standing in 1972 and second in 1973 before winning the title in 1974, by the largest margin ever compiled. He won 30 races out of 37 starts.

Jerry passed his Indianapolis driver's test in 1975, but made no attempt to qualify. He was unable to land an Indianapolis ride in 1976.

In 1977, Jerry qualified for 16th starting spot in the 500 and finished in 10th place, earning selection as Stark & Wetzel Rookie-of-the-Year. He finished only 18 laps in 1978 and 1979 before being side-lined with mechanical problems. He was seventh in USAC points the latter year, finishing fourth in the Pocono 500.

Jerry and wife Kay have two children, Trevor John and Shelby.

Tom Sneva

You could hardly blame Tom Sneva if he is getting just a little tired of playing the "bridesmaid" role in the Indianapolis 500. After all, this is his third second place finish in the last four runnings of the event.

But, the feat which he performed on May 25, 1980, will live in Speedway annals. He started in 33rd — and last — position and passed 31 cars to move up to the runner-up finish. That was the greatest position advance in Speedway

history, eclipsing Jim Rathaman's job of moving from 32nd to second in 1957.

How Tom got back there at the rear of the final rank is a story in itself. He qualified on opening day for the fifth row in an unfamiliar Phoenix/Cosworth. Tom made it clear that he didn't care much for the way the car handled, so he was not exactly devastated when he crashed in practice during the week after qualifying.

But, that did mean that under USAC rules, he had to go to the back of the pack in the five-year-old McLaren chassis they substituted for the Phoenix.

But Tom stood on the throttle from the time the green dropped and had moved all the way up to lead the race by the 75-lap mark. And, it took a supreme effort from that "other yellow car" (driven by Johnny Rutherford) to relegate him to his accustomed second spot. But this was a far more satisfying runner-up finish than those of 1977 and 1978. In both of those, Sneva had started on the pole and moved back one spot.

Certainly among the most intelligent of the 500 drivers, Sneva is a graduate of Eastern Washington State College and served as a high school teacher, coach, and principal before turning to a racing career. He also played high school and college basketball.

The edges looked pretty rough when we saw Tom run his first USAC Championship race, a 300-miler at Trenton, N.J., in 1971. He went on to run seven Championship races, with a 10th at Ontario, CA. being his best finish. But he was something of a sensation on the USAC Sprint circuit, winning six features in a rear-engined Sprinter.

Fastest rookie qualifier for the 1974 Indianapolis 500 in 1974, Sneva started

in eighth position and was running fourth at 50 miles. But transmission trouble put him out after 94 laps. He caught the eye of Roger Penske and joined Penske's team for the 1975 season. Starting fourth in the Indianapolis race, Tom ran over the left front wheel of Eldon Rasmussen's car in the second turn, touching off one of the most spectacular accidents in Indy history. Tom's car hit the outside wall, right in front of the V.I.P. suites, caught fire and disintegrated. Sneva miraculously escaped with minor burns, which caused him to miss only one Championship race.

Starting on the outside of the front row in 1976 at Indy, Tom took the lead on the 38th lap and finally finished in sixth position.

Sneva ran the first official 200-miles-an-hour lap in Indianapolis history on May 14, 1977, with a 200.535 circuit on his opening qualifying lap. He slowed to a four-lap average of 198.884, but that was good for the pole. He was runner-up to A.J. Foyt as the master scored his history-making fourth victory. Sneva went on to win his first to two consecutive USAC National Championships, winning the Pocono 500 and the first Texas 200 on the way.

In 1978, Sneva set the existing Speedway track records of 203.620 for one lap and 202.156 for four laps and finished a mere 8.19 seconds behind winner Al Unser. Starting on the front row for the fourth straight year in 1979, Tom was running sixth after 188 laps when he crashed on the northwest turn.

Residents of Spokane, Wash. in the off-season and an apartment-dweller in Indianapolis during the racing period, Tom and wife Sharon have two children, Joey and Amanda. Tom is 32 years old.

George Snider

Having apparently settled comfortably into his role at A.J. Foyt's "backup driver," George Snider qualified just a fraction slower than the "Boss" and exited the race just one position earlier than A.J., almost as if it was pre-ordained.

Snider's 15th place finish was not one of the better performances by the 39-year-old driver from Bakersfield, CA., who now makes his home on Foyt's Texas ranch. But, at least, it kept alive George's record of appearing in 16 straight Indianapolis 500's. Nine of those were in Foyt backups.

"Ziggy" Snider has been driving race cars for nearly 20 years and is always a top contender when he straps on a

helmet. At his best on the dirt, George won USAC's first Dirt Car Championship back in 1971.

He started out driving Modifieds at Fresno, CA., in 1961. His USAC career began in Midgets in 1964 when he finished 14th in point standings. His Speedway debut was in 1965 when he started 16th and exited after 64 laps with rear-end trouble, placing 21st. His best Indianapolis finishes were eighth places in both 1975 and 1978. He started outside on the front row in 1966 and was leading going through the first turn, when the race was red-flagged due to the first-lap pileup happening behind him.

The father of two children, George is married to Debbie Snider.

Al Unser

Al Unser probably could be forgiven if he were heard to curse the luck that saw him leaving the "Yellow Submarine" and switching to an untested, new Longhorn car for the 1980 Indianapolis 500.

That he did nothing of the kind but quietly and manfully bore up under the burden of having an obviously not-fully-developed mount is to his credit.

A three-time 500 winner (1970-71-78), Al could probably have joined A.J. Foyt in the elevated echelon of four-time winners if he had been willing to swallow his pride and stay with the Jim Hall Chaparral. But, Al had some honest differences of opinion with Hall, which resulted in his switching to the Longhorn team of Bobby Hillin.

It was a struggle for Al to get the Longhorn going but he gained ground in small but steady chunks and made the field with a tidy 186.442 average good for

the outside spot in the third row.

But the car lasted only 33 laps before dropping a cylinder and dropping Al to 27th place in the final standings.

Al started driving modifieds around Albuquerque when he was 18. He finished second to brother Bobby in the 1960 Pikes Peak Hill Climb in 1960 and again in 1962. In 1964, Al broke Bobby's long string of triumphs at "the Peak" and set a new record in the process.

After driving CRA and IMCA Sprint cars, Al switched to USAC Sprints and Midgets in 1964 and also ran his first Championship race at Milwaukee that year.

He made his Speedway debut in 1965, driving an A.J. Foyt backup car to ninth place. He again won the Pike's Peak Hillclimb that year. He was dueling for the lead with Gordon Johncock in 1966 when he spun into the inside wall on the main straightaway. Al finished second in the 1967 "500" behind Foyt and after wrecking in 1968 and missing the 1969 race when he broke his leg in a playful motorcycle accident, put together successive victories in 1970 and 1971 in the famed Johnny Lightning Specials.

Also Al has won two 500's each at Pocono and Ontario. His seven victories put him behind only Foyt in 500 triumphs. A.J. has eight.

Al and wife Karen live in Albuquerque. He is the father of three children by a former marriage, including Al Jr. who is now racing Sprint cars in the Southwest.

Bobby Unser

When Bobby Unser's #11 Norton Spirit bit the dust after 126 laps due to an ignition coil problem, Johnny

Rutherford's toughest competition went out the window.

Had it not been for that mechanical failure, it might well have been the 46-year-old elder Unser rather than Lone Star J.R. who would have joined the exclusive ranks of three-time winners of the 500.

Bobby, who won the 500 in both 1968 and 1975, could well be right up there with A.J. Foyt as a four-time winner, because he had the race in his back pocket in 1979 before gear problems dropped him back to a fifth-place finish and gave victory to his teammate, Rick Mears.

One of the hardest chargers you will ever find, Bobby also excels as a test driver. He has probably logged more miles testing both tires and cars than any other driver around the Speedway.

After starting out in modified stocks, progressing to Midgets and Sprints and winning the Pikes Peak Hill Climb seven years out of eight, Bobby came to the Speedway as a rookie in 1963 and drove the Hotel Tropicana Las Vegas Novi. He hit the wall on the southwest turn on the third lap and was eliminated. In 1964, he was involved in the second-lap accident in turn 4 which claimed the lives of Eddie Sachs and Dave MacDonald. Bobby escaped with minor injuries. After finishes of eighth in 1966 and ninth in 1967, Bobby won the 1968 classic at 152.882 mph after pushing turbine failure with seven laps to go.

Bobby was third in 1969 and second in 1974 before posting his second victory in the rain-shortened 1975 race which went 435 miles. He was sixth in 1978 and 1979.

Bobby and wife Marsha live in Albuquerque, N.M. He has four children by a former marriage.

Billy Vukovich

Another of the Speedway's outstanding second-generation drivers, Billy Vukovich is a steady performer who was runner-up to A.J. Foyt for the USAC National Championship title in 1979.

Vuky had one second place finish and two thirds last year. He drove an Offy engined machine, which appeared down on straightaway power all month, to a 12th place finish in this year's 500.

Also a talented golfer and baseball player who might have made his mark in either of those sports, Vukovich decided instead to follow in the tireprints of his famous father, Bill Vukovich, who won the 1953 and 1954 "500's" and was killed in an accident while leading the 1955 running.

Starting out in Super Modifieds near his Fresno, CA. home in 1963, Billy was named NASCAR Rookie-of-the-Year for California in 1964 and started driving BCRA Midgets in 1965, also winning rookie honors in that competition.

He broke into USAC Championship racing in 1967 and drove to a fourth place finish in the Hoosier Hundred, winning another Rookie-of-the-Year title for that. His initial Indianapolis 500 was in 1968 and he took seventh place and — you guessed it — was named Stark & Wetzel Rookie-of-the-Year.

His other up front finishes at Indianapolis were fifth in 1971, second in 1973, third in 1974, sixth in 1975 and eighth in 1979. His only Championship victory came at Michigan International Speedway in 1973.

Vuky and wife, Joyce, who now make their home in Coarsegold, CA. have two children, Billy Jr. and John.

Bill Whittington

Bill Whittington had finished only nine laps of his first 500-mile race when he crashed against the wall in the southeast turn and glanced off, taking fellow rookie Dick Ferguson out with him.

Born in Lubbock, TX., Bill attended high school in Hawaii and studied at Broward Junior College in Florida.

Running his first race in 1978 at Sebring, FL. in a Porsche, Bill went on to finish second in the Camel GT Series for sports cars, winning the finale at Daytona Beach, FL.

Co-driving to victory with brother Don Whittington in the 24 Hours of Lemans and in several other endurance events, Bill finished third in the World Challenge for Endurance Drivers.

Bill made his debut in Championship auto racing in the 1979 California 500 at Ontario, CA., finishing 12th. Bill won the Road Atlanta GT event in April of 1980 at the track he and brother Don own.

Bill's hobby is horseback riding and he is active at his ranch when not racing. He

and wife Pat have two children, Keely and Nerrissa. He is 30 years old.

Don Whittington

Don Whittington spent a great deal of the 1980 Indianapolis 500 in the pits and a brief and terrifying portion on the wall in the northwest turn. But he kept rolling and finally finished in 13th position.

A pair of brothers from Texas who now reside in Florida, Don and Bill Whittington who was eliminated from this year's race by an early crash, posted victories in Eundurance races in the 24 Hours of LeMans (France), and events at Daytona Beach, FL. and Watkins Glen, N.Y. the same year. All of this they accomplished in 1979 en route to Don's winning the World Challenge for Endurance Drivers in their first full season of racing.

The Whittington's own the Road Atlanta road racing course at Flowery Branch, GA. and also own a large recreational vehicle dealership.

Don became interested in racing in 1978 and ran his first race that March at Sebring, driving a Porsche. He finished fourth in points in IMSA competition.

Don tried his hand at NASCAR Grand National racing in February of 1980 with some equipment purchased from A.J. Foyt and finished 16th in the Daytona 500. Don and his wife, Sherry, live at Fort Lauderdale, FL. He is 34 years old.

James McElreath Barbecue

by John Pell

Lloyd Ruby used his famed chef talents to please over a thousand race fans.

Long ago someone said the racing fraternity takes care of its own. This was taken one step farther when not only people connected with auto racing, but race fans themselves, got together on May 22, 1980 at Indianapolis Raceway Park to pay tribute to James McElreath, the late son of Jim and Shirley McElreath. The occasion was a Texas-style barbecue with the proceeds going to the James McElreath Children's Park in Arlington, Texas. As the large crowd (more than a thousand) so clearly indicated, the McElreaths are highly thought of by their counterparts and fans alike.

The real recipients of this outpouring of love and respect for the McElreaths are children who, over the coming years, will visit the park in Arlington. The $7,200 netted at the cook-out will be spent on playground equipment for the park.

The story behind the park began at the Winchester, Indiana Speedway on October 16, 1977. Young James McElreath's star was just beginning to shine when he lost his life. This ended what promised to be the first father and son team to race together at Indy. Grief-stricken, Jim and Shirley returned to their home in Arlington. Looking out over the land on which James had planned to build his home, Jim and Shirley decided to memorialize their son's name by building a park for children. Why a park? As it was explained to me, Jim and Shirley love children. What better way to show this than build a park where they can play? As so many people, who knew James, said, "He would have wanted his land put to this use."

Their friends heard about the plan for the park and how, by themselves, Jim and Shirley were clearing the land. These friends included Lloyd Ruby, Buck Pendland, H.P. Looper, Tim Phillips, Ronnie Palmer, Ed Berryman, Sam Rowlett, and Stan Benge. They got together last December, and, as they put it, started "kicking around" ideas on how they could help the McElreaths raise money for the park. Due in no small way to Ruby's and his friend's ability in organizing and preparing large Texas style barbecues, they decided to do exactly that — stage a barbecue. Through hours of hard work, these men treated everyone who came to delicious food and all the beer anyone could consume.

All of this can be summed up by a fan's remark, "I am glad that I can be a part of something that shows that we still care for our fellow man."

Jim and Shirley McElreath were happy with the turnout.

The Larry Rice family depict the mood of the event.

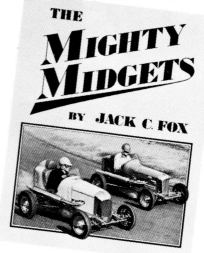
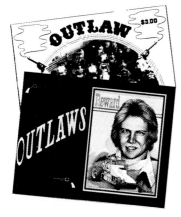

221

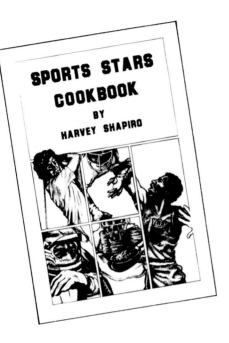

Speed Reading

Eddie Called Me Boss
by Dick Sommers

The True Story of a Car Owner's 14 Years at the Indianapolis 500

Dick Sommers' "Eddie Called Me Boss" is one of the most refreshing racing books to come along in quite some time. We cannot recall another Indianapolis 500 car owner who has put his humor and heartache on paper in such a revealing and entertaining fashion. Sommers tells not only of his personal feelings in dealing with some of the sport's greats, but reveals many of the financial aspects of his involvement as well.
$12.95 pp Immediate Delivery

STAY TUNED FOR THE GREATEST SPECTACLE IN RACING
Ron Dorson

Our new book on Sid Collins, better known to millions of race fans world-wide as The Voice of the Indianapolis 500, is nearly finished. Author Ron Dorson had been working with Sid on a biography for two years, then Sid learned he had a fatal disease and took his own life. Dorson finished the book on his own and the result is an in-depth study on one of racing's most famed personalities. While some chapters are in Sid's own words, you'll soon believe as we do, that Ron Dorson should write more racing books. $10.95 pp Immediate Delivery

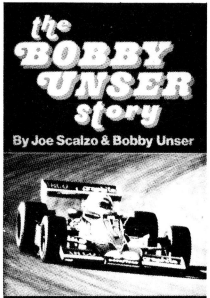

the BOBBY UNSER story
By Joe Scalzo & Bobby Unser

Joe Scalzo is one of the nation's most respected auto racing writers and in collaboration with Bobby Unser has turned out another memorable book. Bobby Unser, known to racing journalists as confident and outspoken, has finally turned a bit introspective about his involvement in the sport. Unser's brash style tells you of his feelings for not only the sport in general, but his feelings about fellow drivers and virtually everything else that surrounds racing.
$11.50 pp Immediate Delivery

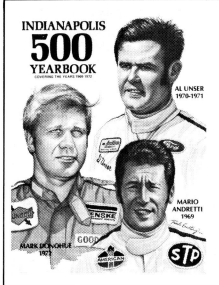

1969-1972
500 YEARBOOK

Here's the book collectors have been waiting for. The 1969-72 "500" Yearbook is actually four Yearbooks combined in a library casing. There are 292 pages, over 1,000 photographs. Inside you will find all the usual feature stories you've come to expect in our regular Indy Yearbook: Day-by-Day coverage; Complete race report; In-depth statistics; Driver Biographies; Qualifying photos; Feature Stories; and More.

The new book is actually four Yearbooks bound in a library casing, so it will stay readable for years to come. As with all our other Yearbooks, none will ever be re-printed so when the initial print order is run they are gone forever.

Price (Hardbound Only) . . . . $24.95 p.p.

Carl Hungness Publishing   P.O. Box 24308-Y   Speedway, IN 46224
• Master Charge and VISA accepted.   • Indiana Residents add 4% sales tax.

223